Women's Activism in the Transatlantic Consumers' Leagues, 1885–1920

Nineteenth-Century and Neo-Victorian Cultures

Series editors: Ruth Heholt and Joanne Ella Parsons

Recent books in the series

Domestic Architecture, Literature and the Sexual Imaginary in Europe, 1850–1930
Aina Martí-Balcells

Assessing Intelligence: The Bildungsroman and the Politics of Human Potential in England, 1860–1910
Sara Lyons

The Idler's Club: Humour and Mass Readership from Jerome K. Jerome to P. G. Wodehouse
Laura Fiss

Michael Field's Revisionary Poetics
Jill Ehnenn

Narrative, Affect, and Victorian Sensation: Wilful Bodies
Tara MacDonald

The Provincial Fiction of Mitford, Gaskell and Eliot
Kevin A. Morrison

Women's Activism in the Transatlantic Consumers' Leagues, 1885–1920
Flore Janssen

Forthcoming

Lost and Revenant Children 1850–1940
Tatiana Kontou

Olive Schreiner and the Politics of Print Culture, 1883–1920
Clare Gill

Literary Illusions: Performance Magic and Victorian Literature
Christopher Pittard

Pastoral in Early-Victorian Fiction: Environment and Modernity
Mark Frost

Spectral Embodiments of Child Death in the Long Nineteenth Century
Jen Baker

Life Writing and the Nineteenth-Century Market
Sean Grass

British Writers, Popular Literature and New Media Innovation, 1820–45
Alexis Easley

Oscar Wilde's Aesthetic Plagiarisms
Sandra Leonard

Reading Victorian Sculpture
Angela Dunstan

Mind and Embodiment in Late Victorian Literature
Marion Thain and Atti Viragh

Drunkenness in Eighteenth- and Nineteenth-Century Irish Literature
Lucy Cogan

Philanthropy in Children's Periodicals, 1840–1930: The Charitable Child
Kristine Moruzi

Violence and the Brontës: Language, Reception, Afterlives
Sophie Franklin

The British Public and the British Museum: Shaping and Sharing Knowledge in the Nineteenth Century
Jordan Kistler

Queer Desire in Aesthetic Literature: Form and Experiment in Late-Victorian Print Culture
Frederick D. King

Dickens and Decadence
Giles Whiteley and Jonathan Foster

Women's Activism in the Transatlantic Consumers' Leagues, 1885–1920

Flore Janssen

EDINBURGH
University Press

Edinburgh University Press is one of the leading university presses in the UK. We publish academic books and journals in our selected subject areas across the humanities and social sciences, combining cutting-edge scholarship with high editorial and production values to produce academic works of lasting importance. For more information visit our website: edinburghuniversitypress. com

© Flore Janssen, 2024

Edinburgh University Press Ltd
The Tun – Holyrood Road
12(2f) Jackson's Entry
Edinburgh EH8 8PJ

Typeset in 11/13pt Sabon
by Cheshire Typesetting Ltd, Cuddington, Cheshire, and
printed and bound in Great Britain

A CIP record for this book is available from the British Library

ISBN 978 1 4744 9798 5 (hardback)
ISBN 978 1 4744 9800 5 (webready PDF)
ISBN 978 1 4744 9801 2 (epub)

The right of Flore Janssen to be identified as the author of this work has been asserted in accordance with the Copyright, Designs and Patents Act 1988, and the Copyright and Related Rights Regulations 2003 (SI No. 2498).

Contents

Figures

Acknowledgements

This book has had a long gestation and therefore has come to owe much to many.

It developed from my PhD project 'Women Writers, World Problems, and the Working Poor, c. 1880–1920: "'Blackleg' Work in Literature"' (Birkbeck, University of London, 2018), supported by a Birkbeck School of Arts Research Studentship. The inspiring supervision of Ana Parejo Vadillo led me to discover new, inter-disciplinary angles for the work, while my wonderful examiners Nadia Valman and Linda K. Hughes gave encouraging prompts for next steps and Carolyn Burdett helped me to think through other incarnations of the consumers' league research project. The mutual support of my wider Birkbeck community also continues to mean a lot: I particularly wish to mention Alexis Wolf and the truly heroic Sasha Dovzhyk.

My new community at Utrecht University has offered valuable opportunities to move this project forward. I have gained so much from speaking to colleagues at the Modern and Contemporary Literature research seminar and at ReAct meetings, especially Sophie van den Elzen, Anna Poletti, Barnita Bagchi, Michela Borzaga, Ann Rigney, Daniele Salerno, Clara Vlessing and Duygu Erbil.

I have been endlessly lucky to work with Edinburgh University Press on this project. Editors Susannah Butler, Michelle Houston, Emily Sharp and Elizabeth Fraser were all marvellously accom-modating and supportive through a pandemic and an interna-tional move. The incisive and encouraging comments of my peer reviewers were brilliantly helpful; I can gratefully name Rachel Bowlby. Many heartfelt thanks are also due to the generous Lisa

C. Robertson, Terry Elkiss and Richard Kaplan for their useful suggestions and corrections on the manuscript in its final stages.

Then, for support and interest, always: my thanks to Austen Saunders, Clementa Veldman and Johan Janssen.

Thank you all.

Series Preface

Nineteenth-Century and Neo-Victorian Cultures
Series Editors: Ruth Heholt and Joanne Ella Parsons

This interdisciplinary series provides space for full and detailed scholarly discussions on nineteenth-century and Neo-Victorian cultures. Drawing on radical and cutting-edge research, volumes explore and challenge existing discourses, as well as providing an engaging reassessment of the time period. The series encourages debates about decolonising nineteenth-century cultures, histories and scholarship, as well as raising questions about diversities. Encompassing art, literature, history, performance, theatre studies, film and TV studies, medical and the wider humanities, Nineteenth-Century and Neo-Victorian Cultures is dedicated to publishing pioneering research that focuses on the Victorian era in its broadest and most diverse sense.

Abbreviations

USA

CLNY   Consumers' League of New York
GFWC   General Federation of Women's Clubs
NCL   National Consumers' League
NLC   National Labor Committee

UK

WIC   Women's Industrial Council
WIN   *Women's Industrial News*
WPPL   Women's Protective and Provident League
WTUA   Women's Trade Union Association
WTUL   Women's Trade Union League

Introduction

Gender, Wealth and the Rhetoric of Ethical Consumption

Consumer activism has an enduring appeal. The concept combines ideas of collectivism linked to the perceived universality of the act of shopping with the potential to make a social, economic or political difference through individual actions. It inspires a sense of people power that can function within the status quo, so its attraction can work across political boundaries. It can shapeshift to fit a range of situations and reformist agendas, targeting issues from labour conditions to environmentalism, from animal welfare to public health, and any intersections between them. It can be made to apply to different socio-economic groups, from the ethical consumerism that calls on shoppers to pay more for ethically produced goods to structures of cooperative buying. It can work at levels from the hyperlocal to the global, from neighbourhood shop to stock market. It serves many aims to many activists, from increasing community influence to appeasing individual guilt. It can even change its own identity to fit these models, not least because, as sociologist Jeffrey Haydu remarks, 'it demands less time and carries less risk than does collective public protest'.[1] The notion of ethical shopping allows some proponents to avoid the label of activism altogether, while it enables others to embrace an activist identity based on their consumer choices.

Historicising consumer activism

Much of this book was written during the coronavirus pandemic that grew to global proportions in 2020.[2] The first months of the emergency pandemic response raised their own unique calls to consumer activism while also bringing to the fore many of the socio-economic problems that have inspired consumer activism since the eighteenth century. Mutual aid groups organised the neighbourly action of shopping on behalf of local vulnerable people. Meanwhile, attention was drawn to conditions in service industries, particularly delivery services, on which individuals suddenly became more reliant than ever – including those who had previously used them as a convenience or luxury, as well as those who had always depended on them because of disabilities, for instance. The already long-standing call to boycott specific online retailers and large-scale delivery services was renewed as news emerged that workers in this industry might lack such protections as sick pay and, as a result, were prevented from self-isolating if they were infected or vulnerable to the virus.[3] While some responses to the personal, social and economic impact of the pandemic were underpinned by political philosophies, such as trade union initiatives to support casualised service industry workers or mutual aid groups working on anarchist principles, individual consumers were also called on, not least through pressure from other individuals through social media, to support small, local and independent businesses and cultural institutions to help them survive the financial hit caused by lockdown closures. While all these different initiatives offered opportunities to counteract feelings of powerlessness in the face of global crisis, the limitations of individual action also quickly became clear as substantial injections of cash from governments were needed to keep businesses afloat.

To some extent it is logical that both consumer campaigns and individual consumers striving to shop more ethically have found themselves repeatedly reinventing the consumer activist wheel: of course the basic point of where and how to spend one's money exists within particular and changing contexts that influence what the best and most effective approach will be at any given time. It is striking, however, that a movement with as long a history as consumer activism is generally not widely historicised. Certainly cooperatives and mutual societies are often strongly aware of their own histories and use these narratives to reflect their growth from local to national or international, to demonstrate their adaptability over time and to inspire confidence in new members.[4] Specific boycotts will often be aware of and build on earlier campaigns; individual organisers may also bring previous activist experience. The National Consumers' League (NCL) of the USA is conscious of its roots in the history that this book also explores, and its official literature reflects this, albeit in limited ways. Over the last two decades, historians of consumption have been significantly expanding the important work of highlighting the history of consumer movements, including more problematic aspects of their aims and practices. The work of scholars such as Frank Trentmann, Lawrence B. Glickman and Matthew Hilton is key to this study. As Trentmann warns:

> It can be tempting to trace back today's ethical consumer movements to the boycotts of slave-grown sugar around 1800. Historical reality was less straightforward and progressive. Liberals dreamt of a world where trade connected people and continents in webs of interdependence. But by 1900, few people in the affluent north troubled themselves with the conditions of the millions in the south who sweated to procure the ingredients of their comfort. [...] it was at the very time that Westerners discovered the consumer [...] that they forgot about the African consumer. In the inter-war years, caring at a distance meant privileged British housewives buying Canadian apples and Kenyan coffee to support their white cousins in the empire.[5]

This kind of historicised and problematised thinking tends not, for obvious reasons, to be written into present-day consumer campaign narratives, however. Where these movements mobilise historical context it is generally with the aim of building a sense of cohesion and legitimacy through historical roots.

Largely due to the lack of historical awareness about the backgrounds to consumer activism, many proposed large-scale campaign strategies therefore find themselves running into the same essential problems. How can individual consumers obtain sufficient information to make ethical decisions? How can they keep abreast of new developments with a multinational reach? When mass signals, such as labels certifying ethical production, are evolved to help individual consumers in their decisions, how can the underlying principles and controls be maintained as these projects are scaled up in a global context? How can the impact of consumer actions be measured? And who decides what the aims and desired outcomes of these initiatives are? As activist journalist Naomi Klein asked in her investigative campaign text *No Logo* in 2000, in which she addressed the human rights violations of multinational fashion brands, how can we ensure that they do not function merely 'to protect the right of Westerners to buy branded goods without guilt'?[6]

This book does not pretend to be able to offer answers to these difficult and recurring questions. It presents a case study of the so-called consumers' leagues in the UK and the USA between about 1885 and 1920: only one consumer activist movement in the long history comprising, in the UK alone, both such momentous campaigns as the Sugar Boycotts organised by Abolitionists in the 1780s and 1820s and the founding of the Women's Co-operative Guild in 1883, and also the campaigns to buy goods produced in the British colonial empire that Trentmann pointed to. The consumers' league movement gained significant national and international influence around the turn of the twentieth century but has now largely disappeared in its original form. While ambitious, it was also highly limited in both its focus on a specific group of potential activists and its intended sphere of influence. Different consumers' leagues evolved their campaign strategies through trial and error, including unsuccessful and sometimes troubling initiatives such as whitelisting and labelling campaigns as well as exhibitions of goods produced by sweated labour and, indeed, of the sweated labourers themselves. In spite of the sometimes hit-and-miss style of their activities, the movements and their leaders reached wide audiences, raised awareness of important social and economic problems and drew widespread support. While the individual leagues – with the notable exception of the NCL in the US – can no longer be said to be part of the popular historical consciousness, it is worth noting that this is in part due to the fact that some of their underlying ideas and the campaign strategies they evolved are now so established as to be taken for granted.

The history of the consumers' leagues is particularly relevant to consumer activist initiatives today because of its engagement with the question of consumer guilt and its more and less successful attempts to develop a proactive response with a broad support base. As this book will show, the leagues pioneered consumer activist strategies and rhetoric that continue to be used in the present day, particularly in their representation of specific problems and of the people affected by them, and in their communication with potential activist audiences. My examination of the movement's successes and failures, its appeal to its audience, and its precarious balance between progressive aims and conservative, paternalistic and sometimes exclusionary politics will provide a foil to present-day campaigns and give an insight into the difficulties of trade-offs between principles and wide appeal in the attempt to build a mass campaign.

The narrative of consumer guilt

Of all the different campaign narratives around consumer activism, the consumers' leagues were specifically focused on what I will term the narrative of consumer guilt. The concept relates to a still familiar argument that gained in popularity over the course of the nineteenth century and is particularly strongly associated with the figure of the exploited woman needleworker as a symbol of sweated labour.[7] In essence, the narrative of consumer guilt hinges on assigning to specifically leisured middle-class women consumers the responsibility for the low wages of exploited producers of luxury goods and clothing above all. It was argued that customers made unreasonable demands for cheap clothing to be produced and delivered quickly and that this forced workers to submit to underpayment and overwork. There are obvious parallels with the systems of demand, production and supply behind the present-day problem of fast fashion, a shorthand term for clothing produced almost directly to online order and shipped immediately, either to be returned straightaway or to be worn no more than a handful of times before being discarded. Appeals to consumers are again asking them to desist from adding their demands to these systems as they enable poor labour conditions in production and shipping, particularly (though not exclusively) in the global south, and have a high environmental cost.

The key argument of the narrative of consumer guilt presented prices as in direct correlation with wages and conditions, with the latter entirely dependent on what consumers were willing to pay. This foregrounded the consumer's role and influence in market processes, but in doing so it erased other socio-economic complexities. As a result, it presented the problem of labour exploitation as one that might be easily resolved, but could not be, unless consumer behaviour changed to reflect greater compassion and generosity. Like the consumers of fast fashion today, these mid-nineteenth-century consumers were being urged to look beyond their own desires to the wider impact they might have.

Linked to broader social trends such as the rise of the middle class and the associated growing number of women with more leisure time and disposable income to substantiate the desire for more smart clothes, this narrative of consumer guilt became a cultural staple.[8] It connects directly to the growing awareness and developing perception of the social problem typified by the evocative term 'sweating'. From the mid-nineteenth century this had become well-known shorthand for unregulated and exploitative labour characterised by long hours, low pay and poor conditions that was particularly associated with an urban environment. Historian of labour Sheila C. Blackburn divides historical understanding of sweating in the mid-nineteenth to early twentieth century into three phases: what she calls its 'discovery' in the 1840s, its 'rediscovery' in the 1880s and 90s, and finally the understanding of sweating as resulting from an unregulated economy. She identifies this final phase as following from the 1906 London 'Sweated Industries Exhibition', which will also be discussed in Chapter 3 of this book. Specifically alert to depictions of workers in these narratives, Blackburn highlights questions of class and gender in their characterisation. For instance, between the 'discovery' and 'rediscovery' phases, she notes that, having been '[p]reviously depicted as weak, passive and prone to prostitution, sweated female homeworkers were now viewed as hapless breeders of a casualized residuum'. She also addresses racist and xenophobic assumptions that were woven into representations of sweating, from the 'mistaken insistence that the exploiting middleman sweater was frequently Jewish' to the ways 'newly arrived immigrants and, later, women homeworkers were portrayed as the chief victims as well as the key perpetrators of sweating'. After 1906, however, she argues that

> reformers stressed that sweating touched both factory and outdoor workers. The explanation for sweating was not necessarily to be found in personal characteristics, such as 'race' or gender, but in a capitalist system which failed to regulate low pay legally.[9]

In the campaign texts examined in this book it will become clear that there were frequent crossovers between the rhetoric of these different stages and that campaign literature regularly reached backwards for emotive and regressive arguments about gender and race that Blackburn identified as belonging to the 'discovery' and 'rediscovery' stages.

In the consumer guilt narrative originating in the 1840s, the two key figures of the thoughtless consumer and the victimised worker were virtually always women, distanced by circumstance and experience. Blackburn traces the blaming of 'unthinking females looking for a bargain' for the state of wages in the garment industry back to 1842.[10] Cultural and political historian Rohan McWilliam notes how the gendered pattern of exploitation was reflected in the Second Report of the Children's Employment Commission, also known as the Grainger Report, in 1843. For example, it offered

> evidence that aristocratic special occasions (such as weddings and funerals) caused young girls to stay up all night sewing. The manager of a clothes shop thought that 'the only means of preventing the late hours of work, is by the ladies who employ dress-makers being more considerate by allowing more time, and not being so very pressing in their orders'.[11]

From this expression of thoughtlessness or privilege on the part of wealthy customers ordering hand-made clothes, unaware of or unconcerned by the impact of their demands on workers, evolved a cultural trope that lasted for decades, even continuing to resonate in the present day. This was at the heart of the consumers' leagues' engagement with their potential activists and supporters.

The most famous cultural expression to develop from this narrative is Thomas Hood's poem 'The Song of the Shirt', published in the Christmas issue of the popular satirical entertainment magazine *Punch* in 1843, the same year that the Grainger Report cited above was compiled. In an echo of the clothes shop manager quoted in the report, the appeal of the poem was clearly directed against consumers and their excessive demands:

> O, men, with sisters dear!
> O, men, with mothers and wives!
> It is not linen you're wearing out,
> But human creatures' lives![12]

The emotive imagery and sentiment of the poem, reportedly based on the true story of destitute seamstress Mrs Biddell, inspired a series of visual artworks portraying romantically pathetic needlewomen.[13] Nineteenth-century paintings by John T. Peele (1849), Pre-Raphaelite Anna E. Blunden (1854) and William Daniels (1875) echoed the poem's title. Later works such as the painting 'It is not the linen you're wearing out, but human creatures' lives' (c. 1907–17) by Beatrice Offor, as well as the 1908 US silent film 'The Song of the Shirt' directed by D. W. Griffith, illustrate the long cultural reach of Hood's poem into the twentieth century. In 1979 Sue Clayton and Jonathan Curling used it as inspiration for an anti-capitalist feminist history documentary about women's sweated work in the garment trade, which also shared the title of the poem.

'The Song of the Shirt' thus began an influential strategy of representation of consumer guilt by seeking to show consumers the misery and hardship suffered by the workers exploited to meet their desires. Unsurprisingly, these representations quickly expanded to portray the woman needleworker as vulnerable to sexual exploitation, both because her income was insufficient and because her long working hours left her to make her way home alone at night through dark and deserted streets. These themes are explored in politicised fiction such as *Woman's Wrongs* (1852) by the Chartist Ernest Jones and the deliberately sensational *The Seamstress* (1853) by G. W. M. Reynolds, but also surface in Elizabeth Gaskell's social novels *Mary Barton* (1848) and *Ruth* (1853).

How embedded the connection between consumer demands and worker exploitation was as a reference point in popular culture becomes clear from a still well-known cartoon, again for *Punch*, by John Tenniel, who would soon go on to find fame as the illustrator of Lewis Carroll's *Alice's Adventures in Wonderland* (1865) and *Through the Looking Glass* (1871). 'The Haunted Lady, or "The Ghost" in the Looking-Glass' (1863) shows a woman looking at her reflection as she tries on a magnificently crinolined ball gown (see Fig. 0.1). Behind her stands the witch-like 'Madame la Modiste', who tells her: 'We would not have disappointed your ladyship, at any sacrifice, and the robe is finished *à merveille*.' The sacrifice she was willing to make is visible in the dark background of the reflection in the mirror: a seamstress, herself in a very plain dress that shows how skeletally thin she is, lying in a straight-backed chair with her eyes closed, sleeping the sleep of exhaustion or death. Casting the customer as 'your ladyship' makes the relationship of exploitation uncomplicatedly clear, as in McWilliam's

Figure 0.1 John Tenniel, 'The Haunted Lady, or "The Ghost" in the Looking-Glass', *Punch*, 4 July 1863. © The British Library Board o P.P.5270.

example from the Grainger Report: the aristocratic lady could surely have afforded to pay a higher price for her exquisite gown, and it is suggested that she only required impossibly rapid delivery to avoid disappointment before some social event. Madame la Modiste features as the unscrupulous intermediary sweater who facilitates consumer ignorance by making promises that obscure the real impact of her ladyship's demand; but the placement of the seamstress in the mirror clearly suggests that the customer could find out more about the conditions under which her clothes were produced, and indeed has cause to be suspicious at the price and speed of production. Without the desire of her ladyship for new outfits, it is implied, there would be no scope for the sweater to institute her systems of exploitation.

The themes of the Haunted Lady would become key for the consumers' league movement. The focus of British consumers' league pioneer Clementina Black on consumers' awareness of the unfair prices of ready-made garments, and the Consumers' League of New York's calls for shoppers not to contribute to the overwork of shop assistants by failing to respect closing times and requesting deliveries at short notice, were direct responses to this narrative. The argument was that, if consumers created these conditions through their demands, they could similarly ameliorate the situation by amending their requirements and desires to be more reasonable. Calls for adjustments to consumer demand were also at the heart of the exposure of the sweatshop boom in the 1990s and 2000s, just as they are now a significant part of appeals to resist fast fashion. Awareness-raising campaigns aim to help consumers put bargains into their socio-economic context by alerting them to the fact that overly cheap goods and services may, for instance, be indicators of modern slavery.

The rhetoric of the consumers' leagues led the way for these modern campaigns with a conscious inversion of the consumer guilt narrative to produce a narrative of consumer influence. In developing this campaign argument the consumers' league movement used precisely the same representative structure and components that also illustrated consumer guilt. Central to this was an understanding of gender, used in these narratives virtually exclusively in binary terms and connected to social roles assigned to narrowly defined gendered identities. The gendered experience was further split along class lines, with working-class women seen as producers and middle-class women as consumers; but it was also used to appeal for sympathy on the basis of gendered understanding. Both narratives also relied strongly on judicious use of genre and publishing platforms in developing strategies of representation that were as influential as those of Hood and Tenniel in the widely read and socially prominent magazine *Punch*. The strategies of both cast the reader as consumer and the consumer as reader. The consumers of popular writing were also the consumers of luxury goods. Targeting them through the reading material they consumed for their entertainment gave unique access to this wide-ranging audience base.

Where the narrative of consumer guilt relied on blaming middle-class women for working-class women's suffering, the consumers' leagues recruited women members by appealing to ideas of gendered sympathy. These might rest on pointing to comparable experiences across social classes of work and care, or to threats linked to gendered identity such as the fear of sexual assault. Campaign leaders worked in a range of genres from journalist articles, books and pamphlets to events and exhibitions, but a thorough knowledge of audience was always crucial and persuasive pieces were often inserted into popular settings, from magazines to shop windows, to reach a wider readership instead of preaching to their choir. Black published consumers' league proposals in mainstream, women's and Fabian periodicals; the 'Sweated Industries Exhibition' in the Queen's Hall in central London, which she co-organised, became a society event; but she also engaged directly with economic theory in designing and defending her campaign aims. The National Consumers' League of the United States used both popular and academic publications to make emotional and scientific cases for consumer activism and sought to influence legislature. In these ways the consumers' leagues worked to bridge the perceived social, cultural and economic distance between producers and consumers that was held responsible for emotional and practical thoughtlessness or callousness about worker exploitation.

Many activist women also used these processes to reach across the distance that kept them personally from exercising political influence. This, too, rested on gendered representation: by portraying women workers as victims and themselves as uniquely placed to understand their situation based on their shared gendered experience, they put themselves in the position of intermediaries who could convey these women's circumstances to the lawmakers of their own social class. In this way their strategies of representation could also be deliberately designed to advance themselves and women of their own class while keeping workers, and specifically working women, in a clearly defined place in their activist narrative.

The influence of these strategies for campaign communication is still central to consumer activism in the present day. Communication through a range of platforms is key to capturing the attention of potential activists and alerting them to the harmful impact of their consumer choices. Strategies of representation depend on impressing the reader with an emotional as well as a rational sense of this harm. It is also important that the impact of individual consumer choices is exaggerated in order to give consumers the sense of their own influence that will prompt them to change their behaviour. For better or worse, then, the consumers' leagues helped to set the tone for still familiar narratives of consumer empowerment to respond proactively to feelings of guilt, but also for the problematic implications of exaggerating consumer influence and simplifying the socio-economic structures underpinning exploitation.

Scope and terminology

The title of this book defines my focus as 'women's activism in the transatlantic consumers' leagues'. In this introduction so far I have used the terms 'consumer activism' and 'consumer movement' as practically interchangeable. The question of terminology can be complicated and has been specified by scholars in particular contexts. For example, Glickman, in discussing the history of consumer politics in the USA, distinguishes between 'consumer activism' as 'bottom-up protests by non-state actors', 'consumer movement' as 'efforts through advocacy and lobbying to protect and advance "consumer interests"', and 'consumer regime' as 'the often overlooked state politics of consumption'.[14] In the same edited volume, Hilton contributes a discussion of what he calls three types of 'consumer movement': firstly, the 'mobilization of consumers around the concerns of other types of person: for instance, the slave, the worker, the child'; secondly, movements that see 'consumers organize both to protect their own self-interest and to campaign for the rights of all consumers'; and lastly, movements 'associated with ethical consumerism, green consumerism and fair-trade'.[15] The activities of the two different iterations of the consumers' league movement I address in this book both stretched across these separate categories as they developed: they campaigned on behalf of 'other types of person', most notably women workers, but also represented consumer interests. They encouraged forms of ethical consumerism on individual as well as group bases and also lobbied state bodies. To embrace the broad categorisation of the leagues' activities, therefore, I will continue to refer to the leagues as a consumer movement and to their practices as consumer activism, accepting that this encompasses a wide spectrum that I will define more specifically in the different examples I present.

While gender and class emerge as clearly identified themes both of consumers' league rhetoric and of my analysis of it, what is missing from the structures explored in this book is a separate category addressing the roles of race and ethnicity. The reason for this is that this topic is not generally explicitly articulated in the campaign texts I consider in this book as the key factor that it was (and is), and I am therefore unfortunately unable to present here the required evidence for a detailed study of the subject. Such a study would be a very necessary and welcome contribution to scholarship in this field. This is not least because it would pose an important challenge to a tendency that persists in the UK but also in the USA to accept by default what scholars including Caroline Bressey have called an 'imagined Whiteness' of history, simply because the stories of people of colour may be less readily accessible in specific historical and archival contexts – which is itself of course the result of systematised racism.[16] Meanwhile my failure to include race as a separate central category of analysis in this book should in no way be taken to suggest that consciousness of and engagement with race and ethnicity was not implicitly present throughout the consumers' leagues' discourse. Jewish and migrant communities were at the heart of narratives of labour exploitation, particularly in the garment industry. The shared identity and experience of these communities often provided a rallying point for worker organisation as well as philanthropic initiatives including, for example, Jewish trade unions and social clubs in both the UK and the USA. Unsurprisingly, however, marginalised identities could equally be used as a basis for exclusion and a reinforcing of the sense of emotional and cultural distance which the consumers' leagues did their best to bridge in other circumstances.

Clementina Black's philosophies of labour organisation in England were sometimes explicitly inclusive of migrant and Jewish workers, as illustrated, for instance, by her reference to the specific circumstances of Jewish women workers in the *Rhyme of the Factory Acts* (1900), the pamphlet she published to help workers understand the impact of the eponymous legislation; she also worked with campaigners for the interests of Jewish workers, such as Lily Montagu. While her campaign for a national minimum wage drew on research and initiatives from other countries including France and Australia, however, she nevertheless also presented internationalism as a threat to the effects of consumer activism as it complicated production processes beyond the information and influence of consumer activists. She accepted without question that it was impossible and indeed pointless to attempt to improve working conditions in other countries such as China or India, which she held up as examples of exploitation that were too extreme to be contemplated for English workers but also taken for granted in situ. The influence of British imperialism in India is not taken into account in this part of her analysis.[17]

Among the leaders of the US consumers' leagues, affluent and educated Jewish women including Josephine and Pauline Goldmark and Maud Nathan took prominent places. The extra precarious positions of Jewish and migrant workers are sometimes acknowledged in US campaign writing but did not significantly influence campaign aims or policies such as protective labour legislation to curb women's working hours. With regard to the US leagues' attitudes to Black women workers, historian of labour and gender Nancy Woloch notes that protective labour legislation of the kind the US consumers' leagues were dedicated to implementing 'rarely reached Progressive Era black women'. Because 'industry rejected them', Black women workers predominantly ended up in less regulated or unregulated sectors such as agriculture and domestic labour. As '[h]ousehold labor and black women's long workdays fell outside the realm of consumers' leagues or protective laws', Woloch explains, 'black women (involuntarily) eluded the protectionist gaze'.[18]

Direct racist exclusion also bleeds through into the US consumers' leagues in themes such as the association of migrant workers with disease which posed a threat to middle- and upper-class consumers' households, the adoption of campaign strategies from strands of labour organisation deliberately aimed at excluding Chinese migrant workers, and the eugenicist focus on women workers as propagators of a specific working-class type that conformed to standards set by a more influential social group. For instance, in her study *Fatigue and Efficiency* (1912), in which she explores the impact of overwork specifically on women workers, NCL leader Josephine Goldmark explicitly sets the negative impact of the night-time employment of Black women in the furnace rooms of glass factories, resulting in what she describes as 'coarseness and immoralities', against the 'perils and alarms of refined women' forced by their working hours in night restaurants to return home around midnight.[19] Her phrasing suggests the assumption that she and her readers will agree that the impact on the latter group of women is necessarily greater and a matter of more concern. She later also expresses apprehension 'from the physiological or racial point of view' regarding what she sees as an influx of 'young laborers of new immigrant races' into the USA to replace workers who have been run into the ground by overwork.[20] As part of the intersectional feminist framework I use within this book I will identify the points in the campaigns discussed where race plays an explicit or implicit part and explore the impact of the activists' approaches to the issue. I will similarly highlight and question the consumers' leagues' engagement with problematic discourses around disability and gender essentialism.

Unfortunately, there is no scope within this book for a detailed interrogation of how the middle-class women-led consumers' leagues compared to and interacted with working women's consumer initiatives such as the contemporaneous Women's Co-operative Guild. Consumer activism from the period as well as in the present day tends to assume a division between consumers and workers that is demonstrably fictitious. It enables the necessary exaggeration of consumer influence but leaves unaddressed those consumers who want to participate in consumer activism but cannot afford to pay more to ensure their purchases are ethical. During the period covered by this book, cooperative ventures launched and supported by working-class women were highly successful in influencing the provenance of their purchases at local levels, as several participants in the consumers' leagues, including the long-term socialist General Secretary of the NCL Florence Kelley, were aware. I will highlight parallels between the movements where relevant, both when they are recognised by consumers' league activists and when acknowledgement of working women's movements is conspicuous by its absence.

This book also echoes the focus of the consumers' leagues on urban centres. Within the UK, this is almost exclusively on London, where Black was based and carried out her labour investigations; in response to her original whitelist, which only featured businesses situated in the affluent West End of the city, correspondents asked for wider investigation including shops more local to them.[21] The 'Sweated Industries Exhibition' included workers from across the country, but a London focus remained as this was where most of the activists involved operated and had their contacts. In the US leagues, the focus shifted from the affluent shopping districts of New York City to identify flagship cases in other states; but the consumers' leagues' prominent members were primarily city-based. Large cities such as Chicago, Illinois, and Portland, Oregon, remained focal points as acknowledged centres for labour exploitation, attracting migrant workers and facilitating anonymity. It would be very worthwhile for future studies to expand scholarship in this area by examining more geographically wide-ranging examples of consumer activist campaigns and other local consumers' league initiatives.

Structure

This book's two-part structure is intended to reflect the evolution of the consumers' league movements by tracing the two parallel strands in the UK and USA from their early establishment from the mid-1880s to roughly the end of the nineteenth century, to the consolidation of their campaign strategies around the first decades of the twentieth century. The four chapters are organised broadly chronologically within a contrapuntal framework alternating between case studies of consumers' league activity in the UK and USA. This demonstrates the importance of international communication and mutual influence in the movements' development as well as highlighting diversions in the different national contexts. To reflect the importance of the writing of women activists at each stage of the two movements, every chapter is constructed around the close reading of one or two campaign texts, exploring how they communicate key aims and ideas to specified audiences of potential activists. These central texts are contextualised historically using a methodology that incorporates interdisciplinary approaches including economic history and the history of law. In analysing their arguments I give special attention both to their emotive and affective impact and to their conceptions and depictions of the body, including as representative of specific individual and collective identities. My examination of the consumers' leagues' campaigns and the strategies for representation and communication used in the texts examined will evaluate their success and draw out parallels with present-day consumer responses to social problems.

Part I of the book explores the roots and early beginnings of the two mutually influenced movements in the UK and the USA with particular reference to their use and revisions of the narrative of consumer guilt. Chapter 1, 'Let the Buyer Beware', explores the work of labour organiser and professional writer Clementina Black to establish the first consumers' league in the UK between 1887 and 1890. It shows how she evolved the idea out of her parallel careers in activism and literature to mobilise the middle-class audiences her writing gave her access to in support of the working-class women whose organisation she supported. Her initiative existed separately from working women's consumer action through the cooperative movement and essentially adhered to the class-based distinctions between producer and consumer on which the narrative of consumer guilt also relied. Nevertheless, her proposals were based on soundly explained socio-economic analysis and carefully identified achievable short-term goals as she harnessed the consumer guilt narrative to help her readers find practical ways of making their individual purchases count towards a collective aim. In explicitly empowering the consumer to resist the implications of guilt, Black set the tone for much contemporary consumer activist rhetoric.

Chapter 2, 'An Epoch-Making Movement', traces the movement to the USA to follow its growing influence and evolution between 1890 and 1900 from the Consumers' League of New York at city and state level to the still active National Consumers' League. Like Black's initiative, the New York league emerged from a collaboration between middle- and upper-class women consumers and working women's organisations; its rhetoric also made shrewd use of elements from the narrative of consumer guilt. Unlike many other nineteenth-century consumer initiatives, however, its initial focus was not on the garment trade but on the service industry and on retail workers in particular. The arguments this produced regarding need, desire and the thoughtlessness of wealthy consumers have strong echoes in the discourse around the online purchase and delivery of unessential goods while all but designated essential shops were forced to close in COVID-19 lockdowns in the spring of 2020.

Part II explores how the two movements diverged in their aims and strategies as they were consolidated in their specific contexts. Activists on either side of the Atlantic concluded that the actions of individual shoppers could not achieve the influence they hoped for and soon turned their sights to legislative change instead, but their conclusions on how to achieve this differed substantially, with Black renouncing the idea of a consumers' league altogether while the NCL set out to become a legislative force. Chapter 3, 'Encounters with Sweating', explores Black's move away from her original proposed consumers' league towards a campaign for legislative influence and a legal minimum wage between 1900 and 1910. Her book on the subject, *Sweated Industry and the Minimum Wage* (1907), followed her usual proactive approach based on socio-economic reasoning in arguing for an enforceable minimum wage. The high-profile event that preceded its publication, the 'Sweated Industries Exhibition' of 1906, however, involved her in significant trade-offs in her usual strategies of worker representation as the project put living workers on display to show the reality of sweated work to a wealthy and influential audience in what self-consciously became a society event.

The impulse for social reform that the NCL represented emerged particularly strongly in the period of US socio-political history known as the Progressive Era, which may be roughly dated from the 1890s to the 1920s and is characterised by social activism and reforms to challenge entrenched corruption in the political system which had caused widespread disillusionment with party politics.[22] In its pursuit of a legislative agenda through the courts during this period, the NCL did not escape involvement in difficult politics to attain broad and influential support and short-term victories. Chapter 4, 'The Health and Welfare of the Republic', considers the NCL's influence in the Progressive Era between 1895 and 1920, with a particular focus on its legal interventions. Central to this chapter is the NCL's role in formulating the legal case in *Muller* v. *Oregon* (1908), where a laundry owner was tried for overworking his employees in contravention of the state's maximum hours law for women. The so-called Brandeis Brief submitted for the state of Oregon presented research carried out by NCL members and is recognised as a landmark in US legal history for reshaping the received idea of legal precedent with its use of international sources including medical texts. In spite of this bold approach and the successful outcome of the case, however, the argument of the brief rested in large part on the physical and biological welfare of working women as potential mothers of a healthy working class, bringing it into uncomfortable dialogue with politics of class and gender hierarchies, gender essentialism and even eugenics.

The concluding chapter, 'Afterlives', draws together the comparative strands of the chapters to evaluate the developments in organised consumer activism brought about by the consumers' league movements in the UK and the USA and the impact they have had on consumer activism up to the present day. The early incarnations of both movements correspond to the idea of ethical shopping – that is, not buying products that are known to have an unethical provenance, and not putting overdue pressure on staff in service industries. While this concept is ubiquitous in modern-day discourse, it is interesting to note that both of the campaigns explored in this book in fact quickly moved away from this type of individual action. The legislative change that they chose instead to pursue created the basis for labour legislation defining maximum hours and minimum wages in the present day. While the NCL achieved immediate legislative victories, the minimum wage Black proposed did not come into national law in the UK until 1999, although 1909 had seen the passing of the Trade Boards Act to begin wage regulation in some underpaid industries. I argue that a key common factor between consumer campaigns at the turn of the twentieth century and in the present day is the notion of citizenship and its responsibilities, concepts that both historian Trentmann and journalist Klein use to make the connection between shopping and politics.

The modern economy is even more globalised than that analysed by Black, creating increasingly complex production and market processes which may be opaque and impenetrable for individual consumers. Examining the consumers' leagues as part of the rich history of consumer activism can shed light on our own understanding of and engagement with this widespread and multifaceted form of activism. It reveals the potential of individual action as well as its limits, such as the exclusion from consumer activist discourse of lower-income consumers. We can learn from the social and economic assumptions underpinning these historical campaigns that limited their engagement with workers; but we can also consider how the impact of these international networks of women and their campaign writing laid the groundwork both for the investigations into product provenance and for the rhetoric of ethical consumption that still inform our consumer choices.

Notes

1. Jeffrey Haydu, 'Consumer Citizenship and Cross-Class Activism: The Case of the National Consumers' League, 1899–1918', *Sociological Forum*, 29.3 (2014), 628–49 (p. 628).
2. My personal experience of the pandemic was limited to western Europe.
3. See for instance Paola Peralta, 'Why some gig workers are struggling to access their sick pay', *Employee Benefit News*, 9 February 2022 <https://www.benefitnews.com/news/delivery-drivers-dont-have-access-to-their-covid-sick-pay> [accessed 10 September 2022].
4. See for instance 'Co-op Group History', *Co-op Legal Services* <https://www.co-oplegalservices.co.uk/about-us/the-co-operative-group-history/> [accessed 10 September 2022].
5. Frank Trentmann, 'The Politics of Everyday Life', in *The Oxford Handbook of the History of Consumption*, ed. Trentmann (Oxford: Oxford University Press, 2012), pp. 521–47 (pp. 545–6).
6. Naomi Klein, *No Logo* (London: Flamingo, 2001 [2000]), p. 429. I am grateful to the peer reviewers of the proposal for this book for suggesting the comparative analysis with the contemporary texts *No Logo* and *Fashionopolis* (2019).
7. See for instance Beth Harris, 'Introduction', in *Famine and Fashion: Needlewomen in the Nineteenth Century*, ed. Harris (Aldershot: Ashgate, 2005), pp. 1–10 (p. 3).
8. There are obvious connections to be made here with what Thorstein Veblen called 'the duties of vicarious leisure and consumption', especially as he saw them to 'devolve upon' non-wage-earning, married women expected to use consumption to signal household status. See Veblen, *The Theory of the Leisure Class: An Economic Study in the Evolution of Institutions* (London: Macmillan, 1899), pp. 80–1.
9. Sheila C. Blackburn, '"Princesses and Sweated-Wage Slaves Go Well Together": Images of British Sweated Workers, 1843–1914',

International Labor and Working-Class History, 61 (2002), 24–44 (p. 25).

10. Sheila Blackburn, *A Fair Day's Wage for a Fair Day's Work? Sweated Labour and the Origins of Minimum Wage Legislation in Britain* (Aldershot: Ashgate, 2007), p. 16, n. 10.

11. Rohan McWilliam, 'The Melodramatic Seamstress: Interpreting a Victorian Penny Dreadful', in *Famine and Fashion*, ed. Harris, pp. 99–114 (p. 107).

12. Thomas Hood, 'The Song of the Shirt', ll. 25–8, *Punch, or The London Charivari*, 16 December 1843, reprinted on *The Victorian Web* <https://www.victorianweb.org/authors/hood/shirt.html> [accessed 15 February 2021].

13. *The Times* had reported with horror on Mrs Biddell's case earlier in the year, noting that, according to the magistrate, 'the affair was one of *very common* occurrence in that part of the metropolis [Lambeth]'. The article strongly echoed antisemitic notions eliding the identity of the sweater with Jewishness. *The Times*, 27 October 1843, p. 4, emphasis in original.

14. Lawrence B. Glickman, 'Consumer Activism, Consumer Regimes, and the Consumer Movement: Rethinking the History of Consumer Politics in the United States', in *Oxford Handbook of the History of Consumption*, ed. Trentmann, pp. 399–417 (p. 400).

15. Matthew Hilton, 'Consumer Movements', in *Oxford Handbook of the History of Consumption*, ed. Trentmann, pp. 505–19 (p. 508).

16. See for instance Caroline Bressey, 'Invisible Presence: The Whitening of the Black Community in the Historical Imagination of British Archives', *Archivaria*, 61 (2006), 47–61.

17. Clementina Black, *Sweated Industry and the Minimum Wage* (London: Duckworth, 1907), p. 268.

18. Nancy Woloch, *A Class by Herself: Protective Laws for Women Workers, 1890s–1990s* (Princeton: Princeton University Press, 2015), pp. 18, 19.

19. Josephine Goldmark, *Fatigue and Efficiency* (New York: Russell Sage Foundation, 1917 [1912]), pp. 275–6.

20. Ibid. p. 286.

21. Clementina Black, 'The Morality of Buying in the Cheapest Market', in *The Woman's World* (London: Cassell, 1890), pp. 42–4 (p. 44).

22. See for instance Rebecca Edwards, *Angels in the Machinery: Gender in American Party Politics from the Civil War to the Progressive Era* (New York: Oxford University Press, 1997), p. 151 and *passim*.

Part I

Establishing the Movement,
1885–1900

'Let the Buyer Beware': Clementina Black and the Consumers' League in the UK, 1887–1890

The consumers' league movement originated in the UK as a consumer activist project directed against labour exploitation. It was spearheaded by London-based labour activist Clementina Black from 1887. Black's initiative was not the first of its kind: there are several earlier and contemporary examples of organised consumer campaigns that sought to improve living and working conditions, including middle-class activity on behalf of exploited workers but also initiatives led by workers to improve their own situations. The impactful cooperative movement, for instance, had emerged in the mid-nineteenth century, in order to give working-class consumers greater control over the quality and prices of the products available to them. Black proposed her Consumers' League within a few years of the formation in 1883 of the Women's Co-operative Guild, a collective which had grown out of the Co-operative Society with the aim of allowing married working-class women to exercise their purchasing power as a pressure group within the cooperative movement.[1]

Black was a middle-class woman but was deeply involved in trade unionism and later suffrage campaigns, and her work shows that she was strongly cognisant of working-class women's organisation to defend their own community and class interests. Her Consumers' League occupies an unusual intermediary position between campaigns fought by workers and on their behalf, as she tried to involve middle-class consumers in a project that was separate from, but designed to support, the organisation of workers for better wages and conditions by directing their purchasing power towards businesses that adhered to trade union standards. For several years from 1887 onwards, Black invested significant energy into developing her proposals for a consumers' league, with considerable emphasis on publishing her ideas in a range of periodicals. The scheme achieved a wide appeal that led to versions of it being adopted by different organisations in several countries. Black herself, however, rapidly grew disillusioned with the idea, finding it insufficiently impactful, and by the twentieth century she was putting her efforts into alternative schemes and campaigns aimed at effecting legal change to combat labour exploitation. This chapter explores both how she designed her proposals to appeal to readers, and how this targeting of popular success sits alongside her conclusion that the scheme itself was not viable after all.

Black's campaign grew out of her combination of careers in popular literature and labour activism and this experience gave her the tools to identify and appeal to her readership. Her activist networks, including both her own direct contacts in London and a wider international circle of mutual influence, fed into her project and it went on to inform similar campaigns by other organisations. Central to this chapter are two of Black's key consumer campaign texts: 'Caveat Emptor' (1887), in which she set out her blueprint for a functioning consumers' league, and 'The Morality of Buying in the Cheapest Market' (1890), in which she offered specifically middle-class women consumers a strategy for turning the narrative of consumer guilt on its head through proactive application of their own skills and understanding. These two texts show the development of a scheme that was ambitious and far-reaching but was nonetheless only ever intended to work as a parallel project to her wider activism in the labour movement. They also show the shifts in Black's engagement with the existing narrative of consumer guilt and her own relationship to it as well as that of her readers.

Greater practical successes were achieved by other organised consumer activist campaigns begun around the world shortly after Black's, some of which are considered in this volume. Nevertheless, Black's Consumers' League marked both the beginning of this movement and an important development in the longer history of consumer activism that reaches into the present. What Black proposed was a forerunner of the ethical consumption that is widespread today. Her strategies for drawing readers of popular publications into an accessible form of activism, and the way she engaged with her audience through carefully crafted, reader-centred representations of the social problem of labour exploitation, set the tone for many appeals for comparable forms of activism in popular publications.

Uniting consumers

While Black harnessed several key points of recognition from other contemporary consumer campaigns and their associated rhetoric, her scheme stands out from other consumer activist projects from the period in three important ways. Firstly, it pursued what June Hannam and Karen Hunt, in their analysis of the role of consumer activism in women's socialist campaigns around 1880–1920, describe as 'the use of consumption as a lever in a broader political campaign' – namely that of the amelioration of wages and conditions for workers subject to exploitation. In this way it differed from organisations such as the Women's Co-operative Guild which sought to organise consumers solely or specifically 'to achieve consumerist goals'.[2] Black's Consumers' League also pre-dated proposals with comparable political aims and campaign strategies which were directed primarily at working-class women, such as the formation of the National Women's Council by socialist and labour activist Margaretta Hicks – daughter of Black's close associate, the trade unionist Amie Hicks – and the publication of *The Consumer in Revolt* (1912) by workers' and women's rights activist Teresa Billington-Greig, which called on consumers and workers to unite their interests against unscrupulous profiteering that took advantage of them both.[3] Secondly, it consciously set out to bridge the perceived distance between workers and the middle-class consumers of the goods they produced by proposing a form of consumer activism designed to work alongside labour activism to achieve a common goal. This sets Black's campaign apart from earlier initiatives focused on ethical consumption such as the Sugar Boycotts which involved the mobilisation of wealthier consumers of a luxury product on behalf of enslaved people. Thirdly, it made a point of centring its arguments on the potential for positive influence linked to consumer power. This distanced Black's scheme from the narrative of consumer guilt that blamed thoughtless consumers looking for bargain prices for bringing down workers' wages. In contrast to the accusatory representations familiar from 'The Song of the Shirt' and 'The Haunted Lady', discussed in the introduction to this book, Black's proposals focused on a recognition of consumers' goodwill and offered a channel for these sentiments through achievable collective action. This final point is crucial to Black's strategy of appealing to consumers as potential activists.

When Black began to pursue organised consumer activism as a campaign strategy she already had an established public reputation built on two joint careers, as a writer of popular fiction and as a prominent activist with specific expertise on conditions of women's labour. At the time that she first proposed the Consumers' League Black was beginning consciously to combine these two strands of her work in the style of the many 'women of letters' who, throughout the nineteenth century, used periodical writing in particular to expound their moral, religious, political and social agendas. Barbara Caine, who coined the term, sees this tradition of 'women of letters' as ranging from Mary Wollstonecraft and Anna Wheeler via Harriet Martineau to Millicent Garrett Fawcett.[4] For Black, her experience of labour activism meant that she was able to participate in the growing public discourse around sweated labour and especially its disproportionate effect on women, whose gender and class position limited their access to fairer work opportunities. Over the course of an activist career spanning more than thirty years, Black would work with different organisations towards better representation and conditions for working women. Her methods included supporting the formation of women's trade unions, pursuing legislative improvements to working conditions and wages, and campaigning for women's suffrage. Many of these initiatives involved the mobilisation of potential activists across social classes in solidarity with and in support of working women. Her choice of different publishing platforms to communicate these campaign strategies reflected her deliberate targeting of readerships who were already familiar with her work as a writer as well as an expert in a field that was drawing increasing public concern.

The Consumers' League that Black presented to her broad readership rested on a simple argument: while workers combined to demand better pay and conditions, consumers could unite in paying fairer prices for goods and services and in patronising businesses that treated workers fairly. While this formula closely parallels the assumptions that underpin the narrative of consumer guilt, Black based her ideas on a sophisticated understanding of the economic problem her campaign was directed against. She articulated this analysis in her article 'The Ethics of Shopping' which was published in *Seed-Time*, the organ of the Fellowship of the New Life, in October 1890. The article followed a lecture on the subject that she had given to the fellowship in April of that year. Black was a member of the fellowship and its splinter group, the socialist Fabian Society that had been formed in 1884.[5] As such she was very familiar with *Seed-Time*'s readers' commitment to social, political and economic transformation, and the responsibility of individuals to work towards achieving this. In this context, she could acknowledge that

> [i]t is not the dictum [of fair payment], but the application, which is difficult, and the difficulty lies in our ignorance of what the real expenses of production are. The whole system of manufacture tends to become more complex, more specialised, more differentiated, and, at the same time, more wholesale.[6]

She hastened to point out, however, that the best solution to this was not to reject this new economic reality out of hand by seeking a return to idealised pre-industrial conditions of production. This course of action might be particularly tempting to some members of the fellowship who already aimed for a simple life that valued manual labour and spiritual pursuits over material interests. To show why this was not a viable alternative, Black explained:

> Division of labour, rightly understood, is nothing more or less than a bearing of one another's burdens, and the simplicity, to which I look, lies forward in a community where each shall do some one sort of thing for everybody, not backward, in an isolation where each did everything for himself [sic]. Our business is not to deplore the new system, but to harmonise and develope [sic] it. We need not aim at weaving, spinning, and dyeing for ourselves; our business is to see that those who do our spinning, weaving, and dyeing, shall be enabled to have a really human livelihood. How are we to do that under the present methods of industry? That is the problem which we really have to solve, and perhaps it would have been solved sooner if so many would-be reformers had distinguished the idea of division of labour, which is beautiful, humanising, and social, from the practical misapplications of it to purposes of mere personal aggrandisement, which are ignoble, oppressive, and anti-social. The modern industrial system needs to grow and enlarge; the modern commercial system needs to be abolished.[7]

While at times paternalistic towards 'those who do our spinning, weaving, and dyeing', this passage involves the reader in intellectual engagement with a pressing socio-economic question. Though Black acknowledges the matter to be a difficult one, she insists clearly that it will not be resolved by a retreat from contemporary economic realities, but rather argues that participation in existing systems is the only way of humanising them.

There is a strong echo in Black's words of John Ruskin's 'The Nature of Gothic' (1853), a text with which many members of the fellowship were likely to have been familiar. According to Ruskin, 'the great civilized invention of the division of labour' in fact divided not labour but workers, 'so that all the little piece of intelligence that is left in a man is not enough to make a pin, or a nail, but exhausts itself in making the point of a pin, or the head of a nail'.[8] The chosen examples of the pin and the nail are clear references to the opening chapter of *The Wealth of Nations* (1776), where Adam Smith explained the manufacturing processes behind precisely these items to show how the division of labour speeds up production.[9] While the high production levels that the division of labour made possible were beneficial in themselves, however, Ruskin argued that workers' dignity and humanity should not be sacrificed to achieve this. What was needed to resolve this issue, he stated, was a better understanding of

> what kinds of labour are good for men [*sic*], raising them, and making them happy; [. . .] a determined sacrifice of such convenience, or beauty, or cheapness as is to be got only by the degradation of the workman; and [. . .] equally determined demand for the products and results of healthy and ennobling labour.[10]

Black clearly sets out to continue to build on the observations and theories of Smith and Ruskin. Her key advance on Ruskin's analysis, besides the incorporation of women workers into a discourse he focuses exclusively on men, is her acceptance of what she calls the 'modern industrial system'. While Ruskin saw this kind of specialisation as a negative development in a modern economy that precluded dignity in work through its focus on repetitive and unoriginal production, Black pointed to its potential to benefit workers. In Black's view, the division of labour that was 'good' for both workers and consumers – who are presented as distinct categories in this article aimed at a society of middle-class

intellectuals – involved specialisation in a context of cooperation and just reward for labour. This efficient but humane system
would allow workers to produce at their best, thereby also giving
consumers access to good-quality products at fair prices. The consumers had a role in ensuring the success of this system: it required
them to see their interests as connected rather than opposed to
those of workers, and to collaborate to ensure that their buying
power supported fair wages and conditions. Black's line of reasoning here is not dissimilar to Karl Marx's grander theories: she both
evolves existing interpretations of socio-economic development
and identifies a form of social revolutionary potential in these historical and economic processes. This approach was likely to appeal
strongly to the socialist Fabian contingent of the fellowship.

Black's echo of Ruskin in addressing the Fellowship of the New
Life is one of many examples of how she adapted her campaign
arguments to her readership. Her long experience of producing popular fiction for a defined literary market had shaped her
interaction with readers as consumers of her writing and gave
her considerable expertise of writing to the demands and desires
of different readerships. Her proposals for a consumers' league
read as a very deliberate intervention by an accomplished woman
of letters in the growing body of popular writing responding to
the contemporary economic situation and its increasingly visible
excesses. Depending on her publishing platform, her campaign
texts engaged directly and tangentially with a variety of well-
known sources ranging from the intellectual, such as Marx and
Ruskin, to the popular and bang up to date, including Walter
Besant's social novel *Children of Gibeon* (1886). Tailoring the
context of her argument to her readership helped Black to appeal
directly to her readers and engage them in ways that were relevant
to their specific experience.

In connecting the experience and interest of consumers and
workers, Black used a strategy typical of the rhetoric of 'long-
distance solidarity' that Lawrence B. Glickman sees as common to
many consumer activist movements.[11] He describes how

[c]onsumer activists, in effect, proposed a new physics of time and
space, highlighting the real-time effects of consumption and suggesting
that in an increasingly global market economy, the moral impact of
one's actions was not determined by physical propinquity but by the
market-based effects of one's economic actions.[12]

In other words, the fact that goods might have been produced at a great distance from the consumer – whether in terms of geography or socio-economic experience – did not mean that consumers should feel morally or emotionally disconnected from workers. In order to make this point in her campaign texts, Black positioned herself in three different roles in relation to her readers. She was the trusted writer who brought this social question to her readers' knowledge, the labour activist who had observed the impact of sweating at first hand, and the concerned middle-class consumer who sought ways of imbuing her own purchasing power with activist impact and invited her readers to join her in this venture. To reinforce this idea, Black chose language that deliberately ranged her with the readers of her campaign texts. She consistently wrote from the perspective of a collective 'we' that implied that her readers shared her concerns regarding their consumer choices. Thus, by removing the sense of distance between herself and her reader, as well as between her reader as consumer and the workers whose conditions she described, she ensured that she would not be cast in the moralising role of earlier propagators of the narrative of consumer guilt. This would make it more likely that her readers, instead of taking a defensive attitude to an accusation of unwitting and even inevitable wrongdoing, would accept the information she provided and give consideration to the arguments and appeals she made. Her strategy suggested change to her readers in a gentle way that invited their own participation in their change of mind, anticipating the style of much persuasive consumer activist writing today. On the other hand, this approach may also be considered to reinforce divisions: acknowledging that the experience and interests of workers and consumers needed to be brought together hinged on the assumption that they belonged to separate social columns, when in fact, as organisations like the Co-operative Guild illustrate, workers were also consumers and many consumers were workers. In addition, by positioning herself as an intermediary between these two apparently distinct groups, Black put herself in a position of claiming to speak on behalf of workers. There is no indication in her proposals that she incorporated ways of feeding back her ideas and achievements to the workers whom the scheme was designed to benefit. In this way, the interests of her readers as consumers, both of her work and in a wider context, seem to transcend the aims of her original scheme, foreshadowing some of the more uncomfortable trade-offs she would go on to make in her campaigns to resist worker exploitation.

Women and work in Black's writing and activism

Women's experience of work and exploitation were central to Black's career, both as a writer of fiction and as a campaigner. This may easily be seen as a reflection of her own preoccupation with the opportunities open to her as a middle-class professional woman dependent on the proceeds of her own productive labour as a writer. During the early 1880s this preoccupation began to find practical expression in her growing involvement in the women's labour movement. Her literary production slackened at this time as she devoted her energies to her activist project instead. As well as being her first campaign text to promote consumer activism, in many ways 'Caveat Emptor' marks the start of Black's combination of her careers as a writer and activist, as she began to make use of her access to publishing platforms to expound her campaign strategies.

At the time of the publication of 'Caveat Emptor' in 1887, Black had a decade of experience of writing in diverse genres of popular fiction. She began publishing short stories in 1876 and her first novel, *A Sussex Idyl* [*sic*], appeared in 1877. Her prolific publications ranged from contemporary pastoral romance to historical fiction. While her professional identity placed her under economic pressure, it also gave her the freedom and independence to pursue her own activist aims. Writing popular fiction and journalism for broad readerships, she was conscious of her own relationship to her readers as consumers of her work which ensured that her success relied on her ability to create marketable products. On the other hand, while working within the structures of popular writing, her publications frequently managed to challenge preconceptions regarding genre and character roles, especially as they pertained to gender. Many of her works of fiction reflect forward-thinking ideas regarding the social position of women. Black's women characters act on their own initiative and seek practical alternatives to the confines of their prescribed roles. In this way she acknowledged the reality of the consumer market, but resisted the mindless consumption of her work, instead using this palatable format to suggest new ideas to her readers. Her writing regularly challenged the assumption and even ideal of women's ignorance of many aspects of practical life and economic and moral self-reliance, arguing: 'We do our best to blindfold our maidens, and then we make it an article of belief that our women are too helpless to walk without a guide.'[13] These opinions also clearly informed her involvement in the campaign for women's suffrage in the early twentieth century. Her understanding of gender always took into account the experience and needs of working women. For example, the plot of *A Sussex Idyl* revolves around middle-class characters learning from the young working-class woman protagonist, with the strong implication that her middle-class readers could learn from the experience and knowledge of working people too. She carried this approach forward from her fiction into her campaign writing with articles such as 'Something about Needlewomen' in *The Woman's World* (1888) and 'A Working Woman's Speech' in *The Nineteenth Century* (1889), and it is frequently visible in her attempts to enlighten consumer ignorance of working people's conditions.

Much of Black's adult life reflects her personal attempts to find the most productive attitude towards her own position within contemporary class and gender relations. Living independently in London from the late 1870s, Black and her sisters 'circulated in the various radical and literary clubs open to men and women alike that sprang up in the capital' including, as we have seen, the Fellowship of the New Life and the Fabian Society.[14] They were drawn to socialist politics and quickly became part of the city's anarchist and socialist networks including the international circle of political exiles around Black's close personal friend Eleanor Marx and, later, through Black's sister Constance Garnett, Russian-speaking exiles such as Ukrainian anarchist Sergei Stepniak. Ana Parejo Vadillo notes that Black became 'a well known and highly respected socialist' and goes on to show that the Black sisters went further than many of their contemporaries in the practical pursuit of their political aims, living their convictions through a 'daring household arrangement [. . .] dictated by their political attitudes'. She explains:

> Living by themselves and doing their own housework was first of all a rejection of bourgeois attitudes they so much criticised, in so far as they rejected the comfort of the middle classes. But it was also an attack on the division of classes, because they refused to have servants. And thirdly, and most importantly, it was a frontal attack on Victorian gender attitudes.[15]

Black and her sisters, then, tried to create for themselves in their independent and politicised urban household a version of the same ideals symbolised in her early fiction, such as *A Sussex Idyl*. Taking responsibility for their own lives through labour, they sought to imbue with meaning those household tasks that it was often possible to disregard, including for the middle-class socialists with whom they associated, because of the ubiquitous if invisible presence of servants in any household that could afford them at all. Ruth Livesey notes that Black's paid labour, her writing, 'offered [her] material freedom from sexual difference', but her own experience of work also counteracted assumptions of class difference, fostering her sense of shared experience with working women across class boundaries.[16] For the Black sisters, their household structure functioned as a practical incarnation of this identification with working women which Black repeatedly tried to convey to her middle-class readerships.

Through her political connections Black rapidly became involved in labour activism, focusing specifically on working women. Particularly in London, the effects of the Long Depression of the 1870s to the 1890s on Britain's labour economy resulted in increased competition for lower-skilled labour. This in turn facilitated casual work, payment at piecework rates, overwork and hazardous working conditions; and growing popular awareness of these practices also revealed their heightened impact on women. It was clear that very large numbers of women in different social positions worked for wages, out of choice as well as necessity, whether to supplement a family income or to support themselves and their own dependants. It was not generally recognised, however, that women had a claim to a living wage or to pay at equal rates to men, and women tended to be excluded by the longer-standing men's labour movement which still advocated for men to be paid a family wage. Supporting women's claim to higher pay, many men trade unionists felt, would serve to undercut men's wages. These arguments were generally supported by middle-class commentators promoting nuclear family structures in which women were assigned an exclusively domestic role. In *Difficult Subjects*, her analysis of representations of working women around the turn of the twentieth century, Kristina Huneault explains that

from a middle-class perspective there was an inherent incompatibility between the identities of 'woman' and 'worker'. For many working-class men, however, women and paid employment were understood to be only too compatible. Fears of job-loss and undercutting were constant factors in working men's relation to their female co-workers. Considered from this perspective it was not the identity of 'worker' but that of 'trade unionist' that often came to exclude women.[17]

The unofficial status of women's labour further enabled exploitative conditions. As Andrew August points out, 'women formed a convenient surplus of labour on which the sweated system of production depended'.[18] Women's work also suffered from a relative invisibility as it might be carried out in unregulated workshops or at home to allow them to combine it with domestic or caring responsibilities. In the precarious economic climate of the 1880s, demonstrations of unemployed men and crowds of men seeking casual work at London's docks were common sights and regular reporting on these issues provoked widespread social concern. In sharp contrast, the extent and conditions of women's labour were not widely known or acknowledged and it was largely through the efforts of social investigators such as Black that the realities of home-based sweated labour and exploitative conditions in factories, unregulated workshops, bars and shops reached a wider audience.

Much of Black's work was geared towards counteracting the levels of alienation between classes as well as genders that resulted in the levels of exploitation that women workers faced. The early women's trade union movement differed from the more established men's trade unions in the significant involvement of middle-class women such as Black. This was, in large part, a direct result of the specific conditions of exploitation to which women workers tended to be subject. Overwork, the prevalence of home-based work, and many women's domestic and caring responsibilities often hindered collective action: isolated workers had fewer opportunities to compare conditions with colleagues within and between workplaces, and long hours left less time to meet and plan. A notable exception to the invisibility of women workers was the high-profile Matchwomen's Strike of 1888; this was followed by a number of comparable strikes of women workers in urban factories. While several of these received extra publicity through the efforts of campaigning writers such as Black, Annie Besant and Eleanor Marx, they usually arose from workers' own organisation and initiatives. This type of union activity was more achievable in a factory setting than in small workshops or domestic workplaces. Factory workers tended to be younger and more independent – it was easier, for example, for a young single factory worker to share accommodation with other workers rather than live in a family home, and this would generally mean fewer caring responsibilities. At least as importantly, their shared workplace enabled them to meet, confer and plan.

Middle-class women, who were supposed to have more leisure time, often supported workers' initiatives by sharing some of the practical business of organisation for which workers might not have enough time or opportunity. With greater mobility and connections across classes, furthermore, they were able to promote the benefits of working women's organisation. Black became a leading member of the Women's Protective and Provident League (WPPL), a body founded in 1874 to support women's labour organisation. It had increasingly come to focus on London, where over half of its membership was based by 1886, the year Black became its secretary.[19] In the two years following her appointment, Livesey notes, Black 'researched the conditions of female labour and attempted to unionize women workers in various London trades in affiliation with the League'. Livesey goes on to explain, however, that

> [a]midst the increasing momentum of strike activity in the late 1880s, Black became frustrated at the reticence of the League's leadership in engaging with the wider labour movement. The renaming of the organization as the Women's Trade Union League [WTUL] in September 1888 seems to have only paid lip-service to such collaboration for Black and she resigned from her post [as secretary] in May 1889.[20]

With her close associate, the labour activist John Burns, Black then went on to found the rival Women's Trade Union Association (WTUA), an organisation that included both working- and middle-class women. Primarily under Black's leadership, the WTUA gave active support to the organisation of working women and the setting up of women's trade unions.[21]

In each of these capacities Black also generated publicity for working women who wanted to improve their pay and conditions. 'Caveat Emptor' was published when she was secretary of the WPPL, and from its appearance until the end of her writing career she would continue to use publishing platforms to expound and promote her activist aims, both independently and on behalf of the various bodies she represented and collaborated with. Her transition from the WPPL/WTUL to the WTUA in 1889 was reflected in a change in her activist publications to focus explicitly on the development of women's trade unions and strike activity. During this period her articles included accounts of women's strikes and the formation of trade unions such as 'A Working Woman's Speech', already mentioned, and 'The Chocolate Makers' Strike' in the *Fortnightly Review* (1890).

Over the course of the 1890s the WTUA grew disillusioned with the practical potential of women's trade unions and refocused again, this time on socio-economic investigations to provide evidence of the disadvantages faced by women in work. The WTUA Annual Report for 1892–93 stated:

> The organisation of workers who are paid actually below a reasonable living wage – as many women workers are – is only possible in times of unusual hopefulness, such as that which immediately followed the Dock Strike. Of course, meetings can be got up and members enrolled, but unless this attempt at organisation is very spontaneous, it may do more harm than good, and inspire in the long run rather a distrust of Trade Unionism than a faith in it.[22]

As a result, in 1894 the WTUA reinvented itself, this time under the new name of the Women's Industrial Council (WIC). Now a virtually exclusively middle-class body (with some notable exceptions such as trade union organiser Amie Hicks) putting its proposals for change to the political establishment, it focused on 'the investigation of the social and economic condition of women workers as a prerequisite to any reform efforts'.[23] Its investigative publications included volumes such as *Married Women's Work* (1915), edited and introduced by Black, which highlighted how many married working-class women engaged in work for wages for many different reasons. The WIC also published its own quarterly periodical, the *Women's Industrial News*, which reported on investigations and promoted ideas and campaigns that the organisation endorsed, such as the 'Sweated Industries Exhibition' that forms the central topic of Chapter 3 of this work.

The relative timings of Black's publications show that she was regularly at the forefront of these changes in campaign direction and organisational strategy. She certainly had a leading role in conveying them to a broad reading public of potential supporters. With her professional access to a range of publishing platforms, she was uniquely well-placed to take on this promotional work, transferring the skills of her writing career to appeal to her readership on behalf of the working women she sought to represent. The texts considered in this chapter show how she carried her plan for a consumers' league forward from the WPPL/WTUL into the WTUA, but she abandoned it around the time of the WTUA's development into the WIC. The change in her perception of consumer activism, further explored in Chapter 3, reflects the priorities of the WIC as an investigative organisation putting pressure on governments and pursuing legislative change. Nevertheless she continued to use the promotional strategies that originated with 'Caveat Emptor' across these different campaigns.

Clementina Black, 'Caveat Emptor', *Longman's Magazine*, 1887

'Caveat Emptor' is reflective in many ways of the experimental nature of this first venture on Black's part to combine her literary and activist careers. The family monthly *Longman's Magazine* was in no way an activist platform: in style and scope it was far removed from the numerous political periodicals circulating during the period, from *The Link* published by Fabian and freethinker Annie Besant to *Justice*, the organ of the Social Democratic Federation. At 6d *Longman's* was aimed at a relatively wide readership but, although its price was only half that of well-known shilling monthlies such as *Temple Bar*, it was still high enough to make it primarily available to a middle-class readership.[24] While it had a large social reach, therefore, the price suggests that its readers were more likely to see themselves as consumers than productive workers. On the other hand, while it 'was dedicated to a non-partisan political stance and studiously avoided controversy', even steering clear of realistic fiction, the publication did show an interest in social problems as, for example, it sponsored food provision for struggling dockworkers.[25] As Black sought to achieve broad support for a proposal intended to exist in tandem with her trade union work, the scope and readership of *Longman's* probably seemed more suitable to the purpose than a radical political publication with a specified audience. The fact that the magazine was issued by a literary publisher, furthermore, may well have made it easily approachable for Black on the basis of her own literary reputation.

In view of Black's role and aims as a public-facing campaigner with extensive experience of the literary market, it is unsurprising that 'Caveat Emptor' reflects a sophisticated publicity strategy, even if its proposal for a consumers' league itself is to a degree underdeveloped. The article shows an early but very conscious connection of Black's two careers in its concerted effort to promote understanding and sympathy between workers and middle-class consumers to counteract the detachment of consumers from the provenance of the goods and services they bought. In doing so, Black sought to create a common cause for workers, labour organisation and consumers.

The well-known Latin phrase 'caveat emptor' translates as 'let the buyer beware'. It encourages the buyer to examine goods prior to purchase to avoid the risk of later disappointment. Black, however, redefined the phrase, in a sense that referred clearly to the narrative of consumer guilt that held the buyer paying a low price for a product directly responsible for the wages paid to the worker who produced it. Black was asking the buyer to beware, not of disappointment with the product, but of the potential harmful consequences attached to their act of purchase. Rather than the quality of the product, she called on consumers to examine the conditions under which it was produced, and to consider how realistic was the price for which it was being offered in view of the materials and particularly the labour likely to be required for its production. Placing her consumer-readers on their guard regarding these matters relied on explaining to them some of the workings of the market economy and its excesses with which her own research and trade union work had familiarised her.

Black's argument rested on the involvement of the consumer as a participant in market processes, showing their connection to the producers of the goods they bought. Recognising the fact that the structure of the market tended to make the worker less and less visible to the consumer was an important part of this project. Strategies for visualising the hidden iniquities of sweated work had developed alongside the emergence of the narrative of consumer guilt, as Beth Harris shows with reference to the figure of the sweated needlewoman. She explains that reformers reacted against the appeal of cheap and attractive garments as it obscured the conditions under which they were produced. As she states:

> The job of the reformer, it was claimed, was [...] to uncover, especially for the female consumer, what could not be seen beneath the gilded façade of the show shop. [...] if they [consumers] could see through the gilding of the show-shop then the life of the seamstress would be improved.[26]

In other words, consumer goods were deliberately presented by sellers in a way that obscured production processes to the consumer who was dazzled by the shopping experience and, quite probably, by the low prices at which the goods were offered. This structure created degrees of separation between worker, seller and consumer which cast them in a mutually exploitative relationship: while the seller tried to maximise their profit by minimising labour costs and raising retail prices, the consumer sought out low-cost goods, all of which contributed to reductions in workers' wages. Exploited workers, furthermore, would not be able to break this cycle for themselves as they were reliant on work for survival. Black, however, distanced herself from this way of framing the argument; her article suggested that her readers were likely already to have internalised these ideas based on the awareness-raising campaigns of the previous decades. Instead, she focused on a shared sense of compassion, implying that consumers were naturally concerned about the realities they saw and would like to help. Merely instilling feelings of guilt in consumers would not in itself help workers, however; so 'Caveat Emptor' presented itself as a response to the need for a practical direction to unite consumers' compassionate impulses in order to contribute in a tangible way to the improvement of workers' conditions.

As she would go on to do again in 'The Ethics of Shopping' three years later, Black acknowledged that the continual emphasis on the idea of consumer guilt might cause consumers to feel a temptation to abandon the increasingly complicated market and seek instead to conduct transactions solely on a local and personal scale. This solution was intended

> to eliminate the middleman and deal with the worker direct; to get our carpentering done by a man who works for himself, our clothes made

by a sewing-woman whom we pay ourselves, and then fixing in our own mind a standard of cost according to which these people could live comfortably by working not more than eight hours a day, pay them at that rate without regard to the market price.[27]

This resolution, however, could only be abandoned as impractical. As Black went on, 'we cannot always, in our complicated ways of life, deal at first hand. Some things can only be got at shops, and most things are (to own the truth) got there better.'[28] If virtually all consumers were thus obliged to make some purchases in a wider economic system, she asked her readers to acknowledge that this meant that 'there are three parties to most trading transactions – namely, the worker, the employer, and the consumer – and [. . .] we who are consumers do in most instances help to make work bad and workers underpaid'.[29] Her phrase 'we who are consumers' deliberately ranged her with her readers, diverting the emphasis away from an accusatory tone to the idea that her article addressed a shared concern. The influence of the consumer in the trading transaction, she explained, derived from 'the inexorable economic law about cheap buying' or 'the inevitable consequences if we buy in the cheapest market', namely:

Where buyers give the lowest price they can, employers will try to produce at the lowest price they can, and the wages of the worker will tend to the lowest point at which it is possible for him [sic] to live.[30]

This representation of the relationship between prices and wages certainly does not tell the whole story of the different interests involved in market production, but it is effective here because it represents the consumer as holding a position of economic power. Using precisely the same argument as that underpinning the notion of consumer guilt, Black repositioned the moral influence in this equation. She argued that, while the worker was subject to the decisions of the consumer as well as the employer and seller, who in turn responded to the market, the consumer had the choice and the means to reject their implied guilt and instead use their influence for good. She contrasted the negative tendency of prices and wages as an inevitable consequence of consumer passivity and worker disempowerment with the possibility of a positive tendency as the result of active consumer involvement through responsible and ethical consumption. The consumers' league she went on to describe provided a way for consumers to support both their own and workers' empowerment through an activist project to change the market status quo.

As she developed her ideas in 'Caveat Emptor', Black's emphasis was on the practical application of the scheme, designating roles for consumers, trade unions and workers. By way of example, she pointed to one initiative by the Knights of Labor, a large and prominent labour federation in the United States. The organisation used their organ, *John Swinton's Paper*, to publish a black-list of 'employers who paid badly, had unsanitary workshops, or oppressed their employees'. Black noted that this model would have to be adapted for use in Britain, as 'proceedings for libel would probably follow' if the practice of blacklisting were copied; her proposed adjustment was a system of whitelisting, providing details of good employers and encouraging consumers to shop at these firms.[31] This subtle change, put down to national differences and practical circumstance, distanced her proposal from the radical and combative approach that readers might associate with the Knights of Labor. Instead, like her refiguring of the consumer guilt equation, it fostered the idea of a common cause between workers and consumers through its focus on positive action and consumers' ability to effect change for good rather than to fight iniquity.

Black proceeded to give examples of whitelists of shirtmakers, upholsterers, dressmakers and milliners. The lists had been collated by the WPPL based on information provided by trade union representatives. Instead of exposing poor working conditions, the whitelists worked as advertisements for ethically run workshops, as well as for the investigative methods of the WPPL. This proposal for positive cooperation between unions, employers and consumers was designed to negate any sense that the interests of each of these groups were opposed to one another. Emphasising the possibility of mutual respect and collapsing class barriers, Black stated:

> The employer after all is not one of a race of malevolent man-eating ogres; he [sic] is one of ourselves; he would rather, if he were not to lose by it, make his employees happy than miserable. But a single employer cannot permanently raise the rate of wages any more than the single consumer can.[32]

As 'The Ethics of Shopping' echoed Ruskin, Black's language here around the image of employers as 'man-eating ogres' may be read as engaging with that of Karl Marx and Friedrich Engels in their representation in *The Manifesto of the Communist Party* (1848) of the bourgeoisie as a vampiric force indiscriminately destructive of people and social structures in the interest of free trade.[33] It is likely, however, that it was intended in this case, like her response to the Knights of Labor's blacklists, to remove the threatening context of class struggle by substituting a narrative of cross-class connection. Making a point of giving everyone their due, Black indicated that the harm which different participants in transactions did to one another was involuntary, but that it was possible for individuals to apply their goodwill and work together towards the amelioration of the position of each.

Black's closing paragraph, however, firmly directed responsibility back to the consumer, as she indicated that her proposal required the broad support of consumers to develop into a successful scheme. She wrote:

> With more time and wider means of inquiry, these [white]lists might doubtless be much increased. To keep them as nearly as possible complete and to see that they were republished at frequent intervals would be one part of the business of a Consumers' League [. . .] But can there and shall there be a Consumers' League? That is a question to be considered by the consumers themselves, that is to say by all of us.[34]

Building on the implication that an enlightened consumer would wish to take action to improve working conditions, this conclusion laid down a challenge to the reader to act on the information in the article. The phrase 'all of us' seems, furthermore, to indicate a recognition of the unifying force of the consumer identity as a reference to anyone who shops, perhaps to emphasise that readers did not need to be unusually wealthy to participate in her scheme; on the other hand, it also has the potential to exclude workers and people in poverty who could not afford to spend more on ethical goods. 'All of us' seems, in this case, to indicate the broad middle-class readership of *Longman's*, who are equated by implication in Black's writing with concerned consumers ready to act on behalf of the working class.

'Caveat Emptor' highlighted the connections between the local and the international in the evolving discourse around consumer activism. Black's reference to the Knights of Labor points to an international exchange of strategies of representation, based on shared economic problems. The proposed solution, however, was thoroughly local: all of the firms that appeared on Black's whitelists were based in London, where the WPPL was able to carry out its own research. Her closing paragraph did suggest that consumers could expand the project independently by adding to the existing whitelists, but this cast the consumer in a far more advanced role than merely that of an ethical shopper, as it required the consumers' league itself to take on the investigative work previously done by the WPPL.

Black's initial proposal in 'Caveat Emptor', therefore, was simply not extensive enough to gain large-scale influence by itself. This was admittedly part of its appeal for support: it served primarily to lead by example, showing consumers how their concern and goodwill could be used for a practical purpose. But the form of consumer activism that it presented also had unacknowledged limitations. For example, it failed to account for the complexity of systems of production that outsourced many elements of the production process, a reality against which the investigative power of the WPPL/WTUL, WTUA or a future consumers' league would struggle to guard. The fragmentation of production processes with a view to increasing economic efficiency increased opportunities for the undercutting of prices and wages by underpaid and exploited workers at the stages in the production process that took place before the materials reached the WPPL-approved workshop, or after the final products left it. In terms of its intention to publicise a campaign and lead by example, however, 'Caveat Emptor' was not unsuccessful: other activists internationally took up the ideas of consumer organisation and of the whitelisting of ethical businesses. Many adapted it for their own purposes, including the Consumers' League of New York and the National Consumers' League in the USA, which are the subject of the next chapter.

By focusing on the positive potential of consumer power, 'Caveat Emptor' discovered a novel approach to the narrative of consumer guilt that was likely to have become highly familiar and possibly frustrating and tiresome to its readers. The article was clearly carefully directed to its readership and strongly suggested that it spoke to a specific and widely shared social concern. It responded to this by offering a practical solution and the suggestion that this was a start to a movement that might be independently taken up and developed by different social groups and organisations. Black's argument itself was in many ways presented for its readers' consumption: it flattered the reader by appealing to their understanding and emphasising their potential to effect practical changes for the better. It was already evident from the proposal, however, that it would need to be considerably scaled up to be effective, and that this was likely to become largely the responsibility of the Consumers' League and its membership. This implication revealed the limitations of the idea that consumers need only adjust their shopping habits to make a real difference – an idea with which Black continued to engage directly in her subsequent campaign texts.

Clementina Black, 'The Morality of Buying in the Cheapest Market', *The Woman's World*, 1890

Longman's Magazine offered Black an extensive and non-politicised audience for her consumer activist campaign and 'Caveat Emptor' set out a scheme intended to be widely expanded. In 1890, 'The Ethics of Shopping' showed no sign that Black intended to scale down her proposal: the examples she gave still touched on a wide range of different trades. Her publication in *Seed-Time* following her speech to the fellowship also showed that she did not shy away from engaging a politicised audience with the campaign. It may be surprising, therefore, that another article from the same year telescopes back to a much narrower focus in its advocacy of consumer activism. Indeed, 'The Morality of Buying in the Cheapest Market' reverts to the consumers at the heart of the original narrative of consumer guilt that she had deliberately inverted in 'Caveat Emptor', namely the middle-class women buying clothing at bargain prices. These articles again show a strong sense of their readership as they find effective ways of exercising moral pressure but, unlike many other campaign texts aimed at this group of consumers, they also reflect a detailed understanding of the economic quandaries faced by concerned consumers.

'The Morality' was one of two articles on the subject of low prices and wages in the garment trade that Black published in *The Woman's World*. While this illustrated miscellany, founded in 1886, was aimed at middle- and upper-class women, it had rapidly evolved from *The Lady's World: A Magazine of Fashion and Society* to its more democratic moniker under Oscar Wilde's editorship in 1887. Writing to Thomas Wemyss Reid, the general manager at Cassell, which published the periodical, Wilde had suggested that it ought to 'deal not merely with what women wear, but with what they think and what they feel'.[35] As Stephanie Green puts it, the periodical became the site of 'an exchange of ideas about femininity, dress, aesthetics, literature and society' which 'addressed an élite but expanding readership of middle and upper class educated women with literary and social credentials'.[36] Black's pieces thus brought together the dual interests assumed in its readership: the fashion that adorned *The Lady's World* and the social concern of the periodical's new incarnation.[37] The period of Wilde's editorship had ended by 1890, but it is clear that Black tapped into the direction he had given to the magazine and the readership he had attracted with the two articles she published in 1888 and 1890, 'Something about Needlewomen' and 'The Morality of Buying in the Cheapest Market'.

Both pieces spoke to the long-standing idea of the needlewoman as the victim of women's attraction to new clothing and rapidly changing fashions as well as the expansion of cheap garment production to meet increasing disposable incomes in the growing middle class. As the making of women's clothing was primarily associated with women workers, women consumers were accused of betraying working women, who were often cast as their poor sisters, by fostering their exploitative working conditions to provide for their own materialistic desires. No comparable parallels were drawn between tailors and the production of men's clothing despite the fact that men also worked in the sweated garment trade; indeed, 'The Song of the Shirt' goes no further than addressing the men who buy clothing as presents for their 'sisters dear', 'mothers and wives'.[38]

While examples such as the Women's Co-operative Guild show that women across social classes were repeatedly told that their principal socio-economic power lay in their consumer choices, these types of accusations of consumer guilt were specifically aimed at middle-class women. As a result, as US social and political historian Landon R. Y. Storrs states in his history of the National Consumers' League, proactive consumer activism 'offered moral regeneration and economic empowerment to the non-wage-earning woman, whom social critics [. . .] were condemning as an economic parasite and fueler of "conspicuous consumption"'.[39] The term 'conspicuous consumption' is a reference to the work of the influential US economist Thorstein Veblen, who, in his 1899 work *The Theory of the Leisure Class*, would describe 'conspicuous leisure' and 'conspicuous consumption' as markers of status. He discussed how, in his contemporary society, social pressure was exerted on women belonging to more affluent social classes to participate in these processes. He states:

> By virtue of its descent from a patriarchal past, our social system makes it the woman's function in an especial degree to put in evidence her household's ability to pay. According to the modern civilized scheme of life, the good name of the household to which she belongs should be the special care of the woman; and the system of honorific expenditure and conspicuous leisure by which this good name is chiefly sustained is therefore the woman's sphere.[40]

This analysis may go some way towards explaining the trend towards conspicuous consumption which went on to form a basis for the narrative of consumer guilt. It is worth bearing in mind too, however, that part of the appeal of consumer activism for these women was that it allowed them to resist consumer guilt without challenging their class identity. Consumer activists generally did not ask them to change their lifestyle, only to reconsider their consumer choices.

Black's experience in the WPPL/WTUL and even in the WTUA proved that non-wage-earning middle-class women could be helpful to working women's causes, as both organisations were supported by middle-class women's greater access to money, networks and leisure time. She will therefore have been well aware of the benefit of harnessing the goodwill of middle-class women consumers to support her own larger campaign in every way possible. The apparently relatively undemanding nature of consumer activism could work as a way of drawing women into activism who might not otherwise have been inclined to engage with it. Invoking the narrative of consumer guilt and offering a positive alternative would be a helpful spur in such cases. Her articles in *The Woman's World* thus fulfilled a similar function to her fiction by instilling the idea of social change into her readers' thinking while allowing them to feel that they were participants in their own change of mind. Just as her fiction created settings in which women's talents and abilities were recognised, Black's campaign texts in *The Woman's World* sought to show how women could put their abilities to practical use to produce social change.

While 'Something about Needlewomen' and 'The Morality of Buying in the Cheapest Market' are centred on the identity assigned to the periodical's readership as consumers and particularly as consumers of fashion, they used arguments based on a recognition of the abilities and personal experience of middle-class women readers. With reference to this experience Black drew parallels between the lives of women from different social classes in order to make the socio-economic reality of working women's lives intelligible to her readers. Based on the information she conveyed, she stated that

> [i]t remains for those who read to consider – first, whether this state of things is satisfactory; secondly, whether it is inevitable; thirdly, whether it is or is not the duty of every woman who has leisure and education to try and find a remedy.[41]

Utilising a method typical of her arguments in *The Woman's World*, Black here made a point of acknowledging the woman consumer-reader's understanding and used this to conclude that the informed consumer was able to take responsibility for their consumer choices. As in 'Caveat Emptor' and 'The Ethics of Shopping', an implicit sense of guilt is recognised only as it relates to readers' ability to confront it if they chose to.

The first of her two articles, 'Something about Needlewomen', was not explicitly a consumer activist campaign text. Its stated aim was primarily to convey the kind of information about the reality of women's working conditions in the trade in ready-made garments that Black had encountered through her work with the WPPL/WTUL. The overall tone of the article places it in the longer tradition identified by Harris of reformers helping consumers to see beyond the 'gilded façade of the show shop'. Like 'Caveat Emptor', the text suggested that it was understood that consumers' interest and concern was already extant but thwarted by the obscuring influence of market processes. Black reinforced this implication by noting the popularity of other contemporary representations of sweated needlework, such as Walter Besant's portrayal of the seamstress Melenda in *Children of Gibeon*, originally serialised in *Longman's Magazine* in 1886. She wrote: 'Mr. Besant's was most emphatically a song in season. Melenda was precisely the sort of person about whom a great many of us had been wanting to learn something.'[42] This reflects another deliberate sleight of hand on Black's part to pre-empt any resentment on the part of her reader in response to an accusation of consumer guilt. By ignoring the fact that Besant's Melenda had joined a well-established cast of other literary and visual representations of sweated needle-women presented in sources from G. W. M. Reynolds to Elizabeth Gaskell, she was able to remove the implication of guilt linked to these previous representations by framing her article as a response to the interest and concern generated by the fictional Melenda. She then proceeded to draw on her knowledge as a social inves-tigator and her reputation as an activist to offer factual informa-tion to help readers contextualise the fiction they encountered. Understanding the reality behind the fiction would allow readers to make more informed decisions regarding the impact of their consumer choices.

In order to convey a sense of this reality, Black proceeded to give what she states is a real account of the career of a needleworker that she knew. Relayed largely in the working woman's own words, the account detailed the hours and wages she had been used to in her working life since 1852 (inciden-tally, the year in which Ernest Jones had published his nar-rative of an exploited seamstress in *Woman's Wrongs*). The worker's account is marked by a self-confidence that allowed her to resist the worst conditions and wages, moving between employers and asking for promotions; but it becomes clear that in spite of her skill and her ability to stand up for herself she was still forced to accept low pay and had no prospect of retir-ing from work at the time of her conversation with Black, some thirty-five years later. At the end of this woman's story Black asked her readers:

> And what is the prize [of such a working life]? Twenty shillings a week at the highest for hard work every day and all day long. She does not complain, nor do those like her; but is it so well for women whose own lives are easy to be satisfied to have it thus?[43]

In other words, the concern readers might feel over Melenda was all to the good, but awareness of the conditions of the fictional character's real-life counterparts ought to spur readers of *The Woman's World* to examine the injustice of their relative posi-tions and proceed to take real-life action. Black's fairly transpar-ent pretence that reading about Melenda might have been the first prompt for concern regarding their consumer habits in relation to the exploitation of needleworkers played on her consumer-reader's conscience in two ways. On the one hand, it excused the reader for a previous lack of activism: how could they have responded to a situation of which they were unaware? On the other hand, accepting this pretence only left one possible conclusion, namely that the consumer, once enlightened, had a duty to participate in projects to ameliorate the conditions about which they had now learnt.

The tactic of 'Something about Needlewomen' was still primarily focused on explaining the nature and impact of exploitation to women consumers, thus supplying the consumer-reader with information in response to their existing concern. 'The Morality of Buying in the Cheapest Market' used a different strategy: it acknowledged and appealed to the common knowledge of needlework shared by most women across classes during the period. Black suggested that she was helping consumers to understand the case by encouraging them to apply their own knowledge and understanding to cases where garments were sold for surprisingly low prices. This was another string to her bow of subverting accepted narratives of middle-class women's consumer guilt by empowering the woman as purchaser. In this case, she sought to counteract the class-based alienation between consumer and worker through a gendered identification based on shared knowledge and experience, a strategy that harks back to other portrayals of capable working women in her fiction and journalism.

In contrast to her writerly trick in 'Something about Needlewomen', however, in 'The Morality' the assumption of existing consumer concern with which Black opens uses language surprisingly close to the original narrative of consumer guilt. The opening line reads: 'It is difficult for a woman with any conscience at all not to be overcome with occasional qualms when she goes forth on a morning's shopping and observes the prices at which made-up clothing may be bought.'[44] She does not accuse her readers outright of buying these cheap garments, but there is a strong implication that many probably do, simply because of their ready availability. The price itself, however, is enough, Black suggests, to prick the consumer conscience; and this reaction is the direct result of women's shared knowledge of garment production. She states:

We all know, roughly, the amount of time and labour involved in making this or that undergarment, by hand or by machine [. . .], and we know, in the same approximate way, the cost of [. . .] whatever the material may be. The simplest possible calculation shows us that most of the women who make these clothes cannot possibly live in health and comfort upon what they earn by this work.[45]

Acknowledgement of this issue leads Black to discourse on the nature of consumers' ignorance of working conditions, in spite of the fact that they are in principle far from ignorant of the production processes involved. In a marketing system where only the end product and its selling price are available to the consumer, it takes effort to try to understand how the products ended up in the shop. Black adds that the same goes not just for garments, but for a variety of other products of sweated trades, such as the boxes which are included in the purchase of matches, pills and shoes. Returning to the idea of the conscientious consumer, she asks rhetorically:

Is there any woman who reads these lines who would not gladly pay a penny for every box of matches, and some small price for the cardboard [shoe] box, if thus she could make it possible for these other women [box makers] to lead more human lives? It is not that we wish to cause suffering, but we do not know how to prevent it.[46]

This ignorance, Black acknowledges, is not easy for an individual to dispel. Again, as in 'Caveat Emptor' and 'The Ethics of Shopping', she runs through the potential action an individual might undertake to reduce the harmful impact of their consumption by trying to cut out any profit-making intermediaries from their transaction. She mimics the probable thought process of the concerned consumer as follows:

Suppose that we do pay a larger price, how can we be sure that the extra money will go into the pocket of the woman who actually does the work? And while we are not sure, is it worth while to pay the longer price merely to increase the profit of the retail shop at which we buy? [. . .] To escape [this problem], we perhaps make up our minds to have our work done as far as possible at first hand. We give out our sewing to some woman whom we employ direct. Then we find – naturally enough – that that woman is not skilled at all sorts of work [. . .]; and we begin to ask ourselves on the other side whether, after all, it is the proper thing to give our high pay for work which is not really good of its kind.[47]

She goes on to add that it would be impossible to carry this plan through consistently, tracing back the provenance of all consumer goods, from the materials used to make the garments to the ingredients used in the consumer's food. 'And so', Black concludes, 'we go back to the shops, and salve our consciences by subscribing to various charities, nearly all of which are, in fact, a rate in aid of wages, and which help, not to raise, but to depress, the low prices already paid to labour.'[48]

Black's use of 'we' and 'us' here neatly sets up her argument for collective action. She notes that workers had combined into unions to protect wages and employers into syndicates to keep up prices – so, she asks, why should consumers not combine to ensure the money they pay for the things they buy goes into fair wages for the workers who make them?[49] As in 'Caveat Emptor', she points to trade union lists of fair employers as a basis for informed ethical consumption, sharing her own knowledge and information as a concerned consumer as well as an informed activist and appealing to her readers' understanding.

In this way, Black's articles for *The Woman's World* offered women consumers a new way of seeing themselves that was not determined by the shaming strategy of the narrative of consumer guilt but rather by references to their own reason, understanding, goodwill and socio-economic experience. Instead of representing consumer guilt as practically inevitable, she put her readers in possession of the facts of the social and economic context of exploitation and its workings within market processes. This representative strategy also offered women consumers a new way of thinking about the workers who produced the goods they bought. It counteracted a class-based sense of separation and alienation by encouraging women consumers to identify with women workers through their shared experience of gendered work including needlework and household management. Other gendered issues also came into play here, including the lack of remunerative work opportunities available to women and many women's caring responsibilities for dependants. It is worth noting that between the appearance of 'Something about Needlewomen' in 1888 and 'The Morality' in 1890 Black's organisational allegiance transitioned from the

WPPL/WTUL to the WTUA, gaining a more explicit focus on women's trade union organisation. This may be one reason for the greater emphasis on socio-economic conditions and cross-class experiences of work that characterises 'The Morality'. The WTUA mobilised middle-class women to support the organisation of working women, providing an increased motivation for Black to encourage women consumers to identify with women workers.

While Black's explanations of labour exploitation worked to show, furthermore, that a system that facilitated sweating must necessarily victimise workers and women in particular, her matter-of-fact exposition of the mechanisms of exploitation also removed the pervasive sense of victimhood that characterised sweated women workers in previous narratives. Black's portrayals of women workers, based on her own encounters with women subject to labour exploitation, did not rely on the emotive evocation of pathos, but did highlight that they were unlikely to have chosen to work under these conditions. This way of stating the case removed all sense of inevitability from exploitative practices and transactions. If it was acknowledged that workers were not resigned to their exploitation, nor consumers to the fact that their shopping habits must contribute to these conditions, this was an unarguable incentive for consumers to unite in activism to counteract these negative socio-economic tendencies.

'Caveat Emptor' had ambitiously attempted to draw a wide range of consumers into a trial for a consumers' league working to improve a number of different industries. Black's articles in *The Woman's World* had greater specificity of readership and purpose. The underlying assumptions were the same, however: consumers were concerned about the impact of their consumption and Black offered them information to help them understand the situation and proposed a practical solution to which they could begin to subscribe relatively easily. As her articles in *The Woman's World* show particularly clearly, however, the sophisticated strategies she used to approach her consumer-readers sometimes relied on deliberate concealment and simplification of the socio-economic context of which she was herself strongly aware. While suggesting that she was putting her readers in possession of the facts, therefore, it was evident that this only pertained to the facts she felt it necessary for them to know. Sometimes the reader was given the opportunity to acquiesce to these sleights of hand to alleviate their own sense of guilt, as with the example of Melenda; but on other occasions Black deliberately simplified her proposals to divert attention away from the possible limitations of her scheme. Certainly her interactions with her readers were consistently designed to encourage a level of activist participation that would allow the consumers' league to become an effective cog in her activist ambitions, which were conceived on a much larger scale.

Conclusions: Exchanging strategies

In these examples of Black's consumer activist campaign articles, there is no sense that the distance between worker and consumer that she works to bridge is a physical one – rather, it appears as a socio-economic construction, the result of the market processes that hid the worker and their work from the environment of the consumer. This is underpinned by Black's accounts of her own interviews with working women and the role played by organised workers in gathering and verifying the information she lays before her readers. In 'Caveat Emptor' she presented lists of London-based businesses compiled by the WPPL whose membership was so strongly concentrated in the capital. But it soon became clear that even this approach was not local enough: in 'The Morality' Black noted that she had received complaints from women who were eager to patronise ethically run shops but who did not shop in the upmarket West End, where most of the firms on the list were located, but nearer their homes in less affluent neighbourhoods in Clapham, Islington or Kensington.[50]

If consumers already found their influence curtailed by these highly localised issues, it is unsurprising that Black's articles do not touch on the fact that the 'commercial system' she rejected in 'The Ethics of Shopping' was by this time operating in a global market. Initiatives for consumer activism throughout the later nineteenth and early twentieth centuries, from the cooperative movement to the consumers' leagues, were strongly local in their aims, seeking to enlighten potential activists about issues close to their own home in order to persuade them that they could exert influence over these matters – and it was significantly easier to make consumers feel that they could make a difference in their own neighbourhoods and communities than internationally. As the case studies in this volume show, however, the activists who initiated these campaigns were generally extremely well aware of the international context of their campaigns. They recognised the similarities between the economic situations and attendant social problems in their different countries and shared one another's campaign strategies. Black participated in these mutual international exchanges as she both adopted and adapted campaign ideas from abroad and saw her own work presented as an example of successful activist practice in other countries. While 'Caveat Emptor' was initially only able to formulate practical action based on the situation in London, the proposal drew on an idea developed by the US Knights of Labor. Black used this fact to strengthen her argument: her venture was viable because it had been trialled successfully abroad in a country with a comparable economy. Her heightened awareness of the global nature of the economic systems in which the UK participated would go on to influence her eventual move away from the Consumers' League, however, as she acknowledged the difficulties of adequately investigating, let alone influencing, conditions of labour and production abroad.

Preserving a localised feel to consumer activism campaigns in order to persuade consumers of their activist influence may be considered as another sleight of hand on the part of campaigners. As it became clearer that a global market involved complex processes of production and distribution, the role of consumer activists actually became more important. As Black's articles illustrated, it became more difficult for consumers to buy locally as production and commercial processes were scaled up. International markets also made it harder for consumers to discover for themselves the provenance of commodities, increasing the need for consumer organisation to acquire information and take effective action. The parallels between this conundrum and present-day consumer activism are clear, as the growing awareness of sweatshops and exploitation in the 1990s and 2000s which led to ethical clothing campaigns and publicity around fair trade could not fully bridge the distance between consumers in the global north and the places where much of this exploitative labour was concentrated. Even when accounts of working conditions were successfully conveyed to consumers, it proved difficult to design effective action that these consumers could and would undertake to make a material difference to the workers concerned.

Cognisant of these realities around the turn of the twentieth century, consumer activists across borders began to share the results of their investigations, to draw parallels between conditions in different countries, and to adopt campaign strategies and solutions that had proved successful elsewhere. Black's reference to the Knights of Labor was one of the first of regular mentions in her publications of the work of international investigators and activists. The next chapter will more fully reveal the links and mutual influences between Black's consumer activist initiatives and the consumers' league movement that developed in the United States simultaneously with her proposals. In Black's 1907 text *Sweated Industry and the Minimum Wage*, which is examined in detail in Chapter 3, she compared Britain to Germany and the United States and included data gathered in Australia in order to illustrate the similarities in wages and conditions in these different countries.[51] She also referenced foreign researchers into sweated work, such as 'acute French observer' Albert Aftalion and his book *Le Développement de la fabrique et le travail à domicile dans les industries de l'habillement* [The development of the factory and home work in the garment industries] (1906).[52] Her argument for a minimum wage drew on the example of the Trade Boards already regulating wages in some industries in Australia, and on groundwork laid by other 'careful enquirers' including 'Father Ryan, Professor of ethics and economics in the St Paul Seminary, Minnesota' in his book *A Living Wage: Its Ethical and Economic Aspect* (1906).[53]

Makers of our Clothes, the 1909 investigative text Black co-authored with reformer and philanthropist Adele Meyer, included an appendix entitled 'Home-workers in Germany' that compared their own investigative strategy with that used by a researcher from Breslau (present-day Wrocław in Poland). This researcher had deliberately sought contact with the WIC in London in order to share details of their working methods and the results of their investigations. In presenting the data, Black and Meyer pointed out that '[t]he fact that the women visited belong to an organisation has made it possible to obtain very full details – much fuller than is possible when unorganised women are visited by strangers', as was often the case in the WIC's investigations.[54] This suggested that they saw the strategy used in Wrocław as a successful example that could be used to improve their own practices of organisation and enquiry. Black's interest in international activist strategies and victories was also carried forward into the work of the WIC. Representatives of the WIC, as well as its organ the *Women's Industrial News*, kept a close eye on campaign developments abroad and frequently lent authority to their proposed schemes by referring to the success of comparable initiatives in other countries.

These mutual exchanges of information show that researchers and activists felt that knowledge of conditions abroad would help them to understand the situation in their own country, and that the example of international campaign strategies allowed them to improve their own. In this sense, they bridged geographical as well as emotional distance; they identified social problems that were shared across borders; and by embracing successful strategies implemented in other countries to combat these problems they sought to show both other activists and policy makers in their own country that solutions could be found. Although they generally did not share their knowledge with potential activist readers to avoid complicating their own narrative of consumer influence, the awareness of internationalism that underpinned these activists' practices is essential throughout the next chapters of this volume.

A close examination of Black's first series of consumer activist campaign articles shows that the publicity strategy she pioneered with these texts was in many ways more sophisticated than the campaign itself. By 1887 Black was a thoroughly practised professional writer and was rapidly becoming an experienced labour activist. Her role in evolving the WPPL into the WTUL and later in founding the WTUA, all during the development of her consumers' league proposals, shows her readiness to experiment with new strategies in order to pursue her activist aims. Her conscious adoption of the role of a woman of letters to advocate her campaigns reflects a similarly experimental strategy that made good use of her talent for communicating with specific readerships. Her ability to dissect and repurpose existing narratives of consumer guilt works in the same way as her pushing the boundaries of popular narratives to suggest new social ideas to the readers of her fiction, as she both assumed the existence of feelings of guilt in her readers and simultaneously proposed a way of reshaping these into positive action. In keeping with the rest of her work across her long career, she focused on the social and economic value of women, their work and their abilities, and this was an important part of her efforts to connect the experience and empathy of middle- and working-class women, although she was careful not to challenge the class status quo that assumed a divide between women workers and women consumers.

In this context it is particularly important to remain aware that Black never saw or presented consumer activism as a single solution to problems of underpayment. Rather, it was always explicitly intended to work as one of several strands of an activist project to improve exploitative working conditions. As Matthew Hilton puts it in *Consumerism in Twentieth-Century Britain* (2003), her proposal for a consumers' league 'was seen as a support to existing labour concerns'. Her approach of whitelisting, drawing on both the demands and the expertise of trade union activists and researchers, illustrates the fact that she

> recognised that 'such a league of consumers would never be strong enough entirely to remedy the poverty of the worker', but she believed it to be the first step towards a 'natural alliance' between consumers and trade unionists.[55]

Just as her articles connect the experience of workers and consumers, they connect their organisation as activists: consumer decisions would be informed by the investigative work of trade unions, and consumer activism would then endorse trade union-approved working conditions by supporting those businesses that upheld them. Her conclusions pre-empt those drawn by Naomi Klein in *No Logo* more than a hundred years later. Describing her conversations with labour organisers at the Workers' Assistance Center in the Cavite export processing zone in the Philippines, Klein writes that

> organizers don't much like the idea of Westerners swooping into the zone brandishing codes of conduct, with teams of well-meaning monitors trailing behind. 'The more significant way to resolve those problems,' [they say] 'lies with the workers themselves, inside the factory.' And codes of conduct [. . .] have little hope of helping because the workers have no hand in drafting them. As for third-party independent monitoring, [. . .] no matter who performs it, it's just that: third party. All it will do is reinforce the idea that somebody else is looking after the workers' destiny, not the workers themselves.[56]

The potential solutions Klein describes were proposed by multinational companies in response to consumer pressure; but the responses of the workers make clear that external pressures are not in themselves the answer to improving conditions – workers must have a say in what they require in and from their work-place and it is impossible for equivalent satisfactory results to be achieved by third parties on their behalf.

Black herself gradually began to doubt her own assertion that 'consumers, when once the information is put before them, can, *if they care enough about it*, raise the wages of the workers above starvation point' by redirecting their patronage to ethically run workshops.[57] Chapter 3 will show how, by the time she became involved in the organisation of the 1906 'Sweated Industries Exhibition', she was willing to distance herself from the consumers' league scheme as publicly as she had first endorsed it. Her change of mind was motivated by the continued development of her own economic theories and her growing awareness of the global market. Instead of asking consumers to attempt to influence an increasingly complicated system of production, she resolved that the only way of raising wages and ensuring their stability at a living wage level was the implementation of a legal minimum wage. She maintained that the support of consumers was necessary to enforce change, and that this support could be obtained by making them aware of the conditions of sweated labour; but she had altered her view that the consumer's power lay in their acts of purchase and she adapted her representations of market relations accordingly.

While Black's consumers' league plan did not take shape as she wished it to in the UK, however, her ideas proved influential with different organisations and across borders. This chapter has shown, furthermore, that the impact of her decision to unite her careers as a writer and activist in her promotion of the scheme as a woman of letters should not be underestimated. She changed perceptions of the narrative of middle-class women's consumer guilt to show that it could lead to positive action, and while she ultimately discarded the campaign for which she developed it, she would continue to use her distinctive strategy for communicating with her readers as potential activists throughout her later social and political projects. Contemporary examples of working-class women's cooperatives, as well as my own examination of the simultaneous consumers' league movement in the United States, also show that her vision for uniting the interests of consumers and workers as part of a two-pronged campaign that accorded respect to activist participants across classes was an innovative response to the challenge of motivating potential activists in order to address problems requiring structural solutions.

Notes

1. For a history of the Women's Co-operative Guild see Catherine Webb, *The Woman with the Basket: The History of the Women's Co-operative Guild 1883–1927* (Manchester: Co-operative Wholesale Society's Printing Works, 1927).
2. June Hannam and Karen Hunt, *Socialist Women: Britain, 1880s to 1920s* (London: Routledge, 2002), p. 135.
3. On the history of the National Women's Council and *The Consumer in Revolt* see Hannam and Hunt, pp. 142, 157 resp.
4. Barbara Caine, 'Feminism, Journalism and Public Debate', in *Women and Literature in Britain 1800–1900*, ed. Joanne Shattock (Cambridge: Cambridge University Press, 2001), pp. 99–118.
5. See Ana Parejo Vadillo, *Women Poets and Urban Aestheticism: Passengers of Modernity* (Basingstoke: Palgrave Macmillan, 2005), p. 53.
6. Clementina Black, 'The Ethics of Shopping', *Seed-Time: The Organ of the New Fellowship*, October 1890, pp. 10–11 (p. 10).
7. Ibid. p. 10.
8. John Ruskin, 'The Nature of Gothic', in *The Stones of Venice*, vol. 2 (New York: National Library Association, n.d. [1853]), pp. 151–230 (p. 165).
9. Adam Smith, *An Inquiry into the Nature and Causes of the Wealth of Nations* (Oxford: Oxford University Press, 2006 [1776]), pp. 12–13, 15–16.
10. Ruskin, p. 165.
11. Lawrence B. Glickman, *Buying Power: A History of Consumer Activism in America* (Chicago: University of Chicago Press, 2009), p. 6.
12. Ibid. p. 7.
13. Clementina Black, *A Sussex Idyl* (London: Tinsley, 1877), pp. 196–7.
14. Ruth Livesey, *Socialism, Sex, and the Culture of Aestheticism in Britain, 1880–1914* (Oxford: Oxford University Press, 2007), p.50.
15. Vadillo, p. 53.
16. Livesey, p. 51.
17. Kristina Huneault, *Difficult Subjects: Working Women and Visual Culture, Britain 1880–1914* (Aldershot: Ashgate, 2002), p. 169.
18. Andrew August, *Poor Women's Lives: Gender, Work, and Poverty in Late-Victorian London* (Madison: Fairleigh Dickinson University Press, 1999), p. 101.

19. Ellen Mappen, 'Introduction', in *Helping Women at Work: The Women's Industrial Council 1889–1914*, ed. Mappen (London: Hutchinson, 1985), pp. 11–30 (p. 13).

20. Livesey, p. 55.

21. Mappen, p. 14.

22. '1892–3 Fourth Annual Report', in *Helping Women at Work*, ed. Mappen, pp. 45–9 (p. 45). The high-profile London Dockworkers' Strike of August–November 1889 had seen the organisation of highly casualised and exploited unskilled manual labourers into prolonged strike action that achieved a raise in wages and a regularisation of working hours, and was widely accepted as proof that casual workers could be organised.

23. Mappen, p. 12. In the introduction to her edited volume Mappen offers a detailed history of the WIC and its formation out of the WTUA.

24. '*Longman's Magazine* (1882–1905)', in *Dictionary of Nineteenth-Century Journalism in Great Britain and Ireland*, ed. Laurel Brake and Marysa Demoor (Ghent: Academia Press, 2009), p. 378.

25. Ibid. p. 378.

26. Beth Harris, 'All That Glitters Is Not Gold: The Show-Shop and the Victorian Seamstress', in *Famine and Fashion: Needlewomen in the Nineteenth Century*, ed. Harris (Aldershot: Ashgate, 2005), pp. 115–37 (p. 129).

27. Clementina Black, 'Caveat Emptor', *Longman's Magazine*, August 1887, pp. 409–20 (p. 414).

28. Ibid. p. 415.

29. Ibid. p. 409.

30. Ibid. p. 411, emphasis in original.

31. Ibid. p. 415.

32. Ibid. p. 416.

33. For instance, Karl Marx and Friedrich Engels, 'The Manifesto of the Communist Party', trans. Samuel Moore, transcribed from *Marx/Engels Selected Works*, vol. 1 (Moscow: Progress Publishers, 1969), pp. 98–137, 68pp. (p. 16) <https://www.marxists.org/archive/marx/works/download/pdf/Manifesto.pdf> [accessed 9 February 2020].

34. Black, 'Caveat Emptor', p. 420.

35. Wilde to Wemyss Reid, quoted by Anya Clayworth, '*The Woman's World*: Oscar Wilde as Editor: 1996 Vanarsel Prize', *Victorian Periodicals Review*, 30.2 (1997), 84–101 (p. 87).

36. Stephanie Green, 'Oscar Wilde's *The Woman's World*', *Victorian Periodicals Review*, 30.2 (1997), 102–20 (p. 102).

37. I am grateful to the anonymous reader of this manuscript for their suggestions on *The Woman's World* as Black's choice of platform for these publications.

38. Thomas Hood, 'The Song of the Shirt', ll. 25–6, *Punch, or The London Charivari*, 16 December 1843, reprinted on *The Victorian Web* <https://www.victorianweb.org/authors/hood/shirt.html> [accessed 15 February 2021].

39. Landon R. Y. Storrs, *Civilizing Capitalism: The National Consumers' League, Women's Activism, and Labor Standards in the New Deal Era* (Chapel Hill: University of North Carolina Press, 2000), p. 19.

40. Thorstein Veblen, *The Theory of the Leisure Class: An Economic Study in the Evolution of Institutions* (London: Macmillan, 1899), p. 180.

41. Clementina Black, 'Something about Needlewomen', in *The Woman's World*, ed. Oscar Wilde (London: Cassell, 1888), pp. 300–4 (p. 304).

42. Ibid. p. 300.

43. Ibid. p. 302.

44. Clementina Black, 'The Morality of Buying in the Cheapest Market', in *The Woman's World* (London: Cassell, 1890), pp. 42–4 (p. 42).

45. Ibid. p. 42.

46. Ibid. p. 42.

47. Ibid. p. 42.

48. Ibid. p. 42.

49. Ibid. p. 43.

50. Ibid. p. 44.

51. Clementina Black, *Sweated Industry and the Minimum Wage* (London: Duckworth, 1907), pp. 143, v.

52. Ibid. p. 2.

53. Ibid. p. 149.

54. Mrs Carl [Adele] Meyer and Clementina Black, 'Appendix A: Home-workers in Germany', in *Makers of our Clothes: A Case for Trade Boards* (London: Duckworth, 1909), pp. 195–207 (p. 195).

55. Matthew Hilton, *Consumerism in Twentieth-Century Britain: The Search for a Historical Movement* (Cambridge: Cambridge University Press, 2003), p. 47.

56. Naomi Klein, *No Logo* (London: Flamingo, 2001 [2000]), p. 440.

57. Black, 'Caveat Emptor', p. 416, emphasis in original.

2

'An Epoch-Making Movement': Consumers' Leagues in the USA and Beyond, 1890–1900

In his history of twentieth-century consumerism, Matthew Hilton notes that '[b]y 1892, Black seems to have given up on the project [of the Consumers' League] and she would later turn against the idea of the Consumers' League as a potent weapon of the labour movement'.[1] Chapter 3 of this volume will consider in more detail the circumstances and publications Hilton is referring to when he states that Clementina Black 'turned against' the notion that a consumers' league might be a useful tool to support trade unions. It is important, however, not to understand from his observation that Black's brand of ethical consumerism failed to find any fertile soil in spite of her enthusiastic promotion over a period of five years. On the contrary, the work of a number of different scholars of consumer activist initiatives at the end of the nineteenth century suggests that the idea of consumers' league-style activism was not abandoned, and that many concerned consumers retained it as a possibility of wielding socio-economic influence in protest against some of the negative effects of an increasingly complex economy.

For instance, both Hilton himself and Ian Mitchell show that the project, though under a different descriptor, was taken up by the Christian Social Union (CSU) in Britain in the 1890s.[2] This organisation sought to promote an ethical and equitable society on an Anglican religious basis and believed that encouraging its members to deal with businesses that used fair employment practices was one way of working towards this better society. To help its members direct their custom to fair and ethical employers, it produced whitelists of dressmakers and bakers that met their standards in London.[3] The two industries they chose are telling in the wider debate around consumer activism during this period.

Dressmakers are obviously representative of the long-standing concerns about exploitation in the garment trade. By the later nineteenth century, baking had also become central to social concerns about industrial developments, as it was closely associated in the public consciousness with fears about food adulteration as well as poor working conditions. Other responses to poor and sometimes dangerous practices in the baking trade included the Salvation Army's bakery, which began to advertise delivery in and around London from the mid-1890s. For a slightly higher price it guaranteed good-quality bread and employed workers in need of the Salvation Army's social support, and promised that its profits would be reinvested in the organisation's extensive social work.[4] The consumer activism proposed on a Christian religious basis by the CSU and the Salvation Army therefore promised to benefit the consumer as well as the producer as, by paying a little extra, the consumer would receive good-quality products alongside the knowledge that they were acting to promote social improvement.

This chapter, however, is concerned with a much more prominent and long-lived incarnation of the consumers' league movement. Begun in New York City at around the same time that Black put forward her original proposals, this local initiative went on to inspire other consumers' leagues at state level and by the turn of the twentieth century it had grown into the National Consumers' League of the United States (NCL), which survives today; it also became internationally influential in the early twentieth century. While the two organisations on either side of the Atlantic were underpinned by similar ideas and ambitions, were led by and targeted women in comparable social positions, and, crucially, made extensive use of women's published writing to advertise their cause and activities, they quickly developed along different lines.

Taking the consumers' league across the Atlantic

The consumers' league movements in the US and the UK both emerged into the familiar climate of consumer guilt as a response to broad awareness of the exploitations facilitated by the contemporary economic system. Both saw the potential of adapting the consumer identity into an activist one, thus offering middle-class women a way to turn their non-productive and negative socio-economic influence into active, positive social participation. Initially, the state and national leagues in the US used tactics comparable to those proposed by Black, such as whitelisting, but the US consumers' leagues quickly altered their approach to social activism. As Landon R. Y. Storrs states in his history of the NCL and its impact on early-twentieth-century US politics,

> the NCL recognized that the strategy of using public pressure to elicit voluntary compliance by employers had serious limitations [and] concluded that employers would have to be coerced, rather than persuaded, into fair labor practices.[5]

In Storrs's analysis, the success of the US leagues lay in their refiguring of the consumer as a specifically legislative activist. The leagues' leadership quickly began to focus their investigative activities less on informing and advising individual consumers and more on launching legal challenges and lobbying for legal change to reinforce social progress. This transformation from an ethical shopping society into a pressure group was the key reason for the success of what would become the NCL and the influence it was able to wield, particularly in the development of protective labour legislation, during the Progressive Era. The shift from charitable to legislative activity has a great deal in common with the development of Black's personal campaign aims, which also became increasingly focused on instituting labour laws to improve and protect workers' positions. The US consumers' leagues, however, were predominantly made up of women consumers from higher social classes and sought to represent and safeguard the interests of both exploited workers and duped consumers on a model that left out the collaboration with trade unions which Black advocated.

The US consumers' leagues' development of the gendered and classed consumer identity reflects how 'gender-based ideology shaped both the limits and possibilities for women in the political arena' in the USA during this period.[6] It is also worth noting, however, that the idea of a consumer identity as providing activist potential at this time was not regarded as inherently classed. Rebecca Edwards, a historian of gender in US political history, notes that during the so-called Gilded Age Democrats 'articulated a new political identity for women based on their household duties as shoppers and consumers' in a sense that could cross over ideas from the consumers' league to something closer to a cooperative movement.[7] The Gilded Age, named after the eponymous 1873 novel by Mark Twain and Charles Dudley Warner, came to signify roughly the decades between 1870 and 1900, a period marked by economic expansion following the Civil War. Conversely, it also coincided with the stock market Panic of 1873, which sparked an economic depression with a protracted global impact. This period then both precedes and overlaps with the Progressive Era and impacted on its social and political developments. Both of the central texts in this chapter engage with the fact that, in these early stages, consumer activism was not necessarily presented as something that naturally excluded women whose purchasing power was smaller.

The role of women's campaign writing was key to the founding and the rapid development of the US consumers' league movement. The texts considered here are of a slightly different kind than Black's articles to promote the original idea of a consumers' league to its potential membership; but both were obviously intended to be persuasive to clearly defined audiences. The first is Alice L. Woodbridge's 1890 *Report on the Condition of Working Women in New York Retail Stores*. As the cover of the eight-page pamphlet edition published in 1893 states, the report was read at a 'Mass Meeting' held in New York City 'under the direction' of the Working Women's Society in May 1890; this meeting is generally credited as the founding moment of the Consumers' League of New York (CLNY).[8] Woodbridge, herself a retail worker, was the secretary of the New York Working Women's Society and undertook an investigation into the working conditions of shop assistants. Once the report had been produced, Woodbridge took care to present her cause to an audience directly involved in creating the pressured conditions in which shop assistants worked: leisured women consumers, particularly those belonging to New York's influential families whose social position often incorporated charity and philanthropic activities. Her report's insight into the lives of women and children in working poverty is designed to be emotionally shocking to an audience who might themselves be unused to and possibly unaware of such conditions – as members of the Working Women's Society were unlikely to have been.

Woodbridge's initiative and its influence on the formation of the first of the US consumers' leagues will be contextualised with reference to *The Story of an Epoch-Making Movement*, a retrospective of the development of the CLNY and its influence on the NCL and various other international consumer organisations on the same model. It was written by Maud Nathan, who had been well-known as a social reformer since the late nineteenth century and who was a leading member of both the New York and national leagues. She published her personal history of the US consumers' league movement in 1926, when the most energetic social improvements of the Progressive Era were already coming to their close. As well as recounting an origin story for the movement and illustrating the strategies and triumphs that allowed it to become 'epoch-making', therefore, Nathan also offered a form of retrospective persuasion that set out to show the league's continued relevance and the need for its members to continue their work in the changing society of the twentieth century, following the international upheaval of the First World War. Reading Woodbridge's initial report in the context of Nathan's history therefore gives a strong sense of the role of class, gender and national identity in the formation of a consumers' league on an explicitly and self-consciously American model.

The second key text relates to the National Consumers' League. The article 'Aims and Principles of the Consumers' League' was written by the newly founded organisation's influential General Secretary, the prominent socialist Florence Kelley, in the *American Journal of Sociology* in 1899 to advertise the league's ambitions and strategies, including the development of its own label to vouch for the standards under which the goods that carried it were produced. Although no debt is acknowledged to Black's initiative, Kelley's article, the information she provides and the persuasive strategies she uses have much in common with Black's articles, particularly 'Caveat Emptor', in her approach to consumer as well as employer responsibility within a national and international market. As in Black's publications, furthermore, a wider political context is evident in Kelley's article. While they are not explicitly stated, there are clear historical and strategic connections between the Consumers' League label and pre-existing labels issued by trade unions to prove fair production standards.

Black is never directly referred to as an originator of the consumers' league idea in the histories and promotions of the US leagues, but there is a distinct awareness of her influence on wider debates, and of exchange in activist strategies across borders as well as between movements. The stories told by various activists about these cross-pollinations are different, but they often include a sense of pride in their adaptation of particular ideas for their own national and cultural context. In *The Story of an Epoch-Making Movement*, Nathan notes:

The ideas and principles of the Consumers' League originally came to us from England, but tradition and conservatism are forces against which it is difficult to battle, and the League languished in the country which had given it birth.[9]

Nathan, here, paints a portrait of a good idea suffocated by a lack of public support in a country unwilling to adopt the radical new strategies it proposed. *The Story* suggests that the original idea found support in the more progressive United States, but it is clear throughout that the success of the US leagues relied on the repurposing of campaign strategies including Black's to suit a different national environment. Like Black's scheme and its emphasis on the role of consumer activism to support labour organisation, the Consumers' League of New York first developed in connection with the concerns of women workers and the idea that middle-class women consumers could be involved in the movement towards fairer working conditions for women workers in particular.

As the activist priorities of the US leagues took shape, they diverged from Black's wide-ranging campaign against under-payment. The manner in which they addressed potential consumer activists gradually shifted to focus increasingly on the role of middle-class women acting on behalf of working women. Although their methods clearly achieved more successful results than Black's league, they were less interested in pursuing a multi-pronged approach to improve the social, economic and political position of exploited workers more widely.

Telling origin stories: The development of the Consumers' League of New York

We have seen that many nineteenth-century consumer activist appeals to women centred on exploitation in the garment trade, casting women of different classes both as sweated producers and as thoughtless consumers of textile goods. Black mobilised this familiar trope in her articles in *The Woman's World* in 1888 and 1890, framing her appeal in the context of women's awareness of the cost and labour involved in garment-making. While the garment trade in New York City was also well known to be highly exploitative, however, most recorded origin stories for the Consumers' League of New York, including Nathan's retrospective, suggest that this was initially not a primary concern for the CLNY. Woodbridge's report, Nathan's account and other histories indicate that the organisation was formed out of a social campaign that was concerned with the exploitation not of the needlewoman as the traditional symbol of sweated labour, but of the (young) woman retail worker.

The CLNY did go on to concern itself with the New York garment trade on several levels. Daniel E. Bender, in his history of sweated labour practices in the United States, *Sweated Work, Weak Bodies* (2004), shows that the sweated garment industry, and particularly the danger of disease transferred from deprived neighbourhoods and tenement housing to middle-class households via the clothing produced by sweated workers, would become an important issue for the CLNY. He argues that this preoccupation was linked not least to suspicion of the large numbers of migrant workers that the sweated garment trade absorbed in New York City.[10] Florence Kelley's work, among others, shows that fears about pathogens being carried on clothing pre-dated the formation of the CLNY and the NCL, with factory and labour inspectors alert to it as a problem in home-based work in particular. As a campaign priority, however, it is more reflective of later concerns within the US consumers' league movement, when its focus began to highlight consumer interests alongside, and sometimes over, workers' well-being. It should be noted that for the National Consumers' League, the garment trade again became a focal point in an early experiment to test its own reach, as Kelley's article on the aims and principles of the NCL and the introduction of the Consumers' League label indicates.

In the context of existing rhetoric around consumer guilt, it nonetheless seems striking that the first US league, located in a city and state known for its exploitative garment trade, did not use the production of clothing to appeal to its target audience of wealthy, socially influential women consumers. It is worth noting here that the two campaign narratives addressing consumer guilt over clothing or shopping do have significant points in common. The CLNY's focus on retail was as explicitly gendered as Black's appeals on behalf of exploited needleworkers in *The Woman's World*, but was, if anything, more dependent on an understanding of consumer guilt through thoughtlessness, as the still novel phenomenon of the department store was directly representative of the identification of the woman consumer with frivolous desire and with shopping as a hobby for the wealthy and the leisured. Whereas Black's articles had relied on an appeal to the consumer-reader's own knowledge and reason, repeatedly acknowledging the difficulties faced by the consumer who wished to make ethical decisions but lacked both information and influence, the issue of the New York shop assistants was raised with a shock-and-shame approach aimed specifically at what Black would later call 'ladies of wealth and influence' in order to induce them to correct their behaviour as consumers.[11]

Nathan's text treats as a given the perceived necessity of involving women with social influence to improve the working conditions of women workers in particular. On the other hand, she also clearly acknowledges that the grievances of New York's urban shop workers would not have been heard by women in higher social classes if they had not been brought to their attention by the representatives of working women. Both Woodbridge's report and Nathan's reflections indicate that some exploitative practices in retail, such as prohibitions for workers to make use of seats ostensibly installed for them or instructions to workers to continue serving customers even during their break times, were deliberately kept hidden from customers; but it is also strongly hinted that it would have been possible for customers to have discovered some of these problems if they had been more observant.

Nathan's retrospective begins with a summary of women's working conditions in retail around 1890, which in most points echoes the issues raised in Woodbridge's report. The nature of their exploitation had much in common with many contemporary accounts of women's exploitative employment, including evidence collected by Black about conditions in workplaces such as factories and bars in London.[12] Retail workers in New York were paid low wages, were fined for damage to and loss of store goods, and regularly worked long hours in overtime for which they were not compensated.[13] In addition their work was subject to seasonal fluctuations, with rushes, for instance, around the winter holidays, while Woodbridge notes that many were forced to take unpaid leave at slacker times.[14] Workers on the shop floor were kept standing throughout their working day, their mealtimes were often cut short, and no adequate facilities, such as proper bathrooms and changing rooms or clean and comfortable spaces to eat or take breaks, were available.[15] While these conditions were clearly created by an unscrupulous management minimising expenditure on the well-being of staff, Nathan argued that these problems were compounded by the behaviour of shoppers and particularly of wealthy, leisured women who shopped for their own amusement. Issues like unpaid overtime were exacerbated by customers who stayed beyond opening hours or requested deliveries or returns at irregular hours and short notice, to suit their own convenience without regard to the workers who were compelled to fulfil their orders by employers who sought to oblige their paying customers rather than their dependent staff.[16] According to Nathan, Woodbridge 'realized how helpless were the working girls themselves to remedy conditions. She had the vision to perceive that these abuses could be abolished only if the women who patronized the stores knew about them.'[17] In other words, customers were better placed to exert pressure on the shops that relied on their custom than were the workers who themselves relied on their employment. The tone of Nathan's description, however, points to a form of consumer activism that has more in common with charity and patronage than with the solidarity with working women that Black called for in her articles: Nathan is seeking to mobilise 'the women who patronized the stores' to exert their influence on behalf of 'helpless' 'working girls'. As this and the final chapter of this volume will demonstrate, this type of activism on behalf of workers would come to typify much of the NCL's work in the decades leading up to Nathan's retrospective.

Woodbridge's approach was very similar to the social investigation tactics used by Black and the various organisations with which she was involved. It also reflects the campaign steps that would become a motto for the NCL: 'investigate, record, agitate'.[18] She visited a range of shops and enquired about common practices regarding issues such as working hours, fines and hygiene from workers as well as independent commentators including physicians. Having drawn up her report based on a judicious combination of generalisation and shocking detail, she then proceeded, in Nathan's words, to 'cast her eyes about for some public-spirited women who would listen to the reading of the report'.[19] This reading took place at the mass meeting organised by the Working Women's Society in the large and prominent concert venue of Chickering Hall on Fifth Avenue near Union Square. As a result of this outreach work, the cause was taken up by Josephine Shaw Lowell who, as a leading reformer and charity activist working within the Charity Organization Society, was precisely the type of socially influential woman the Working Women's Society is likely to have aimed to engage. Shaw Lowell in turn recruited Nathan, another New York socialite with wealth, leisure and position to devote to charitable work, to help her in the formation of the Consumers' League of New York.[20]

While Nancy Woloch, in her history of protective labour legislation for women in the United States, *A Class by Herself* (2015), adopts Nathan's narrative of the foundation of the New York league from the Working Women's Society's mass meeting on the conditions of retail workers, Storrs gives a different origin story for the CLNY and the NCL.[21] In one section of his history of the NCL, Storrs does state that '[i]n the 1890s affluent women who were appalled by working women's reports of conditions in department stores founded the National Consumers' League'.[22] He appears to see the Consumers' League of New York as developing separately from this, however. He writes:

> The Consumers' League [of New York] emerged in response to an initiative by workers. In 1888 a New York shirtmaker and organizer named Leonora O'Reilly invited some of the city's prominent women to a meeting of the New York Working Women's Society, at which they heard an appeal for assistance from their 'toiling and down-trodden sisters.' The group decided to appoint a committee to assist the Working Women's Society by [creating a whitelist of ethical employers].
>
> In response to this prodding from wage-earning women, the Consumers' League of New York took shape in early 1891.[23]

Storrs's story, then, still presents the Working Women's Society organising a mass meeting in order to involve activists from different social classes, but it has shirtmaker Leonora O'Reilly in the place of Alice L. Woodbridge and the garment trade in the place of retail work. In an intermediary summary of the same events, Eileen Boris, in her history of the New York garment trade, *A Coat of Many Colors* (2005), names garment worker O'Reilly as the leader of the Working Women's Society when it 'called upon Lowell and other activist society women in 1888 to help them win just working conditions, such as seats for department store workers'.[24] Even when it is not explicitly stated that she appealed exclusively on behalf of garment workers, this way of centring O'Reilly and her profession in the Working Women's

Society's attempt to reach out to women from higher social classes links back to the common narrative of the sweated needleworker.

In 1899, the National Consumers' League grew out of the Consumers' League of New York and other leagues at city and state level that followed the establishment and growing success of the New York City league: Syracuse and Brooklyn in New York State as well as Chicago, Boston and Philadelphia.[25] The official website for the NCL does not give information about the development of the New York league, though it does state that to 'protect in-home workers, often including whole families, from terrible exploitation by employers' was a key aim of the NCL in the early 1900s.[26] This broad-brush example connects to the emphasis on the home-based garment industry rather than retail, which by definition was not 'in-home' work. There is a sense here of standing up for workers who are themselves invisible as they work within their homes; a retail worker would have been visible to customers, even though the worst aspects of their working conditions, as Woodbridge's report shows, were not necessarily outwardly evident. It is not illogical that the surviving organisation should choose to stress the potential power of the consumer activist by pointing to the idea that a consumer's actions and decisions could have a beneficial influence beyond the society immediately visible to them. Indeed, in the context of the present-day global economy in which the website exists, consumers may buy products made under exploitative conditions in other parts of the world and the impact of consumer choices on the environment may manifest in climate change and natural disasters elsewhere, and therefore bridging this type of social and experiential distance is crucial in mobilising consumer activists. In contrast to the NCL website, however, the more historicised Guide to the Consumers' League of New York City Records at Cornell University Library follows Nathan's origin story.[27]

Considering the prevalence of sharing activist strategies between organisations as well as across countries and borders, it does not seem inconceivable that the different initiatives described by Nathan, Storrs and Boris to combat exploitation in retail and the garment trade were in fact developed simultaneously. Both types of work employed large numbers of women, whose position in the labour market was inevitably more precarious and made them less able individually to resist poor conditions. For this reason these two trades were necessarily of importance to the Working

Women's Society. In addition they employed two of the organisation's leaders, Woodbridge and O'Reilly, who were therefore well equipped to research the conditions linked to them and identify the needs of workers in these sectors.

Whichever trade was central to the original mass meeting, it is clear from the Working Women's Society's bold and successful initiative in calling and advertising a meeting of this kind that its leaders were well able to organise against exploitative working conditions. Nevertheless Storrs shows O'Reilly, herself a worker in the trade discussed, embracing the trope of the 'toiling and down-trodden' garment worker in order to appeal to wealthier women, and Woodbridge's report shows that she too made use of rhetoric adapted for an audience of middle-class, non-wage-earning women in conveying the conditions of retail workers. In fact many of these different versions of the origin narrative show organised working women reaching for sentimentalised tropes familiar from social novels and shocking news stories to paint a picture of virtuous but worn-down women, rather than presenting testimonies from the real working women who constituted the membership and leadership of the Working Women's Society. The suggestion created is that wealthier, leisured women were invited to act on behalf of an idealised woman worker.

It is by no means improbable that the Working Women's Society determined on a strategy of involving wealthier women as champions for their cause and worked to bring the exploitation in both forms of women's employment to the attention of middle-class reformers, and that this is how both the industries of retail and garment-making came to be linked into the consumers' league project over the course of the 1890s. This interpretation suggests that, at least initially, working women played a key role in setting the agenda of the nascent consumers' league movement. Nevertheless it is also true that what Nathan's, Woloch's, Storrs's and Boris's analyses have in common, and what also resonates with ideas in Black's later work, is the perceived need for women from higher social classes to support the initiatives of working-class women to better their own conditions. Another key element in each of their arguments is the empowering of women as consumers. The process of consumer empowerment that I identified in Black's appeals to middle-class women was adopted successfully by the US consumers' leagues as they developed members' identities from non-productive consumer to legislative activist.

Another key point here, and an important difference between Black's version of a consumers' league and the US model, is the issue of social distance in the process of consumption, as explained by scholars such as Lawrence B. Glickman, and touched on with reference to present-day consumer activism. Throughout her campaign Black sought to reduce or collapse the sense of social, economic, emotional and physical distance between worker and consumer. Bringing the consumer into the triangular relationship of a business transaction was the theoretical equivalent of this, while her persuasive writing and portrayals of workers in poverty provided the emotional angle that allowed her readers to imagine themselves in the worker's place. With the 'Sweated Industries Exhibition' she sought a new way of breaking down this distance by literally placing exhibition visitors face to face and in conversation with sweated workers – although, as I show in Chapter 3, this initiative may in fact be understood as a form of reinforcing social distance and difference. By contrast, in spite of their early and public connection with the Working Women's Society, the US consumers' leagues from the beginning made a focal point of the social distance between consumers and workers as the element that allowed them effectively to mobilise consumers on workers' behalf.

The different accounts of the Working Women's Society meeting suggest that the organised working women, at least initially, intended to make use of precisely this advantage. The words 'toiling and down-trodden sisters' simultaneously function to break down an emotional barrier and to emphasise a socio-economic one, inviting cross-class support based on a combination of gendered solidarity and material aid. As the history of the developing CLNY and NCL shows, the effect of this was to separate, if not the concerns, certainly the approaches and ambitions of activist workers and consumers. Boris points out that what was 'fair' in the eyes of consumer activists

> did not necessarily correspond to the demands of trade unionists. Sanitary manufacturing, proper homes (that is, homes free from manufacturing), and the absence of child labor loomed as important, if not more so, as wages or union recognition in attracting elite women to the cause of wage earners.[28]

Consumers' activism on behalf of workers, then, was at least as much geared towards the convictions and priorities of the consumers themselves and the social and political groups they sought to influence as towards the actual demands, wishes and experiences of the workers concerned. My analysis of the rhetoric used by Alice L. Woodbridge in her report, intended to be read aloud to a well-publicised mass meeting in a smart concert venue, will further illustrate these ideas regarding the role of gender and its impact on socio-economic influence in the origins of the consumers' league project and the development of its understanding of its own role and aims.

Alice L. Woodbridge, *Report on the Condition of Working Women in New York Retail Stores*, 1890

Woodbridge's report is clearly geared towards the audience expected at the public reading. There is little preamble, but the two short lines there are make two important points about the report: that the information it presents is trustworthy, and the improvements it asks for achievable and reasonable. The first line reads: 'The facts contained in this statement have been obtained through personal interviews and sources believed to be reliable, and have been confirmed in many cases by several persons before being accepted.' In other words, this is not a sensationalised report based on anecdotes of excesses and information obtained by hearsay; instead, it records the findings of an investigation carried out with thoroughness and responsibility. The line that follows notes that the report describes hardships to which the investigation found women and child workers to be subjected but 'which we believe can be remedied'.[29] This addition highlights the class position as well as the gender identity of the anticipated audience at the meeting. The Working Women's Society could conduct the investigation and vouch for the accuracy of the facts it uncovered. Based on the society's own experience of workplace activism, it could further make the case that these problems were not inevitable and that conditions described could be improved, and how this might be done. At this point, however, it is suggested, the society's influence ended: it could not resolve these issues without support and cooperation from others. The reasons for this emerge over the course of the report, which throughout is highly aware of, and takes pains to emphasise, the vulnerable position of women and child workers both in the labour market and in a wider social and economic context.

In many ways Woodbridge's report and other strategies of the Working Women's Society may be seen as a forerunner of the so-called 'entering wedge' strategy employed by the NCL in the Progressive Era. Chapter 4 will examine this approach in more detail, but in brief it campaigned for improvements in the conditions of workers who were evidently vulnerable – that is, women and children – with a view to building on progress made to attain better working conditions across the board. Certainly this idea was behind the appeal that Woodbridge made on behalf of women and children working in retail: many of her arguments are focused on the demands of the work and the low wages over-taxing the physical and moral strength of the workers and permanently injuring both their health and what was considered their moral character.

The report foregrounds the physical strength and health of child workers. It is noted that the category of child worker sometimes included children younger than fourteen. They were legally debarred from paid employment but frequently worked anyway because their families depended on the additional wages they could bring home. We may assume that the illegality of their employment enabled employers to pay them low wages on the argument that they ran a risk in giving them a job. In addition to the matter of their physical health and ability, fears of 'immorality' – that is, the risk of sexual exploitation – are already hinted at. Woodbridge indicates that there were effectively no limits on the number of hours that retail workers could be required to work, and no exception was made for child workers. She explains:

> In engaging employees, they are not usually engaged to serve a certain number of hours per day, but for such a time as the firm requires them; thus a child on a salary of $2 per week may be obliged to work for sixteen hours a day at certain seasons of the year, and is forced to go long distances through questionable localities late at night, and is thus rendered liable to insult and immoral influences.[30]

In other words, if the simple fact of children being manifestly over-worked to a length of hours that would be excessive for adults were in itself not enough to shock listeners, these practices did harm to the child workers outside the workplace too by forcing them to make their way home alone through a dangerous city at times when it was not safe for children to be out at all. The problem thus went far beyond physical exhaustion, having the potential to taint these children's futures as well as their present.

As well as this relatively vague sense of moral threat and contagion, more concrete and literal examples of infection also play a part. This becomes clear from a long passage on the low standards of hygiene observed in many shops in the areas reserved solely for employees, and therefore not visible to customers. Bathroom facilities, for instance, often required large numbers of workers to share the same washbasin and towel. Woodbridge notes:

> On visiting one store we were struck by the number of children suffering from granulated eyelids. As this is a disease which is contagious, it is easy to see how it can be contracted by the use of one towel in common.[31]

These examples highlight the disempowerment of child workers who were unable to offer resistance to circumstances which made them physically ill because, young as they were, they were depended on to supply an income and could not risk losing their jobs.

Woodbridge's hygiene concerns for women overlap with those for children, but also focus on different elements. For instance, she notes that several shops imposed measures to control the use of bathroom facilities. In one shop, 'the superintendent held the key' to the only available bathroom, and '[w]omen and children alike had to go to him for it'. There is clearly a reference here to the possibility that the potentially acute needs of menstruating workers could be used to exert pressure on them or subject them to feelings of shame. Eventually, Woodbridge adds, 'at the risk of her position, a saleswoman threated to complain of the firm, and the door was left unlocked'.[32] This seems to indicate that the indignity as well as physical discomfort were felt so strongly that even a worker in a vulnerable position would rather risk her livelihood than continue to submit to them; the firm's failure to resist this challenge, furthermore, indicates that it must have been aware that this practice was an indefensible one.

The matter of depriving workers of the ability to use bathroom facilities is indicative of two points that Woodbridge raises with regard to a large number of firms: a lack of consideration for workers' personal hygiene requirements and attempts to control workers' time. As she points out, employers placed 'a value upon time lost that is not given to service rendered'. Salaries were consistently low, but workers were subject to strict timekeeping on their few available breaks and were fined for lateness as well as for any errors in the stock. In other words, while the firms kept very close control on the workers' time, workers were unable to protest against issues like unpaid overtime, as the limit of their working hours was not stipulated. This was one matter, Woodbridge suggests, in which customers could exercise some influence – not because they made the rules to which workers were subject, but because, through greater awareness of these rules, they might avoid certain behaviours likely to put additional pressure on the workers. For instance, Woodbridge writes:

> We find in one fashionable house saleswomen are not allowed to leave the counter between the hours of 11 A. M. and 3.30 P. M., except for lunch; and if a saleswoman has a customer when the lunch hour arrives, she is obliged to remain and wait on the customer, and the time so consumed is deducted from the lunch time.[33]

Certainly the behaviour of customers alone would not remove these rules, but it would be easy for a wealthy, leisured listener to the report to conclude that they should in future aim not to occupy the attention of a salesperson at the time when the lunch break was likely to be due. Without explicitly putting these kinds of solutions to her listeners, Woodbridge does introduce several hints intended to draw in leisured consumers and show them that they had responsibility in this situation. From the beginning, she had indicated that these circumstances were not inevitable: they 'could be remedied'. She also repeatedly cited extremely poor conditions in what she refers to as 'fashionable houses'. This ensured that wealthy consumers could not make or sustain the assumption that exploitative conditions belonged to cheap shops, but rather served to illustrate that even expensive shops sought to maximise their profits by exploiting workers who were not in a position to offer effective resistance.

Elsewhere in the report, Woodbridge further points out that dismissal seriously damaged a salesperson's work prospects, so that most retail workers could not risk jeopardising their employment by any kind of complaint, trade union organisation or industrial action. She notes:

> It is extremely difficult, almost impossible, for a saleswoman dismissed from one house to find employment in another. Reference is required

from the firm which last employed her, and if it is found she had been dismissed she is rarely taken again.[34]

Again, the listener was left no opportunity to assume that this treatment was a fair and proportionate response to someone losing their employment through misbehaviour, while good workers would impress their employer and be rewarded accordingly. In fact, as Woodbridge makes clear, employees were routinely dismissed after five years simply because many businesses preferred to keep up their personnel turnover, explicitly in order to prevent their coming to feel that they had any claim on their employer. The poor conditions of employment, then, could in no way be read as a reflection on the work ethic of the employee; instead, the length of service of faithful and experienced employees was a reason for dismissal rather than recognition. Even workers who were acknowledged to be of significant use to a firm were indiscriminately subjected to the iniquities of poor hygiene, low pay and fines. Woodbridge pointed out that '[t]he fines of a saleswoman in a Sixth Avenue house from Sept 1st to Jan. 1st amounted to $15.00; yet she was one of the most valued saleswomen'.[35] In fact, the good performance of one employee could even be held against another, as in an example of a worker whose responsibilities included keeping charge of stock as well as sales. When she was outperformed in sales income by a younger worker who could devote her full time to sales, she was dismissed despite, Woodbridge suggests, having conscientiously carried out the primary task of stock-keeping for which she had been hired.[36]

In her catalogue of iniquities, Woodbridge never loses sight of the vulnerable position of women both in the labour market and more widely. Gender determined workers' ability to command a living wage, but also made women workers more vulnerable to sexual exploitation – often because of the state of their wages. Woodbridge stated: 'It is a known fact that men's wages cannot fall below a limit upon which they can exist, but woman's wages have no limit since the paths of shame are always open to her.'[37] Examples of men's underpayment, particularly in casualised employment, show clearly that there was no real lower limit on men's wages either; but the threat of involuntary sex work here functions as a rhetorical sleight of hand with a strong shock factor, especially for an audience unlikely to be familiar with the insidious reality of poverty conditions. Though cruder than Black's arguments, this strategy has important points in common with her way of addressing her readership with the assumption of goodwill. It may be assumed that many pleasure shoppers listening at Chickering Hall would conclude that they did not wish their leisure activity to force women into sex work because they could not command a living wage through regular work. As with the equation of consumer guilt, in the context of the nineteenth-century garment trade as well as in its present-day incarnation of ethical consumption, this information was designed to make consumers question whether they needed the product or service they were buying and would persist in purchasing it at the expense of the worker, or whether they would be willing to dispense with it in order to reduce pressure on the worker with immediate effect, and possibly remove demand for the item with the result of the objectionable practice ceasing altogether in the longer term.

In addition to astutely making use of moral outrage, however, Woodbridge also offered her audience a more analytical under-standing of how women's social status affected their position in the labour market. Precisely because it was often not admit-ted how many women were obliged to be self-supporting or to support dependants, their wages remained systematically low; and because they could not afford to lose the employment they had, they were forced to submit to low wages and poor conditions. As Woodbridge points out,

> The very fact that some of these women receive partial support from brothers or fathers, and are thus enabled to live upon less than they earn, forces other women who have no such support either to suffer for necessities, or seek other means of support. Cases may be cited where frail, delicate, refined women, unable to exist upon the salaries they earn, are forced to crime or suicide.[38]

As evidence of this statement, she refers to a case that received considerable contemporary press attention, of a working woman named as Mrs Henderson who committed suicide because she 'could not live upon the salaries offered her; she could, if she accepted the propositions of employers' – that is to say, if she consented to engage in sex acts to supplement her wages.[39] It was for these women who were unable independently to find a situation where they could be self-supporting and maintain both their physical health and their moral well-being that Woodbridge sought to enlist the help of the audience at the Chickering Hall meeting.

She also took care, however, to point out that she was not seeking this aid on behalf of women who already were or would inevitably become sex workers, pointing out 'how few, out of the thousands of working women, do fall'.[40] Instead, she held up the image of the honest working woman, starving and exhausted yet steadfastly virtuous, as a US ideal of courage who could stand comparison with the country's respected military heroes. In fact, Woodbridge argues, working women bravely facing the 'living death' of continuous work under starvation conditions might be considered braver than soldiers falling on the field of battle. She holds up the United States and its people as 'prid[ing] ourselves upon our respect for honest toil' and points out that as such it is disgraceful that these women's labour could not command a liveable life. It is for this reason, she argues, that the working woman facing systematic exploitation in order to earn her living should be regarded not as inadequate or inherently sinful but rather as 'the brightest jewel in our country's diadem'. It is because of the risks working women faced up to that it was the responsibility of those in a better position to 'guard her that her light may glorify the pages of the history which we make to-day'.[41]

Woodbridge's appeal to the national identity of a still rela-tively young and recently unified nation establishing a global position of economic and political prominence, and her refer-ences to the present as history in the making, are calculated to engage an audience of the representatives of New York's socially and economically influential class. She evokes American values such as democracy. The ideals she praises are resilience, strength of character, and the possibility of forging a good life through hard and honest work, which would come to typify the American Dream.[42] At the same time, however, she also highlights that the pursuit of these ideals is out of the reach of many workers whose exploitative conditions preclude any ambition beyond mere survival. Her representation of this harsh reality within a nationalistic philosophical context was designed to prompt her listeners, themselves the beneficiaries of US history and industry, to examine their own conscience as to the role their activities played in the situations described.

Again appealing to a sense of national pride, she also consciously sought to set apart US society as more moral and democratic than countries such as France by noting that '[i]n Paris it is an understood thing that women employed in shops cannot exist without assistance from other sources; and unless something is done soon it must become the case in our own land'.[43] The warning here comes from the common association of Paris with sexuality and sex work; Woodbridge thus implied that the prominent citizens of New York would wish to exert themselves to prevent their own city and country adopting the lax social and sexual norms of a country supposed to be more decadent and to have less progressive energy. A comparable understanding of worker and consumer activism as part of the making of national history as well as policy would arise again in the context of the NCL's case in *Muller* v. *Oregon* in 1908, where the NCL connected present worker well-being with the future health of the nation's working population and set this argument against the claim that the US Constitution codified the freedom to contract labour without state-imposed limitations. In other words, the NCL sought to plead for consideration of the nation's future as opposed to a short-sighted and damaging interpretation of its founding principle of individual liberty.

As with Storrs's representation of Leonora O'Reilly, it is clear that Woodbridge and the Working Women's Society were not and did not regard themselves as typifying the 'frail, toil-worn woman' portrayed in the report; but rather that this figure functions as a means of engaging wealthier classes with the plight of people in poverty. Harking back to the stereotype of the sweated needlewoman, this helpless character illustrates why the Working Women's Society and its membership were unable to remedy conditions alone, and why they appealed for help to a mass meeting. It is important to note here that, unlike Black, Woodbridge does not offer practical suggestions for how she and the society believe the hardships they describe can be remedied; the report stopped at simply raising awareness of the conditions she and her associates had observed. The society did not, for instance, as Black did, call for consumers to support trade unions. While it is very unlikely that the published report recorded the full proceedings of the meeting and it is distinctly possible that practical approaches and solutions were discussed, it is telling that the Working Women's Society seems to disappear from the official US Consumers' League narrative at this point. In her retrospective, Nathan introduces Shaw Lowell and herself as responding to the meeting by taking up the cause of retail workers on behalf of the Working Women's Society and the workers they represented and making it the specific cause of the new Consumers' League of New York. It is unclear whether these developments were what Woodbridge and the society had in mind; certainly the matter seems to have been largely taken out of their hands to be subjected to the new and experimental approach of an organisation made up of the wealthy, leisured and influential audience they had set out to involve. Although some of the new US Consumers' Leagues, including the NCL under the leadership of socialist Kelley, remained preoccupied with the conditions of working women, the Working Women's Society would not lead the Consumers' Leagues' initiatives again following the meeting at Chickering Hall.

From this point, based on the promptings of consumers' conscience that Woodbridge had so sagaciously inserted, the newly formed Consumers' League of New York also developed its own understanding of consumer guilt and responsibility and the appropriate activist response. With reference to the working conditions of shop assistants rather than productive workers, it seems logical that the CLNY's understanding of consumer guilt differed slightly from Black's identification of the consumer as one party in a trading transaction. The exploitation of shop assistants was indisputably and directly linked to the shopping habits of consumers – and specifically of wealthy and leisured women who shopped for pleasure – in a way that the link between prices paid for goods and wages paid to workers was not, as Black recognised in 'Caveat Emptor' and in her devising of consumer activism as one aspect of a wider activist project. If matters like the unavailability of seats, hygienic bathroom and eating spaces and other provisions for the workers were definite signs of employers cutting costs at the workers' expense, the fact that workers were kept beyond their contracted hours and had breaks cut short was demonstrably also related to the inconsiderateness of their customers. It required little extra effort on the part of the leisured shopper, for instance, to remember not to enter a shop at lunchtime or closing time. With reference to these concerns, it is logical that Woodbridge and her fellow worker-activists would seek to enlist the help of women with social influence, who could set an example of considerate shopping to ameliorate the shop assistants' working conditions at least in that respect. The issues of underpayment, lack of facilities and so on, however, were well beyond the influence of well-meaning consumers doing their best not to shop after hours or arrange urgent deliveries at awkward times.

The limits of the influence that wealthy women consumers could exert simply through considerate shopping soon became evident. Nathan gives one anecdotal example of a particularly socially and economically influential shopper exercising her purchasing power for the benefit of the workers in one of the shops she patronised. This wife of a former state governor, after seeing one shop worker faint from exhaustion, gave the shop owner an ultimatum: 'Seats behind counters for salesgirls or I withdraw my account!'[44] While this anecdote served to illustrate the direct influence shoppers could have and thus created a sense of hope and empowerment for consumer activists, it is actually quickly qualified in Nathan's text as she goes on to explain that, while the seats were installed at this particular customer's demand, '[i]t is one thing to provide stools and another thing to permit the use of them'.[45] As it turned out, shop assistants who used the seats would generally be reprimanded, so their working conditions did not change in effect. In one example of how the CLNY's activities should and did extend beyond merely encouraging considerate shopping, it expanded its investigation beyond observing and documenting the conditions in the shop itself to exploring and evaluating existing legislation, and found that there was already 'a city ordinance providing for seats behind counters, but as it had been so loosely drawn and there were no inspectors to enforce it, it was a dead letter'.[46] The same fact was also evident from Woodbridge's report, which notes: 'In our investigation we find the law requiring seats for saleswomen is generally ignored; in a few places one seat is provided at a counter where fifteen girls are employed, and in one store seats are provided and saleswomen fined if found sitting.'[47] This example demonstrates how employers could and did make use of subversion and deception in response to legal requirements as well as consumer enquiries, relying on their workers' inability to make public or otherwise resist the reality of their working conditions.

It was this simultaneous identification of the inadequacy of existing legislation and its enforcement, and of the influence consumer activists could potentially have if adequately channelled, which led to the CLNY's development from a group of ethical shoppers to a body of legislative activists. Following Woodbridge's example, they began to collect evidence through investigation, contrasting requirements and assumptions with the reality of the conditions they found in different workplaces. The information they thus amassed, combined with the wealth and influence of the women involved, allowed the league to develop into an effective pressure group lobbying to have their recommendations enshrined in law. The Consumers' League was thus able to mobilise further-reaching influence than the Working Women's Society could have done, but only once it had also realised the limitations of the strategy of merely changing their shopping habits and proceeded to explore different and more concrete applications of their activist energy.

The result of this first campaign on retail work was the 1896 Mercantile Act enacted in Albany, the capital of New York State, to limit working hours, prohibit child labour and make stipulations about hygienic facilities for workers and seats behind counters. The Act was hailed by Nathan as

> mark[ing] an era for the Consumers' League. Before that, our work had been formative, in a sense, experimental. We had succeeded in arousing the public conscience as to the existence of certain evils and the sense of responsibility for these evils. We had created a public opinion which finally crystallized in legislation. We were no longer a doubtful experiment; we were a force and a power, and we had to be reckoned with.[48]

This legislative victory showed how the motto 'investigate, record, agitate' could be used to 'arouse the public conscience', and the weight of 'public opinion' used to exert pressure on governing bodies. In this sense, the US consumers' leagues brought together the kind of appeals to public consciousness made by investigators such as Black and the Women's Industrial Council, with ambitions for legislative change, which Black would also adopt and develop. Nathan points out, with pride, that British labour activists including Black used the success of the Mercantile Act to have a similar bill passed by the House of Lords in 1899 to combat the exploitation of shop assistants.[49] It thus rapidly became evident that the practice of lobbying for changes to labour laws at state level could also have an international impact as activist organisations in different countries drew inspiration from the success of other bodies around the world. These developments cemented the success of the

CLNY and furthered the development of comparable initiatives in other states, on a national level, and even internationally.

Although Woodbridge and the Working Women's Society never again had key roles in the consumers' league movement in the US, the rhetoric and argument of Woodbridge's report set an important tone for the subsequent use of women's campaign writing by the organisation. The principles of the CLNY, and the subsequent requirements of the Mercantile Act, clearly drew heavily on the observations in her report. The organisation's articulated principles made clear stipulations on such points as fines, the separation of work-, lunch- and bathrooms, the upholding of laws on seating, recognition for length of service, and the employment of children under the age of fourteen. They also took on board the points Woodbridge had made about gender, acknowledging women's added vulnerability in the workplace. Ahead of their time, the principles insisted on equal wages for equal work regardless of gender, calling for extra vigilance on this matter in industries that primarily employed women. They even set a minimum weekly wage for women's work. To these points, foregrounded in Woodbridge's report, they added an emphatic explication of consumer responsibility, especially as regarded prices and wages and 'buying in the cheapest market' – a probably coincidental echo of Black.[50] Knowing the harmful consequences that were likely to follow consumer choices based primarily on price, the principles noted that it was 'the duty of consumers to find out under what conditions the articles which they purchase are produced, and to insist that these conditions shall be at least decent and consistent with a respectable existence on the part of the workers'.[51] The emphasis here was on consumers exerting their influence on behalf of workers, or at least taking responsibility not to injure workers; but the aim of this was to ensure working conditions that enabled workers to live decent lives. The CLNY's primary concern, then, at this point, was with worker welfare rather than product quality or consumer rights.

Woodbridge's approach of identifying achievable short-term goals, and the issues she raised pertaining to hygiene, health, the ability of low wages to undermine quality of life, employer control and the threat that exploitation posed to women's moral welfare, remained key arguments mobilised by the US Consumers' Leagues both to convince their own membership and to influence policy makers. Like many contemporary social investigators, Woodbridge structured her arguments around a catalogue of common iniquities, regularly drawing attention to specific and shocking examples to bring her message home. Without citing specific sources beyond the short passage vouching for her informants, she still included the occasional verifiable detail, such as the reference to Grace Henderson's suicide or the testimony of a 'well-known physician' who described the bathroom facilities in one 'fashionable store' as 'not fit for a human being to enter'.[52] These details would have functioned to convince her audience of the truth of her other observations too. Woodbridge's references to details of disease contagion, such as the children's 'granulated eyes', as well as the comments of the medical witness, may be considered forerunners of the NCL's own lines of argument. The health of workers went on to be an important point in the 'entering wedge' strategy of activism. It related both to the future labour potential of working-class children and to the ability of working-class women to bear a healthy generation of future workers, in ways that were often reflective of problematic agendas. The NCL would regularly use expert testimonies, particularly from medical sources, to underpin these arguments in order to pursue legislative change, not least in *Muller* v. *Oregon*.

The trajectory of the CLNY and the NCL was a little less straightforward than that articulated by Nathan in *The Story of an Epoch-Making Movement*, of investigation leading almost directly to agitation for legislation, and of progress at state level quickly prompting national and international imitation. The various Consumers' Leagues of the US, including the NCL, experimented with and embraced a number of different strategies to engage and mobilise consumer activism in the run-up to the important developments of the Progressive Era. In evolving these strategies, furthermore, the movement engaged with and borrowed from a number of other activist campaigns, just as Black had done. The next text, an early articulation of the aims and principles of the newly formed NCL written by its first and long-standing General Secretary, Florence Kelley, illustrates some of these influences, experiments and proposed connections between campaigns and social groups.

Florence Kelley, 'Aims and Principles of the Consumers' League', *American Journal of Sociology*, 1899

Kelley's philosophy was more explicitly political than that of Shaw Lowell or Nathan; she was a Marxist socialist who had translated Friedrich Engels's *Lage der arbeitenden Klasse in England* [*Condition of the Working Classes in England*] (1845) into English in the 1880s. A trained lawyer and a member of the bar of Illinois, she had a background as a factory inspector as well as a social justice reformer. Her investment in improving working conditions, especially for women, was long-standing. She had

> drafted the Illinois maximum hours law of 1893, led the campaign to enact it, and, as chief factory inspector, headed the team that enforced it. When an Illinois employer challenged the law [in the *Ritchie* v. *Illinois* case of 1895], Kelley and her colleagues wrote a brief to defend it.[53]

As with Black's consumer activist articles, Kelley's socialist politics are not explicitly referenced in her many publications advertising and promoting the NCL and its work. In fact, she largely circumvents class politics altogether in her efforts to emphasise what she calls the 'universality' of the Consumers' League.[54] It is worth remembering, however, that Kelley's politics did directly enter into both her priorities as a campaigner and what she was and was not able to achieve: for instance, in 1897 she would be 'thrown out of her factory inspectorship [. . .] by the defeat of Illinois' socialist-leaning governor and replaced by a Republican man who was solicitous of employer interests', leaving her 'forced to seek new ways of winning and enforcing labor legislation in the face of GOP [Republican party] dominance at both state and national levels'.[55] Chapter 4 will show how this and her experience of the *Ritchie* case motivated her to pursue legal change through the NCL.

In 'The Aims and Principles of the Consumers' League', Kelley is open about the NCL's vision of itself as an organisation founded on principles that are 'partly economic and partly moral'.[56] The economic analysis she proceeds to apply shows that its concerns and ambitions affect and seek to benefit people across classes, genders and communities because, as she points out, everyone is a consumer. Everyone's purchases therefore have the potential to injure or benefit both others and oneself; and the organisation of consumers for the purpose of collecting information, increasing understanding, and engaging in activism where necessary would work to counteract a large number of unethical practices, from labour exploitation to product adulteration to disease contagion. In view of the direction taken by the NCL and state leagues, focusing on wealthier and leisured women as potential activists, we may wonder here, as with Black, how far the democratic 'everyone' went in practice.

Compared to Black's determination to advertise her project through popular publications in order to engage wide readerships, Kelley's choice to publish through a scientific platform like the *American Journal of Sociology* may seem striking. Demonstrating the academic soundness of the initiative was clearly something to which she attached considerable value, however, and which she used to render her article more convincing for an academic readership. She explains that, '[r]ecognizing that its work must be one of education and organization, the Consumers' League has sought the cooperation of the great educational institutions', and proceeds to enumerate the university departments and learned societies of economics, sociology, social sciences and politics that had shown interest in the leagues and their work, including Harvard and Columbia. In fact, she adds in a footnote that the 'substance of this paper' was read at a meeting of the American Social Science Association.[57] Like Black who sought to underpin her arguments with economic theory to prevent readers from dismissing them as overly idealistic, Kelley seems eager to use these academic endorsements to prove that the NCL and its constituent leagues amounted to a well-thought-out and effective organisation with the potential to attain a reach and influence considerably beyond that of such local reforms as had traditionally been the province of society ladies. Academic connections and research in scientific collections would, furthermore, go on to be an important basis for the arguments presented by the NCL for legislative changes, as for instance in the Brandeis Brief for *Muller* v. *Oregon*.

A key aspect of Kelley's argument is that the issues attendant on individual consumers' inability to obtain and evaluate information regarding their purchases, and consequently to act effectively on this information, affected and injured consumers across all levels of society. She illustrates this by referring to three separate examples of what she calls 'ineffectual' consumers, including those with and without social and economic influence.[58] The first example pertains to Italian immigrant communities who, in seeking to buy food and drink imported from Italy at considerable expense, were often sold products that had been adulterated with cheaper substitutes. The economic influence of these individual communities, primarily made up of working-class immigrants, tended to be small, however, leaving them unable successfully to resist these abuses. On the other hand, Kelley hastens to assure her readers that paying more for goods by no means guaranteed wealthier consumers protection from abuses in the production system. The example she gives is drawn from her own experience as factory inspector of Illinois. It relates to an expensive overcoat ordered from a local shop in Montana, the sewing of which had been outsourced by a central manufacturer in Chicago to a home-based migrant tailor who had not yet been registered with the Board of Health or the inspection department. A case of smallpox was discovered in this worker's household, which had not been reported because the tailor had been fearful of losing work. With reference to the customer who had paid between $60 and $75 for the overcoat in Montana, Kelley explained:

> Essentially, the position of this purchaser did not differ materially from that of the Italian immigrants; like them he was paying a price which entitled him to get clean goods; like them he had neither technical knowledge nor organization to make his demand effective.[59]

This example illustrates the same point made by Black, that while cheap products were likely to be connected to cheap production, paying more for goods did not by any means guarantee that this extra money would benefit the various workers in the chain of production.

Kelley's article also demonstrates that, in the formation of the NCL, lessons had been learned from the early experiments in ethical consumerism of the CLNY, which had tended to suggest that individual informed consumers could make a difference to workers' conditions, provided they had some influence in their community and the shops they patronised. Her third and final example described 'a conscientious shopper of my acquaintance in Chicago' who had become concerned about the conditions of garment workers through reading about sweating practices and 'determined to free her own conscience by buying only goods made in factories'. In this search she started at one of her favourite department stores, asking for a written assurance with her order that the department store did not sell products made in sweatshops. Kelley states that the order was 'never sent, though this was an excellent customer whom the firm was in the habit of obliging if possible'. Continuing her fruitless search for clothing free from sweatshop labour, this particular consumer, according to Kelley, was forced to conclude that 'she could not free her conscience alone and unaided'.[60] This woman reflects the same kind of concerned consumer who features so regularly in Black's appeals for consumer activism: wishing to do what they could to avoid contributing to exploitative labour practices which they condemned from a moral standpoint, they proved to be unable to do so independently with any significant effect.[61]

The problem was not even necessarily that the requisite information was unavailable, Kelley noted. On a national level as well as by individual states and cities, information was collected and made public regarding labour conditions, food adulteration and so on; but none of these reports and statistics, Kelley argued, did much to help individual consumers in their choices, as they did not give information about outsourcing and home-based labour, which carried grave risks of undetectable adulteration and disease contagion. There were also difficulties of access to information: 'Official statements on all these matters, safely buried in official reports, do not reach and influence the great mass of the buyers.'[62] She also explained that there were difficulties inherent in state-level administration; even if a consumer themself lived in a state with high-quality industrial regulation and progressive labour laws, States of the Union were constitutionally prevented from forbidding imports from any other state, so products manufactured under the inadequate legislation of another state would still make their way into the conscientious consumer's local shops. In this way, Kelley's argument looks ahead to the realisation Black would later cite as her reason for abandoning her version of the Consumers' League, namely that production systems had become so fragmented and complicated that it was not possible to vouch for a product and all its constituent parts. In Kelley's view, however, the role of a consumers' league would be to help consumers to access and understand relevant and helpful information regarding matters such as labour standards and product adulteration.

It is interesting to note that Kelley's priority in this article is not the legislative change that, from Nathan's account, the CLNY had already begun to focus on by this point following the Albany Mercantile Act. Instead, she highlights early activities of Nathan, Shaw Lowell and the CLNY to develop a system of whitelisting of specific retailers who treated their staff comparatively well. This initiative had been successful, Kelley stated, because the two ladies [Shaw Lowell and Nathan] proceeded to organize their friends; to bring their growing constituency to the attention of the retail merchant; to circulate their White List, and the Standard upon which it is founded; and to educate public opinion as to the power of purchasers to determine the conditions of labor in retail stores.[63]

Here again is an emphasis on the importance of the organisation's leaders being socially and economically prominent. This may seem unexpected in view of not only Kelley's own politics but also her previous argument that all consumers were affected by poor practices and that individual consumers' activism was ineffectual. In contrast to her example of the single concerned consumer in Chicago, however, Kelley suggests that the early CLNY succeeded because of its ability to organise large numbers of consumers, and particularly influential women who could have an impact on the specific and localised industry of leisure shopping that was strongly geared towards their custom.

The other point that is worth citing in this context is Kelley's acknowledgement of the general goodwill of employers, reminiscent of Black's insistence that employers were not 'man-eating ogres' who deliberately exploited their workers. In the example of the CLNY, Kelley notes that nearly forty shops on Manhattan Island decided to raise their standards to be included on the whitelist. She further states that many employers who already strove to treat their workers ethically despite 'intense pressure of competition of others who have a lower standard' in fact 'greeted the league with cordial welcome'.[64] In this way, then, the organisation of consumers would not only benefit workers but also reward decent employers.

It is telling that Kelley places so much emphasis on what was essentially an organised form of ethical shopping, while other experiments in consumer activism tended to end by finding whitelisting inadequate for various reasons. I suggest that this presentation of events is designed to add weight to the project at the heart of Kelley's own article: the introduction of the NCL label (see Fig. 2.1). This experimental undertaking was designed as an aid to organised ethical shopping based on voluntary compliance of producers and consumers alike, without aspiring to legislative change. The label drew inspiration from pre-existing labels issued by trade unions, a tradition that previously also sometimes worked in a deliberately and discriminatorily

Figure 2.1 The NCL label. VectorStock, Standard
Licence.

exclusionary way, for instance in attempting to privilege the
labour of white workers over that of Chinese migrant workers
in particular.[65] It is worth noting, however, that the NCL label
distanced itself from trade unions; while Black's whitelists explicitly referred to union conditions, 'the League's label encouraged
employers to shorten the workday and improve working conditions, but it made no reference to union wage standards, much
less union recognition'.[66]

The label campaign focused, once again, on the garment trade
as both especially exploitative of women workers and disproportionately dependent on the actions of wealthier women consumers.
In order to test the efficacy of the project, the campaign focused
on a specific branch of the industry: the production of women's
muslin underwear. Serving as a guarantee that the garments were
produced under ethical circumstances, the label indicated

> that all goods must be manufactured by the manufacturer on his own
> premises; that all the requirements of the state factory law must be
> complied with; that no children under sixteen years of age shall be
> employed; that no overtime shall be worked.[67]

In the longer term, the NCL hoped also to include a stipulated
minimum wage for workers. The presence of the label, visibly
proclaiming that the garment was 'made under clean and health-
ful conditions' and 'use of label authorized after investigation'
(Fig. 2.1), would relieve consumers of the individual responsibility to inquire into the details of production. In order to make this
worth the manufacturers' while too, the NCL pledged to advertise the conditions upheld in its approved factories, thus ensuring
that these factories gained sufficient custom to turn a reasonable

profit without compromising on their standards. Jeffrey Haydu notes that there was also an element of self-sacrifice to consumers' participation in this scheme as the certified underwear tended to be of a lower quality than that to which many league members could be expected to be accustomed. He states that '[t]he White Label campaign, accordingly, stressed the importance of renouncing personal comfort and class standards to support poor women and children'.[68]

Kelley's article carries out in detail her indication, in the opening lines, that the project she is proposing on behalf of the new NCL is both an economic and a moral one. Placing the article in the *Journal of Sociology*, within a wider context of participation in academic debates around economics and social sciences, brings this point home and adds to a sense of the project's rational and practical soundness – in other words, making a scientific case for ethical and altruistic behaviour as well as encouraging it for its own sake. It is logical in this context that the NCL would strive to make this type of behaviour easily accessible for both consumers and manufacturers through a clearly comprehensible scheme like the label. Like modern-day equivalents such as the Fair Trade, Rainforest Alliance or Marine Conservation Society labels, the scheme worked on the assumption of the essential goodwill of both consumers and sellers. Schemes like these add to the narrative around consumer activism as collapsing distance. While the breaking down of emotional distance between workers and consumers is taken as a given, the NCL label, through its nationwide application, traversed physical distance too. If knowing about conditions of production in one's own state was no guarantee because of unrestricted imports between states, the label, with its pledge of national standards, reassured consumers across state boundaries. In this way, too, it could effectively work on a much larger scale than the CLNY's whitelist, which referred to shops in a specific area largely patronised by a specific, interconnected clientele.

It is worth noting that the label still appeals to the present-day ethical consumer's imagination. In *Fashionopolis*, Dana Thomas states that '[t]he white label empowered shoppers, pushing them to think ethically about their purchases'. In addition, she demonstrates that shop owners were remarkably supportive of the initiative. She cites the example of 'Philadelphia department store magnate John Wanamaker', who

joined the League's campaign to improve factory conditions, promoted white-label-approved clothes in his store, and had window
dressers fill the Broad Street vitrines with displays that demonstrated
the differences between sweatshops and white-label-approved factories. Photographs of the window exhibit later toured international
trade fairs. Within five years, sixty American manufacturers had qualified to use the white label in their clothing.[69]

This example reflects the NCL's clever use of advertising and high-
profile support to advance its campaigns; but it also shows that
employers and retailers were amenable to the NCL's attempts to
include them in their campaign for social improvement.

In many ways Kelley's article and its indication of the NCL's
ambitions at its inception are surprisingly unambitious. On the
one hand it sought to implement a novel, nationwide scheme;
but on the other this was carefully limited to give the experiment
the best chance of success. It also made a fairly safe bet with an
industry that employed and served primarily women, wielding
the long-standing rhetoric of women's consumer guilt for the
exploitation of needlewomen. It is silent on the achievement of
the CLNY on a legislative front; and while this would go on to
become a key contribution of the NCL, it is impossible to tell
from Kelley's article whether legislative change was already an
ambition for the NCL at this point. Similarly, barring arguably
her emphasis on the cross-class importance of consumer activism and the adoption of a device from trade union activism,
Kelley's personal politics do not come into her article. Unlike
in Woodbridge's report or in Nathan's retrospective, furthermore, she barely dwells at all on details of worker exploitation
in a bid to gain her readers' sympathy. She references available
information about sweating and poor treatment of workers but
gives no detailed examples; the assumption seems to be that her
readership, like the concerned consumer in Chicago, will already
be aware of other emotive and shocking accounts. Writing for a
scientific rather than a popular journal, her approach is carefully
objective.

Like both Black and Woodbridge in their separate ways,
Kelley's article seems eager not to sound threatening or alienat-
ing to the audience she seeks to involve. This is reflective of her
role as a representative of a wider organisation. Boris points out
that

[t]he National League under Kelley embraced trade unionism, although the founding convention had rejected a proposal to make 'the trade union standard of hours and wages' [its own] standard. John Graham Brooks, the first president of the national group, noted its contradictory politics: 'To work with trade unions is to antagonize much of the present [League] membership; to ignore them is to antagonize working people.'[70]

In order to keep readers, potential activists and her own membership on her side, Kelley's article emphasises continually that she is offering a well-thought-through initiative that based its call for action on successful precedents nationally and internationally – as well as the efficient workings of the CLNY, she regularly mentions the success of the cooperative movement in the UK. The enthusiasm of progressive employers showed that the scheme need not impinge on industry or business. Her article demonstrated both consumers' eagerness to do good and the risks they ran of being duped in the present situation. There was therefore an objectively recognisable moral need and desire for the work of the Consumers' League; and her scheme showed how economic action could be undertaken without causing economic problems. The consumer activism she proposed, then, would evidently be beneficial to consumers, employers and workers alike.

Conclusions: Consolidating and spreading the consumers' league model

The various consumer activism narratives put forward by Woodbridge, Kelley and Nathan indicate that the US model of the consumers' league that went on to have a significant impact on the policies of the Progressive Era was the result of widespread and varied experimentation, with potential activists testing their influence through multiple strategies and in retrospect necessarily focusing on those that proved successful. As in Black's case, mutual sharing, imitation and adaptation of campaign strategies formed an important part of these developments. The knowledge of a shared, increasingly global economic system with comparable attendant problems underpinned these exchanges between activists across state and national borders. Nathan deliberately presents the US leagues as a movement 'launched [. . .] in the new world which was destined to mould public opinion the world over', and she relates the influence of the US leagues in the establishment of similar organisations in continental Europe.[71] According to Nathan, she was approached in 1903 about setting up a French league; she states that the leaders of the French movement then took the model to Switzerland. A German league was formed following her address to the Quinquennial Convention of the International Council of Women in Berlin in 1904. These developments paved the way for an International Conference of Consumers' Leagues to be held in 1908.[72]

Marie-Emmanuelle Chessel explains that '[t]he "transfer" of consumers' leagues from the United States to France took place rapidly, in the context of a reforming elite on both sides of the Atlantic already open to international exchanges'.[73] Mitchell's account of the formation of the Ligue Sociale d'Acheteurs [Social League of Consumers] suggests that, rather than following deliberately in US footsteps, it was the product of common ideas that had been circulating in Europe as well as the United States for several years; our foreknowledge of Black's activities in the UK makes this more likely. According to Louis Athey in a 1978 article examining the European history of consumers' leagues, the French Consumers' League was inspired by a display contributed by the NCL to the Paris Exhibition of 1900, and its founder Henriette Brunhes corresponded with NCL members about setting up the project.[74] Mitchell dates the founding of the Ligue to 1902, and both his and Chessel's accounts of its first project show parallels with Black's original scheme as well as the practices of the US leagues: it compiled 'a white list of dressmakers who treated their workers well and encouraged shoppers to refuse to have goods delivered in an evening or to shop on Sundays'.[75] Again, the focus seems to be on the consumer choices of the leisured woman shopper, who decided that she could dispense with cheap clothing and round-the-clock shopping if these benefits could only be had at the expense of workers' welfare. Mitchell notes that, '[a]s in the USA, the *Ligue* sought to educate the middle classes rather than to organize the workers themselves. It also conducted surveys into workers' lives and lobbied for social and labour legislation.'[76]

Although the French league consciously drew on the US model and established contact with the NCL, according to Mitchell, it was 'a much smaller organisation firmly rooted in Catholicism rather than socialism'.[77] Chessel explains that 'at the turn of the century [. . .] consumers' leagues became part of a broader intellectual, religious and political movement that surpassed women's traditional Christian philanthropic activities'.[78] What it shares with other conceptions of the potential influence of a consumers' league, then, is a focus on middle-class women consumers and a search for ways to turn consumer guilt into socio-economic influence. The focus was on the consumer rather than the worker and on the moral rather than the economic implications of the relationship between them.

The expression of these common ideas around consumer responsibility appears to have been relatively short-lived, however: of the consumers' leagues established in the Netherlands, Switzerland, Germany and Belgium in the early years of the twentieth century, 'only the Swiss league survived the First World War'.[79] According to Athey, '[i]n Europe the war years were especially critical for the consumers' leagues. Nationalistic policies replaced international cooperative efforts toward reform.'[80] Tellingly, furthermore, there seems to be an acceptance throughout these international narratives of consumer activism that no consumers' league would be (re-)established in the UK. Kelley points repeatedly to the example of the British cooperative movement as successfully regulating supply and demand through expert buyers working on behalf of consumer collectives.[81] At the International Conference in 1908, Britain was represented by the newly formed Anti-Sweating League which had been set up to campaign for a minimum wage following the 'Sweated Industries Exhibition'.

The analyses of these first two chapters suggest, then, that a central question throughout the international histories of the consumers' league movement is one of cooperation – between classes and movements across borders and cultures. For Nathan it was advantageous to pretend that the European leagues were a direct copy of the successful organisation she had helped to build; this served to bolster US national pride, allowing US activists to feel that they had a share in the growing global prominence of their country and thus hopefully encouraging further activism. In its inception, however, the CLNY had borrowed ideas and strategies from the Working Women's Society, and the NCL from the trade union movement. In addition, throughout the history of the NCL and its sister organisations it is equally possible to trace a continued reliance on investigations abroad to strengthen the case for legislation at home. The example of the short-lived French league shows that this kind of cooperation was imperative for an operation on the scale of the NCL; without it, the initiative could not proceed beyond an organised form of conscientious shopping. Storrs's analysis of the failure of its initial projects including the CLNY whitelists and the NCL label show the need for this kind of cooperation, as Black also highlighted in her proposals for a whitelist. According to Storrs, the failure of the whitelisting and labelling initiatives in the US was due to a lack of the resources required to maintain and develop these certifications. He notes that

> the league could not keep up the inspections required to maintain use of the label. Although not successful in changing employer practices, the league lists and labels were nonetheless effective devices for recruiting middle-class women and educating them on labor issues and the working of state government.[82]

Bearing this in mind, it seems obvious that Nathan would focus so strongly on the success of the Albany Mercantile Act in *The Story of an Epoch-Making Movement*, while this early legislative effort is not mentioned at all in Kelley's first publications advertising the new NCL. After all, legislative change became the route that the CLNY and NCL would go down in the first decades of the twentieth century as it provided them with influential successes and produced evident change.

The combined examples of Black's failed consumers' league and the successful CLNY and NCL suggest that a functioning and effective consumer organisation required both a broad base of support among consumers and a leadership that could sustain this support while looking for a combination of activist strategies that was adapted for the particular local and temporal situation. The presence or absence of explicit politics was relevant here too, not least because consumer organisations were eager not to alienate a potential membership in more affluent social classes who could lend prominent support. Socialists Black and Kelley both pointed to successful examples of worker organisation as models, but both the US leagues and Black herself eventually moved away from worker-led initiatives in order to pursue campaigns more focused on exerting political influence at a higher organisational level. The principle of collapsing distance between worker and consumer, then, morphed over time from encouraging sympathy and fellow feeling with workers – as had even been the case, to a degree, in the mid-century narrative of consumer guilt – to a sense of making use of social distance and divisions to act on behalf of exploited workers. This problematic style of worker representation by activists to engage support is at the core of the UK and US case studies in Chapters 3 and 4. Especially in the context of the 'Sweated Industries Exhibition' discussed in Chapter 3, this type of representation almost became another type of consumer product marketed to the potential consumer activist.

Notes

1. Matthew Hilton, *Consumerism in Twentieth-Century Britain: The Search for a Historical Movement* (Cambridge: Cambridge University Press, 2003), p. 48.
2. Matthew Hilton, 'Consumer Movements', in *The Oxford Handbook of the History of Consumption*, ed. Frank Trentmann (Oxford: Oxford University Press, 2012), pp. 505–19 (p. 510).
3. Ian Mitchell, 'Ethical Shopping in Late Victorian and Edwardian Britain', *Journal of Historical Research in Marketing*, 7.3 (2015), 310–29 (p. 318) <https://doi.org/10.1108/JHRM-08-2014-0021>.
4. 'The Salvation Army Bakery', *Darkest England Gazette*, 20 January 1894, p. 12.
5. Landon R. Y. Storrs, *Civilizing Capitalism: The National Consumers' League, Women's Activism, and Labor Standards in the New Deal Era* (Chapel Hill: University of North Carolina Press, 2000), p. 2.
6. Rebecca Edwards, *Angels in the Machinery: Gender in American Party Politics from the Civil War to the Progressive Era* (New York: Oxford University Press, 1997), p. 4.
7. Ibid. p. 7.
8. Alice L. Woodbridge, *Report on the Condition of Working Women in New York Retail Stores* (New York: Freytag, 1893), 8pp. (p. 1), *LSE Selected Pamphlets* <https://www.jstor.org/stable/60218789> [accessed 30 March 2020].
9. Maud Nathan, *The Story of an Epoch-Making Movement* (London: Heinemann, 1926), p. 89.
10. Daniel E. Bender, *Sweated Work, Weak Bodies: Sweatshop Campaigns and Languages of Labor* (New Brunswick and London: Rutgers University Press, 2004), e.g. pp. 51, 66.
11. Clementina Black, 'Suggested Remedies', in *Handbook of the 'Daily News' Sweated Industries' Exhibition*, compiled by Richard Mudie-Smith (London: Burt, 1906), pp. 22–6 (p. 26) <https://archive.org/

stream/handbookofdailynoomudi_0#page/n17/mode/1up> [accessed 24 July 2016].

12. See, for instance, 'The Grievances of Barmaids' by Black, in *The Woman's World* (London: Cassell, 1890), pp. 383–5.

13. Nathan, pp. 10–12.

14. Woodbridge, p. 7.

15. Nathan, pp. 5–8.

16. Ibid. pp. 2, 4, 9.

17. Ibid. p. 16.

18. Newton D. Baker, 'Foreword', in Nathan, *The Story of an Epoch-Making Movement*, pp. xi–xiv (p. xiii). Storrs gives the alternative '[i]nvestigate, agitate, legislate' (p. 15). The NCL's official website no longer uses either motto; it now uses 'For confidence and safety in the marketplace since 1899' <http://www.nclnet.org> [accessed 12 January 2023].

19. Nathan, p. 16.

20. Ibid. pp. 16–19.

21. Nancy Woloch, *A Class by Herself: Protective Laws for Women Workers, 1890s–1990s* (Princeton: Princeton University Press, 2015), p. 13.

22. Storrs, p. 2.

23. Ibid. p. 14.

24. Eileen Boris, *A Coat of Many Colors: Immigration, Globalization, and Reform in New York City's Garment Industry* (New York: Fordham University Press, 2005), p. 214.

25. See Theda Skocpol, *Protecting Soldiers and Mothers* (Cambridge, MA: Harvard University Press, 1992), p. 383.

26. 'History', *National Consumers' League* <http://www.nclnet.org/history> [accessed 12 July 2022].

27. 'Guide to the Consumers' League of New York City Records', Cornell University Library <http://rmc.library.cornell.edu/EAD/htmldocs/KCL05307.html> [accessed 12 July 2022].

28. Boris, p. 214.

29. Woodbridge, p. 1.

30. Ibid. p. 1.

31. Ibid. p. 4.

32. Ibid. p. 4.

33. Ibid. p. 6.

34. Ibid. p. 5.

35. Ibid. p. 6.

36. Ibid. p. 7.

37. Ibid. p. 8.
38. Ibid. p. 8.
39. Ibid. p. 8. Reporting on the case of Grace Henderson's suicide quotes her suicide note which mentions '[w]idowers who advertise for housekeepers and then gently insinuate that you add wifely duties to domestic arrangements'. See for instance 'She Escaped Starvation' in the New York *Sun*, 21 January 1890, p. 5.
40. Woodbridge, p. 8.
41. Ibid. p. 8.
42. The first citation of the term 'American Dream' in the *Oxford English Dictionary* dates from 1911. See 'American, n. and adj.', *OED Online*, Oxford University Press, September 2021, <https://www.oed.com/view/Entry/6342> [accessed 2 November 2021].
43. Woodbridge, p. 8.
44. Nathan, p. 39.
45. Ibid. p. 40.
46. Ibid. p. 40.
47. Woodbridge, p. 6.
48. Nathan, p. 59.
49. Ibid. pp. 89–90.
50. 'The Consumers' League of the City of New York: Principles', cited in Florence Kelley, 'Aims and Principles of the Consumers' League', *American Journal of Sociology*, 5.3 (1899), 289–304 (p. 300) <https://jstor.org/stable/2761531> [accessed 30 March 2020].
51. Ibid. p. 300.
52. Woodbridge, p. 4.
53. Woloch, p. 12. The Supreme Court of Illinois still proceeded to declare the maximum hours law unconstitutional on the basis of the Fourteenth Amendment.
54. Kelley, 'Aims and Principles', p. 289.
55. Edwards, p. 150.
56. Kelley, 'Aims and Principles', p. 289.
57. Ibid. p. 302.
58. Ibid. p. 290.
59. Ibid. p. 292.
60. Ibid. p. 291.
61. These three poignant examples – the duped Italian migrants, the overcoat with smallpox germs and the conscientious department store patron – are reused verbatim by Kelley six years later in the chapter 'The Rights of Purchasers' in her book *Some Ethical Gains*

through Legislation (New York: Macmillan, 1905); see pp. 214–15, 216–17 and 219.

62. Kelley, 'Aims and Principles', p. 297.
63. Ibid. p. 299.
64. Ibid. pp. 302, 301.
65. See Boris, p. 215, and John Graham Brooks, 'The Label of the Consumers [*sic*] League', *Publications of the American Economic Association*, 1.1 (1900), 250–8 (pp. 250–1) <https://www.jstor.org/stable/2485833> [accessed 30 March 2020].
66. Jeffrey Haydu, 'Consumer Citizenship and Cross-Class Activism: The Case of the National Consumers' League, 1899–1918', *Sociological Forum*, 29.3 (2014), 628–49 (p. 643).
67. Kelley, 'Aims and Principles', p. 298.
68. Haydu, p. 639.
69. Dana Thomas, *Fashionopolis: The Price of Fast Fashion and the Future of Clothes* (London: Head of Zeus, 2019), p. 46.
70. Boris, pp. 216–17. The first insertion is mine, the second is Boris's.
71. Nathan, p. 22.
72. Ibid. pp. 97, 99–100.
73. Marie-Emmanuelle Chessel, 'Women and the Ethics of Consumption in France at the Turn of the Twentieth Century: The *Ligue Sociale d'Acheteurs*', in *The Making of the Consumer*, ed. Frank Trentmann (Oxford: Berg, 2006), pp. 81–98 (pp. 81–2).
74. Louis L. Athey, 'From Social Conscience to Social Action: The Consumers' Leagues in Europe, 1900–1914', *Social Service Review*, 52.3 (1978), 362–82 (pp. 362–3) <https://www.jstor.org/stable/30015641> [accessed 30 March 2020].
75. Mitchell, p. 314; see also Chessel, p. 83.
76. Mitchell, pp. 314–15.
77. Ibid. p. 315.
78. Chessel, p. 83.
79. Mitchell, p. 315.
80. Athey, p. 377.
81. Kelley, 'Aims and Principles', p. 295.
82. Storrs, p. 20.

Part II

Strategic Developments, 1900–1920

3

Encounters with Sweating: Public
Outreach and Political Influence
in the UK, 1900–1910

Well-informed about international developments in activist initiatives and strategies to combat labour exploitation, Clementina
Black was certainly aware of the achievements of the consumers'
league scheme in the US since the 1890s. In 1906 she acknowledged that '[i]n New York, where the Consumers' League is
supported by ladies of wealth and influence, it has been more
successful'; she adds that 'the movement is now being copied,
with some enthusiasm apparently, in France'.[1] As Black and the
Women's Trade Union Association/Women's Industrial Council
became disillusioned with the potential of trade unionism to alter
women's working conditions, they focused more on the need
for influential and official support to achieve changes across the
board. While her own socio-economic analysis had led Black to
reject the consumers' league as a workable model to achieve her
activist ambitions in the UK, the conclusion that she and the WIC
eventually reached had much in common with that of the US
National Consumers' League. She decided that while the goodwill of consumer activism could raise awareness around workplace exploitation, changes to workers' conditions could only
be upheld and enforced if they were enshrined in law. For Black,
however, this meant dispensing altogether with trying to persuade consumers that their individual purchasing choices could
make any substantial difference. Instead, her new strategy was
to confront a broad public with the knowledge that the system
in which they made their purchases was inevitably and inex-
tricably linked with sweating practices. This reflects the thinking that Sheila C. Blackburn identified as the third stage in the
understanding of sweated labour, following its 'discovery' in the

1840s and 'rediscovery' from the 1880s: the idea that sweating was an inherent and entrenched part of unregulated capitalism.[2] The direct aim of campaigns to increase awareness of this reality was to put popular pressure on legislators to eliminate the 'sweating system' altogether. In Black's view, this would be best achieved by introducing a minimum wage to eliminate underpayment, the root problem of the sweating system.

The most high-profile tool Black and her associates used to raise public awareness of sweating in the first decade of the twentieth century was the sensational 'Sweated Industries Exhibition'. It was held in the Queen's Hall in Westminster, London, over six weeks through May and early June 1906. The first exhibition of sweated labour in Britain, it was spearheaded by the Women's Industrial Council and sponsored by the *Daily News*, a liberal paper owned by the Quakers and chocolate manufacturers George and Edward Cadbury. For Black, the event brought together her long-standing commitment to appealing for popular, cross-class support and her new preoccupation with engaging the socially and economically influential in order to shape public opinion. This chapter begins with an examination of the exhibition itself: the previous events which it took for its examples, the activists involved, the planning that led up to it, and the layout, structure and content of the event itself. These details highlight how the exhibition reflects the revision of Black's proposals for consumer activism. The two central source texts are the handbook that accompanied the exhibition and Black's subsequent 1907 volume *Sweated Industry and the Minimum Wage*, which explained, and sought to persuade her readership of, her transition from consumer activism to legislative change as a means of preventing underpayment. My analysis of the handbook considers how it addressed exhibition visitors, represented participating workers and explained its own aims. I place this in the context both of contemporary responses and of different historical understandings of the exhibition. My reading of *Sweated Industry* will contrast the exhibition with the examples of Black's work that formed the basis of Chapter 1. I examine how the exhibition fitted into her personal overarching aims and strategies and consider the trade-offs she made in choosing and appealing to potential supporters and the ways in which she mobilised them and drew on their support in pursuit of her legislative goals.

Rechannelling consumer activism through the *Daily News* 'Sweated Industries Exhibition'

Exhibitions of home work and sweated labour were prevalent internationally in the early twentieth century, modelled on the popular world fairs of which the 1851 Great Exhibition was a prominent early example. Exhibitions were put on by a variety of activist organisations, including the US Consumers' Leagues, based on investigations into home work and sweating conditions. Their usual format was a collection of goods produced by sweated home work presented with information cards detailing the conditions in which they were made and the wages paid to the worker. Placing these everyday products in an exhibition setting defamiliarised them for the viewer, adding to the shock of the unexpected information associated with them. This strategy may be seen as a variant on the investigative texts that many of these organisations published, marshalling data gathered through investigation into a format suitable for consumption by a wide audience of potential activists. Women's campaign writing remained crucial even in this predominantly visual form of communication as activists controlled and directed the impact of the images they presented in the exhibitions through explanatory and persuasive text.

The written evidence around the London 'Sweated Industries Exhibition' is particularly relevant to this question. As many of the discussions around its organisation and aims were widely publicised, it is possible to connect its development to the changing aims and ideas of the activists behind it, including Black. Much of the evidence the exhibition provides to us today is contained within its extensive guidebook compiled by Richard Mudie-Smith, a member of the staff of the *Daily News* and a key organiser for the exhibition. Other published sources such as newspaper articles by Black and other members of the organising committee also sought to influence how exhibition visitors understood what they saw. Like Black's consumers' league articles, they offered visitors channels for their activist impulses. These activities culminated in the publication of *Sweated Industry and the Minimum Wage*.

The London exhibition stood out from many other similar initiatives in one very important way: rather than display solely the products of sweating, it exhibited living workers as they carried out their sweated labour. The workers were placed in settings designed to replicate their usual work environment and were available to answer visitors' questions. This exhibition strategy allowed for more immediate impact on its target audience. The presence of real workers helped to convince visitors of the reality of their circumstances while the representations of their working environment and the nature of their work left visitors in no doubt as to the severity of the problem. Putting living people on display was common in world fairs, where workers often demonstrated machinery, but which also included human beings as exhibits representing other cultures as part of racist spectacle. To modern eyes these problematic parallels suggest that the participating workers were being exoticised or dehumanised; the well-intentioned exhibition thus invites comparisons with the so-called slumming practices familiar from the nineteenth century, which saw people from wealthier social groups visit deprived urban neighbourhoods as tourist attractions. This context seems difficult to reconcile with Black's emphasis elsewhere on cross-class empathy with working women in particular. The writings of the exhibition organisers shed further light on how they saw this strategy and the people it involved.

The 'Sweated Industries Exhibition' brought together a range of activists with different agendas and profiles. It was researched, planned and organised by a council of leading figures in labour, political and anti-sweating activism. The formidable list of fifty-eight names in the exhibition handbook includes, besides Black, numerous members of the WIC, such as Amie Hicks and Gertrude M. Tuckwell, trade unionists and labour politicians such as Herbert Burrows and James Keir Hardie, active socialists Harry Quelch, Robert Blatchford and C. F. G. Masterman, and socially engaged writers George Bernard Shaw and H. G. Wells.[3] The organising council represented a broad coalition of reformers who are likely to have had different motivations for their interest in combating sweating practices, but a significant proportion came from more or less radical political traditions. The exhibition itself was dissociated from radical politics, however: the venue was a prominent concert hall in the City of Westminster, and the event was opened by Queen Victoria's daughter Beatrice and granddaughter Victoria Eugénie, who was at the time engaged to the king of Spain.[4] The royal patronage, and the shilling charged for admission, indicate that the exhibition was intended to attract a socially and economically influential audience. The handbook, which contained details of conditions in the exhibited trades and of the exhibition's programme of lectures illustrated '[b]y means of an . . . Oxy-Hydrogen Lantern', cost a further sixpence.[5] These prices form a sharp contrast with the conditions represented in the exhibition. For many of the participating workers, a shilling represented significantly more than a day's earnings. Details of piecework rates paid to home workers given in the 'Catalogue of Exhibits' included at the back of the handbook show that to earn 6d workers produced such divers items as a gross of 'Beaded Sprays', chocolate boxes, matchboxes or pompoms, a dozen doll's heads, jet drop trimmings or umbrella tassels, 1,000 paper bags or envelopes, or one Mysore underskirt.[6] On the first page of her preface to the handbook, Tuckwell cites the case of a trouser finisher who was paid at a rate of 2d per pair of trousers and had been forced to pawn her work because her family could not afford to buy food.[7] This story is in essence the same as that of Mrs Biddell, the supposed inspiration for 'The Song of the Shirt' more than sixty years before, who had ended in the workhouse with her family when she could not redeem the work she had pawned.[8]

The *Daily News* eagerly emphasised the success of the exhibition's aim of alerting a wealthy audience to the existence and extent of sweating conditions. It described the opening of the exhibition as 'w[earing] much the aspect of a Society crush' and went on to state:

> It has often been asserted by social reformers that, after all the columns and volumes that have been written about sweating, a knowledge of the evil must be universal. No observer at Queen's Hall yesterday could continue to share that illusion. Society came, saw, and shuddered; and in the expressions of sympathy and indignation that fell from those gentle-nurtured folk, one saw – it is surely not too optimistic to surmise – a corrective public opinion in the making.[9]

This description suggests that the exhibition not only targeted but managed to reach a different audience from that at which the voluminous body of writing on sweating, including the work amassed by Black and members of the WIC, had been aimed throughout the second half of the nineteenth century. The socially and economically prominent patrons attracted by the exhibition, the article seems to indicate, could have a genuine impact in combating sweating by leading the shift in public opinion that reformers had been hoping to achieve for decades.

The organising groups of this broad collaborative project brought together a class-based agenda and experience of investigating exploitative working conditions to create a new representative strategy to reflect conditions that were otherwise difficult to document. In this way they sought to reach consumers who had previously failed to seek out information on the products they bought because they found the subject confusing or uninteresting. The *Daily News* worked hard to reinforce this aim. It informed readers:

> do not imagine that because this Exhibition is concerned with hard facts it will not be interesting to you. For here is not only that irresistible logic of facts which supplies material for the statistician, but also that irresistible pathos of facts which supplies material for the novelist and playwright. It is for the readers of 'The Daily News' to help form such a strong body of public opinion on these matters as shall make it impossible, in the years to come, for such an Exhibition as this to be held, which shall remove the necessity for such an Exhibition. By visiting the Exhibition in person they will impress the Facts vividly on their minds. Armed with the memory of that visit, they will strive all the more strenuously for the removal of those evils which it is the business of this Exhibition to reveal.[10]

This passage was published in the final weeks of the exhibition, which was extended beyond its original month into the first half of June. This suggests that it attracted more visitors than originally anticipated and that the *Daily News* was now going on to target an even broader audience of readers who had not previously intended to visit. The *Daily News*, then, was seeking to capitalise on the fact that the appeal of the exhibition as a society event helped to move consumer activism out of a specialist investigative and activist discourse. If consumer interest and activism could become fashionable, this would create a broad base of support in ways that previous publications had been unable to achieve.

Despite the *Daily News*'s claim that the success of the event would 'remove the necessity for such an Exhibition', however, the exhibition itself self-consciously copied a strategy that had been tried and tested internationally. The idea for the 'Sweated Industries Exhibition' was described by one of the organisers, H. W. Smith, as 'frankly borrowed from the authors of the similar exhibition in Berlin in the early part of the present year'.[11]

The Berlin 'Heimarbeit-Ausstellung' [Home work exhibition] had opened on 17 January 1906 in the Alte Akademie, Unter den Linden.[12] It presented visitors with displays of the 'products of various home industries, ticketed with the remuneration of the worker and time spent in the manufacture'.[13] The 'Heimarbeit-Ausstellung' of 1906 'had been preceded in 1904 by a modest effort of the same kind in connection with the Congress for the Protection of home workers', also in Berlin.[14] The success of the exhibition strategy at the congress had prompted organisers to introduce it to the general public.

Although other exhibitions of exploitative labour conditions had taken place before the turn of the century, the 'Heimarbeit-Ausstellung' sparked an international trend, and exhibitions of this kind, organised by diverse groups of activists, became a common feature across Europe and the United States. For instance, the 'Heimarbeit-Ausstellung' was cited as the inspiration for home work exhibitions held in 1909 in Switzerland and the Netherlands.[15] In France, 'Expositions of Economic Horrors' displaying 'lists of prices consumers paid for various articles of clothing, presented alongside hours workers spent making those same items and the appallingly low rates they were paid', with an accompanying programme of lectures, were organised predominantly by women who engaged in social activism on a Catholic religious basis.[16] The strategy was also embraced by consumers' leagues. The NCL presented an exhibition of sweated goods at the Paris Exhibition of 1900; as we saw in the previous chapter, Louis Athey cites this as the impetus for the for-mation of a consumers' league in France.[17] The 1908 International Conference of Consumers' Leagues also included exhibitions of goods produced in sweatshops in contrast to consumers' league-approved factories.[18] Kristina Huneault shows that the 'Sweated Industries Exhibition' in London 'sparked a vogue for such events' in Britain too, and 'between 1906 and 1914 over a hundred towns and cities throughout the United Kingdom held their own civic exposés of sweated labour'.[19] Ian Mitchell notes that the Christian Social Union sponsored an exhibition of sweated labour in 1913.[20] In Berlin, the concept was revived in 1925 in order to test what advances had been made by labour legislation enacted in 1911 fol-lowing the 1906 exhibition in Berlin and a comparable exhibition in Frankfurt in 1908.[21]

The enthusiasm of so many different activist groups suggests that exhibitions were considered a representative strategy that was effective both in engaging a broad audience and in reflecting the conditions of sweated labour. It can be seen as an extension of the strategy of using sample cases to reflect common conditions that is familiar from activist publications such as Black's article 'Something about Needlewomen'. Displaying a selection of consumer goods alongside indications of hours and wages would convey the sense that the hours were too long and the wages too low, while sidestepping the complexities that often made wider data on wages and hours seem confusing and inconsistent. An exhibition required less energy from the audience than the selection, purchase and reading of a volume of investigative data would, and the sight of a range of everyday items in this defamiliarised context was likely to be more affecting and convincing than one investigator's statements. The choice of the exhibits and their presentation, furthermore, allowed the exhibition organisers to mediate the visitor's impressions and understanding.

The attraction of the exhibition format for British anti-sweating activists certainly was its visual appeal. The first tentative suggestions for the 'Sweated Industries Exhibition' appeared in March 1906 in the *Women's Industrial News* (*WIN*), the organ of the Women's Industrial Council. These references show the WIC's interest in visualising the social problem of sweating, in contrast with their familiar strategy of documenting and publishing the facts and figures of wages and conditions that they discovered through their social investigations. The project of motivating a public conscience was central from the beginning. The article stated: 'The [Berlin] exhibition has, at any rate, succeeded in drawing public attention to the evils of these miserable home industries', and asked: 'Might not a similar exhibition here in London have a good effect?' The strategy could successfully be adopted because '[o]ur home industries are probably less extensive than Germany's, but they exhibit unfortunately very much the same characteristics'.[22] The characteristics referred to comprised chronic overwork, underpayment, exploitation and precarity due to fluctuating demand and an absence of worker protection or organisation, all leading to high levels of pressure and stress, health problems related to unsafe working and living environments, and malnutrition linked to poverty.

The initial idea was to repeat the German model: the *WIN* suggested that '[a]n exhibition of the articles [produced by sweated labour], ticketed with the rates of pay, might appeal to the eye and understanding of the public, while the same bare facts stated in print do not make much lasting impression'.[23] A retrospective article on the exhibition by Margaret MacDonald, a member of the WIC and of the exhibition organising committee, however, shows that within the space of a couple of months the organisers had decided that it would give 'even more living interest to the English exhibition' to have 'the actual workers making the goods daily before the eyes of the public, and answering the many questions put to them by the visitors'. Based on nationwide research by the WIC, the exhibition included '[f]orty-four men and women – chiefly women – [...] plying as many different kinds of work'.[24] The normal working environments of the participating workers were reproduced insofar as this was possible in a concert hall, and where possible they did their usual work and 'had their family budgets and personal circumstances printed on cards by their stalls'.[25] This arrangement took the exhibition beyond previously tested representative strategies in anti-sweating activism by showing visitors the workers themselves. A sense of workers' self-representation is evoked, as they were able to interact with visitors who could ask them questions. The possibility of explaining individual cases would preclude reliance on data collected by investigators, which might lack specific details or context. Instead, the participating workers would be able to fill in any gaps in the information provided and thus to tell a more consistent story about home work.

Exhibitions that only showed the products of sweated labour had been less successful in resolving the question of the variable nature of available data on sweating. Organisers were very aware of the implications this had for the collection and representation of exhibition content. With reference to the data presented in the handbook to the 'Heimarbeit-Ausstellung' in Berlin, H. W. Smith pointed out:

These 230 pages of tables are, taken as a whole, a dispiriting record of underpay and overwork. [...] We are warned nevertheless that the impression conveyed by these lists will probably be more favourable than the facts would justify. There is generally a reluctance on the part of the worker to admit the *worst worst*. Moreover the considerable time often lost in fetching and returning the work is not counted, and nothing, naturally, can be reckoned for wear and tear of, for instance, sewing machines.[26]

The collection and collation of data for large national or international surveys and exhibitions such as the 'Heimarbeit-Ausstellung', furthermore, revealed the extent of regional and cultural variations in prices, wages and labour practices that might obscure the reality of the workers' poverty. One pamphlet entitled simply *Heimarbeit-Ausstellung Berlin 1906*, which presented data on a number of common home industries in Germany, summed up the impossibility of calculating regular incomes in home work. The section on glove making attempted to strip away as much confusing information as possible by settling on the example of a single woman worker who had no domestic duties to take time away from her paid labour, in Burg, where glove making was a common trade. A worker like this could make fifteen to eighteen pairs of gloves during a working day of eleven to twelve hours, earning 10 Pfennig (0.10 Mark) the pair.[27] These earnings were scaled up to a weekly total, from which the author then deduced an hourly wage of 13–15 Pf. It was noted, however, that extra time had to be spent on preparatory work, and on fetching the work and delivering it once completed. Even if these more-or-less definite calculations were accepted, however, the author warned:

> If this weekly wage of a diligent average worker is already low, it would still be a grave mistake to multiply these figures by fifty-two in order to reach an annual income of 468 Mark. This would be incorrect, as there is a yearly 'dead season' in the glove trade, during which demand is low, no work is given out for a period of weeks or months, and wages fall considerably.[28]

The pamphlet's recognition of these difficulties in calculating incomes in home industries offered context that showed that the information given in the exhibition, as Smith noted, did not reflect the worst aspects of labour exploitation.

The exhibition of Dutch home industries held in Amsterdam in 1909, at which living workers were exhibited, pre-empted possible irregularities in data provided on hours and wages. The guidebook to the exhibition reproduced a list of questions put to the participating workers that were designed to determine what variations occurred in their working hours. Participants were asked whether their work took place solely at home or partially in a workshop or factory, what their working hours were and whether these applied throughout the year, whether members of the family or others joined in the work, whether they worked on Sundays, and what their average weekly working hours were.[29] This rigorous line of questioning seems intended to eliminate any erroneous preconceptions on the part of the exhibition visitor about Sabbath work, the participation in the work of members of the household and other workers, and overtime; but at the same time these questions illustrated how elusive concrete data was in home work practices.

These uncontrollable variables helped to make the case for across-the-board legislation such as a minimum wage, as is shown in Black's essay in the exhibition handbook which offered 'Suggested Remedies' to the problem of home work and sweating. Noting some of the features of home work revealed by the exhibition that made it particularly difficult to regulate, she stated:

> There are certain evils to which home-work is by its very nature more liable than is work carried out in a factory or workshop.
>
> These evils are: (1) excessive hours; (2) unsuitability of workplace; (3) the employment of child labour; (4) low pay.[30]

She also pointed out the systematic disempowerment of sweated workers, informing the reader that '[t]he poorer the worker the less possible is resistance to any reduction in pay'.[31] The exhibition did not shrink from revealing the use of child labour in home industries; the handbook included photographs that showed children participating in home-based work.[32]

The high profile of the exhibition served to convince a wide audience of the truth of these circumstances and to motivate them to take action to resist the levels of exploitation that pressed children into service and caused excessive hours of work. In 'Suggested Remedies' and a number of subsequent publications, however, Black sought to mediate this impulse to activism in exhibition visitors. She returned to the idea of a consumers' league to suggest that 'the attempt, if renewed in England at the present time, and if headed by wealth and well-known people, might be able to produce some direct results, and might, in any case, become a valuable instrument of education'. Primarily, however, she indicated that consumers' leagues were a well-intentioned 'direct expression of the consumer's uneasiness of conscience'. She stated:

> that a Consumers' League could, in the present stage of social progress, completely fulfil its aims seems impossible. At a later stage of

development, when the workers, being better organised and educated, become able effectively to support it, such a league might conceivably become a very powerful agent.[33]

As matters stood, however, she explained, workers subject to sweating conditions were themselves still in too weak a position to support a consumers' league of the kind she had proposed in the 1880s. Instead, she noted that

[w]hile there is always a possibility whenever home-work is carried on that children may be set to work, the danger of their being kept at work for very long hours, and to their own lasting injury is only really serious where the pressure of poverty is extreme. The real cure for the labour of children lies in the adequate payment of the labour of the parents.[34]

In other words, paying home workers a living wage for their work would offer them an escape from the pressures of extreme poverty that obliged them to accept the negative consequences attendant on sweating practices.

In her typical fashion, Black did not fail to present her readers with what she considered to be a suitable channel for their impulses to activism. On the final day of the 'Sweated Industries Exhibition' she published an article entitled 'A Living-Wage League' in the *Daily News*. Through this platform, which was likely to reach a readership whose interest in the exhibition and its socio-economic aims had been carefully fostered and maintained by the column space the paper had devoted to it over the course of the exhibition, Black set out her new approach to consumer activism. Again, she warned her readers against the temptation of joining a consumers' league; instead, she urged the need for a fixed legal minimum wage in unregulated work. The support of consumers was necessary to achieve this legislative change, as it 'should come [. . .] at the demand of a great majority of the people and as the expression of a national desire to right a national wrong'.[35]

While Black's readjustment of her priorities reflected a move away from community activism to a campaign directly calling for legislative change, this campaign for legal action on the problem of sweated labour clearly still relied on popular support. The exhibition had been intended, like her previously published exposés of working conditions, to touch the conscience of consumers and inspire them with a sense of responsibility for the realities revealed to them. In 'Suggested Remedies' she had stated her belief that 'that growth of a public conscience which is so marked a feature in English life of the last eighty years or so' would work to check the problem of sweating.[36] This public consciousness, however, did require mediation from activists in order to harness it for the specific goal of legislative influence. Where she had previously presented the possibility of a consumers' league as an activist initiative for women subject to consumer guilt, she now encouraged 'the uneasy of conscience' to '[j]oin the Living Wage League'.[37] Black's approach suggests that, as far as she was concerned, the representative function of the exhibition was the same as her previous representations of labour exploitation. The habitual working conditions of the participants in the exhibition would have revealed the strain to which sweated workers were subject, and the workers themselves would have shown visitors that they did not choose the conditions of their work. For those exhibition visitors who were motivated to respond to the conditions they had seen, her articles suggested a practical course of action.

The aim of the exhibition, then, is clear: it sought to use visualisation as an improvement on the type of investigative reporting that was felt to be, in many ways, preaching to the choir. This strategy may be compared to that of Black's consumers' league articles in popular periodicals. The exhibition converted the same information that underpinned the 'columns and volumes' mentioned by the *Daily News* into a format that was more accessible and popular as well as more urgent and shocking. Showing visitors the workers who were subjected to sweating conditions and making these workers available to answer questions allowed the exhibition to eliminate quibbles and confusion linked to inconsistencies in collected data. The active participation of workers who had previously been cast in the roles of passive victims gave them unprecedented opportunities to tell their own stories to a wide audience; however, agreeing to participate as exhibits made these workers equally available to spectators who came in search of titillation as to those who were genuinely seeking information. The surviving evidence of the exhibition, furthermore, strongly suggests that the workers' voices were carefully contextualised by the writings of the organising activists. The exhibition handbook and its portrayals of the participating workers shed further light on this question.

Handbook of the 'Daily News' Sweated Industries' Exhibition, compiled by Richard Mudie-Smith, 1906

The exhibition strategy was designed to meet the triple aims of popular appeal, striking presentation and surmounting the difficulty of documenting the changeable details of sweated work, and the participation of living workers was instrumental in achieving each of these. With this in mind, it is possible to see the event as one of the first iterations in many decades of representations of sweating that allowed sweated workers a voice in their own representation. Of course, their contribution was still mediated by the exhibition organisers; in fact, the *Daily News* suggested that workers whose voices had not previously been heard either by the economic and political establishment or by the wider public could be made heard through the amplification offered by the exhibition platform. There are obvious parallels here to articles by Black such as 'Something about Needlewomen' and 'A Working Woman's Speech' that used her name and access to publishing platforms to convey working women's voices to a wide readership.

On the other hand, whether the exhibits were goods produced under sweating conditions or the sweated workers themselves, the representative strategies employed by exhibitions of sweated labour made no secret of their consumer-centred nature. They served to inform consumers of the conditions under which the goods they bought were produced, but in order to be able to do so they had to attract visitors as consumers of the exhibition. They also had to exert sufficient emotional appeal to persuade visitors to support activist schemes for the amelioration of poverty conditions. While anonymised and possibly fictionalised case studies could be used as typical examples of exploitative conditions, however, the involvement of living workers troubled this use of generalisation as the workers' individuality was compromised. The worker and the consumer may have been brought face to face, but there is no question that the consumer held the position of power in this confrontation with workers cast to depict their victimhood in an appeal for rescue by other social classes.

As a result of these complicated contexts and implications, the representation of sweating in the *Daily News* 'Sweated Industries Exhibition' prompted widely diverging views among both contemporary commentators and modern-day scholars. The exhibition strategy proved successful for the organisers, as it fulfilled its aims of engaging broad support for its campaign for a legal minimum wage. By September 1906, the *WIN* reported that '[a]n Anti-Sweating League, to secure a legal minimum wage, has been formed' and '[a] circular has been issued by the League asking for subscriptions to a guarantee fund, and announcing that a Conference will be held in October'.[38] This suggested that they were secure in their belief that the exhibition had attracted economically influential patrons from whom they could expect donations. On the other hand, commentators also expressed doubts about the sincerity of the exhibition visitors as well as about how different visitors understood the information presented to them. For instance, commenting on the exhibition shortly after it had closed in June 1906, Margaret MacDonald wondered in the *WIN*: 'Will it do any good? Many no doubt will go home and forget. Many will be sadder, but by no means wiser. But others may get an insight, and perhaps an inspiration which they have never had before.'[39] These comments reflected a faith in the exhibition's representative strategy as exerting an emotional appeal, but also an acceptance that not every visitor was a potential activist. MacDonald suggested that as far as she was concerned, the exhibition's role was to reach a wide audience, and it was worthwhile if only some of the visitors were enlightened and inspired to support an activist cause. The handbook offers crucial evidence in the disputed matter of the representation and participation of workers in the exhibition.

This strategy of exhibiting sweated workers to a wide audience regardless of its interest and intentions was questioned in the socialist press, which was markedly hostile to the exhibition. Many socialist commentators remained unconvinced that bringing wealthy exhibition visitors face to face with the working poor would serve to bridge the distance between classes. They suggested that the display of sympathy on the part of the spectators that the *Daily News* hailed as hopeful did not in fact betoken any fellow feeling with the workers, as the social and economic interests of the workers and the wealthy exhibition visitors remained intrinsically opposed. *Justice*, the party-political organ of the Social Democratic Federation, attacked the exhibition's decision to pursue popular support for incremental change rather than a more explicitly political agenda. In an article entitled '"Sweated Industries" and High-Placed Hypocrisy' it described the spectators as 'well-meaning people, like philanthropic slave-drivers', and stated: 'we may be quite sure none of the sympathisers of high degree want a social revolution. So they will continue to sweat the workers sympathetically.'[40] In other words, the wealthy exhibition visitors might express sympathy and pity when confronted with the human cost of the excesses of the economic system, but as they benefited personally from the status quo that produced these conditions, they were not interested in bringing about real social change. The *Labour Leader*, the organ of the Independent Labour Party, was similarly sceptical of the exhibition's model for cross-class solidarity. Irish trade unionist Thomas Gavan-Duffy argued that the consumer-centred approach skewed the exhibition's priorities by giving a more central role to the visitors than to the workers. He wrote indignantly about the amount of attention given in the press to the appearance of the royal patrons over the situation of the sweated workers. He stated that, in one report in a daily paper,

> [s]eventy-seven lines of description were given to the silks and satins, the chiffon, and the picture hats, the jewellery and the gloves of third-rate royalty; whilst fourteen lines had to serve for describing the sweated industries and the sweated workers.

As such, he questioned '[w]hether the occasion will prove most memorable as a display of royal stage-play and flunkeyism, or as a means of alleviation of the sweated workers'.[41] For Gavan-Duffy the notion of display as a means to activism was inherently suspect, as he considered it more likely to prompt showing off than sincere engagement with a social problem. He stated that the exhibition revealed 'details with which we have all been long familiar, and it is questionable whether a fashionable social function adorned even by royalty will do anything to right the wrongs of these poor people'.[42]

Gavan-Duffy's calling into question of the efficacy of the exhibition's representative strategy and the audience it sought to engage constituted a criticism of its activist aims: like the article in *Justice*, he felt that there was no real concern for the workers and that exhibition visitors had no intention of changing the position of sweated workers. He stated that the economic progress of the nineteenth century had failed to improve the conditions of workers as they remained underpaid, and suggested that only a reversal of the status quo on socialist principles could effectively change the situations of workers like those who participated in the exhibition. The closing lines of his article read:

> For the human being, for the blouse maker and the brushmaker, there is a lonely dark, damp, ugly garret; there is the penny herring, the dry loaf, and the milkless tea; the endless round of sordid toil; the grim battle for life, the never-ending conflict against poverty and disease. Here are the conditions which in the past have given Socialist agitation its justification, and will to-day and to-morrow provide us with an almost fierce incentive to push on our cause. Let us on, then, with our battle until the wealth now wrung from Labour [. . .] shall be used to rescue the sweated brushmaker and skirtmaker from their dens of pain and pauperism, and endow them with the rights and joys of life in the country which they by their toil have made rich.[43]

It is worth noting here, however, that neither Gavan-Duffy nor the article in *Justice* are particularly concerned with the subjectivity of workers in their critiques of the exhibition. They condemn the organisers' failure to pursue fundamental political change and resist the possibility that the situations of exploited workers might assume a secondary importance to the show of the society patrons; but they still cast the exhibited workers as in need of rescue – though not by high society, but by socialism. There is no sense here that these workers would take part in, let alone lead, this revolution. Like the *Daily News*, the *Labour Leader* addresses its readers on behalf of the sweated workers by emphasising their victimhood. These representations thus have unintended elements in common with the emotional appeal of the exhibition; they take issue primarily with the audience it sought to appeal to.

As the evidence that survives of the exhibition itself, its layout and its participants is very limited, the handbook is now our primary indicator of how the event sought to engage its audience and how this affected its representation of the participating workers. Its contents bring together the result of detailed investigations by experts on the subject of sweated labour, from members of the WIC who had made careers out of visiting the homes of sweated workers to radical Members of Parliament who had experience of representing their conditions to political audiences. In fact, its contents closely resemble the kind of investigative publications the *Daily News* seemed to suggest that the exhibition could replace. The image on the cover of the handbook, however, suggests that the immediate importance of appealing to consumers may have had an impact on the way workers were represented (Fig. 3.1).

Although photographs of real workers were included within the handbook, its cover is an illustration that seems intended to distil the image an ill-informed member of the public might have of sweated home work. It portrays two sweated women home workers engaged in what looks like matchbox making: one is holding a pot of glue, the other pieces of cardboard, and small boxes are stacked around the room. This conformed to the popular understanding that sweated trades were primarily home-based and primarily employed women. Matchbox making, furthermore, had been a symbol of the excesses of the home-based sweating system at least since the Matchwomen's Strike of 1888. Home-based box making was frequently reported on in studies of sweated home work, including Black's 1892 article 'Match-Box Making at Home' in *The English Illustrated Magazine*; the exhibition handbook itself included a section on 'Match Box Making' by Liberal MP Leo Chiozza Money, illustrated with photographs of home-based box making (such as Fig. 3.2).[44] Like the handbook's cover, these images show groups of workers – some of whom may be older children or young adults – working together in rooms that are small, with much space taken up by the materials needed for the work and the products of their labour. The various signifiers of exploitation that these photographs reveal, however, were exaggerated in the cover illustration.

The women depicted in the illustration are stereotyped versions of the victimised home worker: their posture is hunched, their faces look pinched, there are dark shadows under their eyes and their hair is unkempt and possibly greying prematurely. Their surroundings are cramped and untidy; a bare bed may be seen just behind one of the workers. The washing drying overhead – patched and mended like the workers' clothing – and the presence of a baby and a toddler reflect the double shift of paid work and household responsibilities. The image suggests that these women's work causes them to neglect the children: one holds the baby on one shoulder while her hands are busy with the hot glue, and the toddler is sitting on the bare floor. The child looks malnourished and badly clothed; it is holding what looks like one of the matchboxes to its mouth. Its thin legs appear shorter than its arms and the shape and angle of the feet and knees may suggest physical disability resulting from poor food and healthcare.

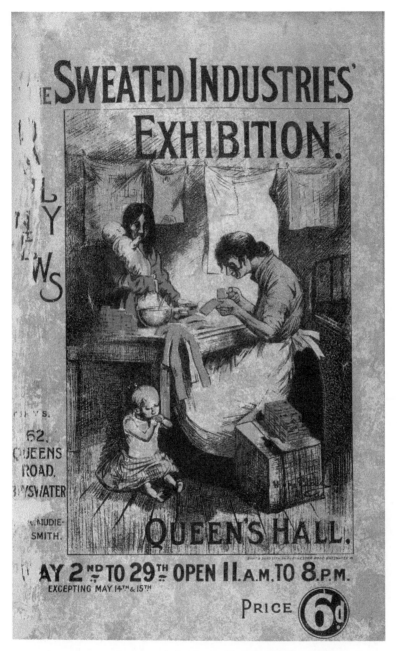

Figure 3.1 Cover of the *Handbook of the 'Daily News' Sweated Industries' Exhibition*. Reproduced with permission from Senate House Library, University of London, Special Collections ([G.L.] B.906).

Figure 3.2 'Match-Box Makers', in *Handbook of the 'Daily News' Sweated Industries' Exhibition*, p. 96. The Women's Library, London School of Economics and Political Science, 331.204 MUD.

The depiction of this working family plays into contemporary discourses about the alleged physical degeneration of the working classes: the adults look unhealthy and old before their time, while the children seem to have little chance of a healthy adulthood. The hunched, overworked figures in the drawing do not give the impression of vocal workers ready to speak to influential exhibition visitors or address a crowd from a platform. This representation, then, seemed designed to strike a chord of recognition with visitors; but much of its emotional appeal derived from its distillation of the problems commonly associated with sweated poverty: squalor, malnutrition and neglect of children. These are matters that, as contributors to the handbook recognised and the photographs within the handbook reflect, most sweated workers were inclined to disguise out of self-respect; we may assume, furthermore, that if the real participating workers had appeared less than neat and clean this might well have repulsed a proportion of the exhibition visitors. The awareness-raising aspect of the illustration, then, seems to have come at a cost of workers' dignity of self-representation. Even if the exhibition itself did offer the workers involved opportunities to speak on their own terms, the cover of the exhibition handbook suggests that its initial method of appeal was complicit in the reduction of individual workers to powerless symbols of the evil of sweating that were recognisable for an audience familiar with fictional and stereotyped representations.

Although the content of the handbook was much more focused on accurate and factual representation than the cover suggests, it also deliberately depersonalised the participating workers. The photographs illustrating the various trades described were captioned with the type of work, but no information about the workers. Occasionally a reference to place was included, but this merely enhanced the sense that the worker portrayed had only a representative function: they were described as a 'Cradley Chain Maker' or a 'Bromsgrove Nail Maker'.[45] The contributions to the handbook describing the different exhibited trades are written by investigators such as Black, Lily Montagu, founder of the West Central Jewish Girls' Club, and Barbara Leigh Hutchins, an active researcher for the WIC and the Fabian Women's Group. While all of these women were personally familiar with the living and working conditions of sweated workers as regular visitors to their homes, none of them had direct experience of sweated work or of these workers' lives in extreme poverty. Even the chapter entitled

'The Home-Life of the Sweated' is written by a visitor from the Shadwell Boys' Club rather than someone who could describe their own lived experience.

In order to entice visitors to explore the problem further, the programme of lectures in the handbook prominently lists the names of famous speakers, from Ramsay MacDonald, who had recently co-founded the Labour Party, to G. B. Shaw. Their names are followed by the title of their talk, many of which are highly specific: local socialist politician George Lansbury spoke on 'The Effect of Sweating upon the Rates' and Margaret MacDonald on 'American Anti-Sweating Laws'. The one exception of a lecture explicitly listed as delivered by a worker was advertised only as '"Sweating." — By one of the Sweated'.[46] The placing of the topic before the speaker, the absence of the speaker's name and the very generalised title emphasise the sweeping representative function of this lecture and the person (or possibly a number of different people) who gave it. A letter entitled 'De Profundis' and signed 'An Ex-Machinist' was included in the handbook 'because it represents the experience of a host of similar sufferers'.[47] The handbook stated that the letter had been anonymised to protect the writer's identity, and it is possible that a deliberate choice was made not to name the participating workers in order to prevent their being stigmatised by employers; but this raises another problem. On the one hand, the role of the participating workers as exhibits and symbols of a system of exploitation is rendered more poignant by the knowledge that they ran significant personal risks to be able to appear. On the other hand, although many of the organisers of the exhibition had extensive knowledge of the conditions of sweated work, none of them personally had to reckon with the concern that their already precarious livelihoods could be imperilled by their participation in a high-profile activist initiative. The anonymous workers thus played the most significant part in the exhibition but also ran the greatest risk in the organisers' project to appeal to consumers.

The danger to their livelihood that the workers incurred by participating in an event that would expose their employers was one difficult question that had to be addressed by the organisers of the exhibitions in both Berlin and London. Smith writes with regard to the Berlin exhibition that 'it was found that many of the workers declined to send articles for exhibition owing to fear of the employers' and he makes clear that the organisers relied heavily on the support of trade unions in obtaining material to exhibit.[48] This problem was necessarily enhanced when the workers personally appeared to show how they were exploited. Margaret MacDonald noted that

> there has been difficulty in many cases in getting the materials for them [participants] to work on, as their work was slack, or they were afraid to do their usual work, and each had to be guaranteed for a certain time against victimisation and loss.[49]

The personal circumstances of the workers, and the risks they ran to be able to participate, thus made it difficult to give a realistic insight into sweated working conditions, as employers were likely to resent their workers for participating or revealing the full reality of their situation, or workers could not do their regular work for fear of involving their employers. These concerns were not addressed in detail in the exhibition handbook, meaning that the full extent of the precarious employment of sweated workers was not reflected.

It is probable that the anonymity of the participating workers should be at least in part ascribed to the risks they ran; but anonymising them for the purpose of the exhibition and the handbook also had the effect of representing them as symbols of a sweating system rather than as individual workers. The section 'Particulars of Workers at Stalls' described the participants in a style more reminiscent of social investigation case notes than a representation of independent individual workers. The 'Remarks' section for 'Worker No. 1', for instance, reads: 'Worker is a widow with four children, the eldest of whom is 9 years and the youngest 3 years. She is in receipt of parochial relief. "The children all look healthy, and are kept very nicely."'[50] No attribution was given for the quotation regarding the appearance of the worker's children, perhaps reinforcing the notion that she and her family, as well as her working conditions, could be freely commented on. It also suggests that the workers selected for participation were among those who managed best on their meagre earnings and who would not offend the respectability of the exhibition visitors. The worst excesses of the sweating system, therefore, were very probably not represented.

Perhaps surprisingly, however, it is Gavan-Duffy's otherwise hostile report of the exhibition that indicates that participating workers did take an active representative role in the event. His descriptions of the way they performed their working practices to the exhibition visitors convey the impression that they were giving demonstrations rather than appearing as passive exhibits. He related how a 'shawl fringer demonstrated how she earned 5s. per week of 102 hours' and a 'female brushmaker was also showing how by filling 1,000 holes she earned 6½d., and totalled up 6s. per week'.[51] In comparison to the world fair format, this was closer to the role of workers demonstrating interesting new machinery than of people from other cultures who were objectified and exoticised. Moreover Gavan-Duffy's comment suggests that participants evaluated and critiqued their own conditions. The participants, then, may have seen themselves as testifying as they might to a formal inquiry or investigation, contributing their personal stories to illustrate a wider problem that impacted on many in a similar way.[52]

Blackburn, an expert on the 'Sweated Industries Exhibition' and its contexts, gives a similar impression of the exhibition when she argues that the workers who took part were 'participants in a dynamic, living spectacle' rather than exhibits.[53] By giving spectators access to living workers, she argues, the educational interactivity of the exhibition worked both ways, as the workers on display could interact directly and personally with visitors to explain their personal experience of exploitative working conditions. They 'answered questions put to them by the crowds [and] spoke on platforms with renowned celebrities of the day'.[54] In other words, participating workers could take charge of their own narrative; and Blackburn suggests that it was precisely the presence of the workers and the opportunities given to them to tell their own stories that lent credibility to the information presented in the exhibition. She notes that this signalled a step forward in the discourse of anti-sweating activism from the stylised representations of sweating that had characterised the mid-nineteenth century: the 'uncomplaining and inert victims' depicted in paintings and poems like 'The Song of the Shirt'.[55]

By contrast, in her examination of representations of working women in the late nineteenth and early twentieth centuries, art historian Huneault is clear in her criticism of the 'Sweated Industries Exhibition' as objectifying the exhibited workers. She describes it as part of 'the basic stratagem of putting the working poor "on show"', one of a 'whole range of late-Victorian and Edwardian exhibiting practices which sought to rehabilitate *for* culture the somewhat peripheral and possibly troubling figure of the woman worker'.[56] Huneault argues that the exhibition relied on making the workers visible and viewable in a specific cultural context in order to gain significant attention. In other words, the exhibition brought the practice of slumming into the West End and licensed spectators' voyeurism under the guise of consumer concern. The de-individualisation and consequent dehumanisation of the workers formed a part of this strategy. Huneault notes that

> despite the unmistakable element of surveillance within sweated industries exhibitions, accounts of the events give very little sense of who these women were. We know almost nothing about what they thought, how they felt or what they experienced as they sat on display. Indeed, the presence of actual women only serves to highlight their absence from any effective contribution to the means of their representation.[57]

Huneault's argument highlights the difference between visualisation and representation: visitors were able to see the workers on display and conditions approaching those in which they worked, but the workers themselves remained largely unseen. Their role was to be part of a cultural tableau rather than to set out their own experience of a flawed system; and this tableau was mediated and shaped by the planning and writing of the organising activists. It is probable that the workers themselves had a great deal to say about their own situations; but as Huneault points out, their words, thoughts, experiences and feelings were not recorded and have not survived among the copious evidence provided by the writings of the organising activists.

Because the exhibition was explicitly intended to engage broad support to ameliorate the position of sweated workers, it is perhaps not surprising that its representative strategy emphasised the powerlessness of the participating workers. In order to persuade potential activists that their involvement was necessary, the workers' inability to change their own position had to be made clear. Both the *Daily News* and Black herself heralded the interest of influential visitors as leading a broad front of support for legislative change; and while he disapproved of the exhibition's appeal to the elite, Gavan-Duffy too presented sweated workers as in need of rescue. Blackburn's representation of the possibilities the exhibition offered to workers to stand up to their conditions also seems to rely on the support of better-placed activists. She writes that the workers, '[e]mboldened by [*Daily News* owner and wealthy chocolate manufacturer] Cadbury's promise to indemnify them if their employers dismissed them', 'implored the Independent Labour Party to intervene on their behalf': in other words, they required support from one third party who could wield social and economic influence to ask another which had political influence to act for them against their employers.[58]

The outcome of the exhibition, as intended, was to strengthen the position of the organisers to lobby for legislative change on the workers' behalf. In her comments after the exhibition had closed, Margaret MacDonald expressed a cautious hope that 'the show may help us to push on our suggested licensing of home workshops'.[59] In fact, as Blackburn shows, significantly greater gains were made following the exhibition, which she describes as the turning point that produced a 'fundamental break in laissez-faire attitudes towards state intervention in the legal control of low pay'.[60] The year 1906 'saw the arrival in power of a New Liberal government prepared to pass laws to eradicate sweating' – it should be remembered here that the exhibition was actively supported by Liberal MPs such as Chiozza Money. Blackburn goes on to note that the same year 'also saw the establishment of an earnings and hours committee to collect systemic data on wages for the first time'.[61] Simultaneously, she states, the exhibition inspired the creation of 'an all-party pressure group, the National Anti-Sweating League', as well as a Select Committee on Homework, which paved the way for protective legislation in the form of the 1909 Trade Boards Act.[62] Thus the shock-and-shame tactics of the exhibition precipitated a move towards the application of direct pressure on government bodies to pass legislation to combat sweating. All of these gains, however, were achieved through the mediation of anti-sweating activists who repurposed the format of the 'Heimarbeit-Ausstellung' and translated the experience of the workers on display to appeal to the audience they had in mind. Although it is difficult to assess based on the available evidence to what extent the workers participating in the exhibition were able to influence the nature of their interactions with spectators, it is certain that this interaction cannot have taken place on the workers' own terms in a setting devised by the exhibition organisers with the exhibition visitors in mind.

The representative strategy of the 'Sweated Industries Exhibition' developed the use of personalised examples and evocative portrayals in studies of sweated work that functioned to illustrate the impact of poverty conditions, enhancing the sense of personal impact by creating the possibility of interaction between different social classes. On the other hand, Maria Grever and Berteke Waaldijk show how the illusion of interactivity could also increase the intellectual and emotional distance between the spectator and the social problem. In their study of another event in which living workers were exhibited, the 'Nationale Tentoonstelling Vrouwenarbeid' [National exhibition of women's labour] held in The Hague in the Netherlands in 1898, they write that spectators looking at living human beings in the context of an educational exhibition 'could publicly indulge in the pleasure of the gaze while remaining anonymous in the crowd'. The exhibition structure, they argue, meant that a balance of power between spectator and exhibited person was maintained, as the exhibition visitor

> could absorb the physical details, shudder in disgust, or identify with what they saw [. . .] At the same time, however, and this is the crucial point, the spectators could maintain their distance. They did not have to relate personally. They could gaze without fear of becoming the object of the gaze. A visitor could flee at any moment, turn around and walk away.[63]

In other words, the personal impact of the exhibition – despite the organisers' best efforts – was ultimately controlled only by the spectator. The exhibited person had no choice but to be equally visible to visitors who genuinely sought information as to spectators who came in search of titillation. Grever and Waaldijk's observations echo the *Daily News*'s hopeful remark that 'Society came, saw, and shuddered' and may be seen as tallying both with Gavan-Duffy's resentment of the social spectacle surrounding the exhibition as a fashionable society event and with MacDonald's more charitable remark that '[m]any [visitors] will be sadder, but by no means wiser' as a result of seeing the exhibition. For some visitors, the workers on display would indeed be no more than exhibits, and the spectacle would not lead to further engagement with the social problem. While the 'Sweated Industries Exhibition' did place sweating inescapably in the public eye, Blackburn notes that there were also other factors which facilitated the introduction

of anti-sweating legislation in the early twentieth century, such as a
new government. Meanwhile, the individual spectator visiting the
exhibition and gazing at the workers on display could keep their
distance and turn their back on the social problem whenever they
wished.

The handbook as evidence of the exhibition's aims and strategies
highlights the trade-offs between appealing to a target audience
and presenting these visitors with the necessary facts and guiding
their responses. It shows the tensions between visualisation as a
strategy intended to surmount some of the difficulties activists had
encountered in their awareness-raising strategies, such as how to
appeal to a wide audience and how to present facts that could be
confusing or contradictory, and the activists' aim of guiding this
emotional appeal into practical channels. This tension is reflected
most strongly in the contrast between the handbook cover and
the photographs contained within it: the organisers were willing
to harness stereotypes that were likely to be recognisable to an ill-
informed public as a bridge to conveying the actual information
that they had built their careers on collecting. These contradictions
speak to the central problem in the exhibition of living workers of
balancing objectification with interaction.

The exhibition allowed the workers themselves to act as examples of the strain of poverty and to explain their own circumstances, but the artificial situation created by the exhibition setting
also meant that the precarious nature and personal impact of their
economic position were not fully reflected. As opportunities for
detailed interaction between participating workers and exhibition
visitors are likely to have been limited, the exhibition structure
meant that the participating workers played the role of representatives of the excesses of an economic system. The part of the
workers in the exhibition was controlled firstly by the organisers
who mediated their appearance in accordance with the narrative
of labour exploitation they sought to create, and secondly by
the exhibition visitors who were free to regard the participating
workers on terms they chose. The exhibition relied on the representation of sweated workers as dependent on the interference
of other activists and the support of wealthier and more influential social groups to effect social change. This representation of
powerlessness is in keeping with Black's opinion that a consumers' league could only be effective once the workers were in a
position to support it; the exhibition sought to demonstrate that

the effects of sweating left workers unable to stand up for themselves. Black's volume *Sweated Industry and the Minimum Wage* explains some of these issues in a context removed from the direct emotive impact of the exhibition setting. Returning to the same detailed socio-economic analysis that characterised articles such as 'Caveat Emptor', she gave her reasons for her pursuit of legislative change in a volume riding on the wave of publicity created by the exhibition without repeating its problematic set-up.

Clementina Black, *Sweated Industry and the Minimum Wage*, 1907

For Black, the 'Sweated Industries Exhibition' marked a culmination of twenty years of experimentation with consumer activism and it reflects the development of her ideas over this period regarding the kind of activism that consumers could initiate and sustain. She shifted the focus of her campaigns from individual to collective action as she became increasingly concerned about the complexities of fragmented production processes and eventually resolved that legal change on a national scale was the only viable solution. This entailed a change in her representation both of the workings of the market for consumer goods and of the influence consumers could wield within it, and she adjusted her appeal to consumers accordingly. In September 1906, as part of an article describing different activist projects established to consolidate the interest produced by the exhibition, the *WIN* noted that Black was 'engaged upon a book dealing with the question of underpayment in relation to a minimum wage'.[64] The result was *Sweated Industry and the Minimum Wage*, in which she developed many of the ideas she had articulated in publications relating to the exhibition.

Alfred G. Gardiner, the editor of the *Daily News* who chaired the executive committee of the 'Sweated Industries Exhibition' and went on to become the chair of the Anti-Sweating League, contributed an introduction to the book. His opening lines give a good sense of how Black and her fellow activists for a minimum wage understood the problem of sweating by the first decade of the twentieth century. He stated:

> The sweating evil has long engaged the attention of social and industrial workers in many fields. Some have approached it from the philanthropic point of view, and have sought a remedy in voluntary means

such as consumers' leagues; others have approached it from the point of view of industrial organisation, and have sought to deal with it by the extension of trade unionism and legislative action. So far all efforts alike have been futile. The evil is too widespread and too remote in its operations to be touched by charity. It involves a class too forlorn, too isolated, and too impoverished to be reached by trade unionism. The cry of the victims has hitherto been too feeble and hopeless to command the attention of Parliament.[65]

This passage addressed a variety of campaigns that Black had supported in the final decades of the nineteenth century, including trade unionism as well as consumer activism. Gardiner suggested, however, that a combination of research and increased awareness of the nature of the problem, and perhaps developments within the economic system itself, had made clear that solutions limited to specific movements, whether philanthropy or trade unionism, could not be strong enough to combat the problem of sweating in the twentieth century.

Gardiner's summary illustrates two crucial themes: the complexity of the sweating system and the socio-economic position of the sweated workers themselves. His description of the sweating system as 'widespread' and 'remote in its operations' showed that sweated work was economically entrenched and the fragmented nature of production made the problem difficult to pin down. The sense of the system as 'remote in its operations' also underlined the importance of long-distance solidarity as consumers' alienation from the production process was increased. What remained from earlier understandings of the sweating system, however, was the sense of the workers as victims, too 'feeble and hopeless' to stand up for themselves. While the perception of the sweating system had developed from the nineteenth-century narrative of consumer guilt, then, the opportunity to interact with sweated workers at the 'Sweated Industries Exhibition' did not significantly alter the perception of the victims of sweating.

Sweated Industry reflects a tension between Black's desire to give a fair representation of sweated workers and their experience and her conviction that these workers themselves were not able to combat their own situation. Like the exhibition, therefore, her representations were still designed to appeal to her readers for help, and therefore remain underpinned by a narrative of victimhood. Her book was divided into two parts based on the structure indicated by its title: part I, 'Sweated Industry', described the conditions of sweated workers in a number of different trades, while part II, 'The Minimum Wage', outlined socio-economic reasons for pursuing the policy with reference to international case studies of activist responses to sweating. This approach was clearly rooted in the long-standing tradition of investigative writing on the subject that Black and the WIC had helped to shape. It may also be understood as combining the two elements of the exhibition examined in the previous section: while the descriptive examples of sweating are comparable to the exhibits, the socio-economic arguments of part II take the role of the publications shaping visitors' understanding of the exhibition, such as the handbook and the accompanying periodical articles. As in the exhibition, the humanity of the sweated workers lent urgency to the issue, but the meaning of and response to their situation was controlled by Black.

Where the handbook may take an objectificatory and even judgemental view of sweated workers, however, the consistent sympathy with women in poverty that characterised Black's work also emerges in *Sweated Industry*. In contrast to the handbook's comments on the appearance of the workers' children, for instance, Black's text immediately asked her readers to recognise the

> cruelly heavy burden resting on the shoulders of the woman who tries to be at the same time mother, housekeeper, and bread-winner, and who in return for her endless exertion seldom receives enough even to keep her properly fed, and never enough to satisfy her own very modest standard of comfort.[66]

On the other hand, it is very clear that the book presents Black's selection from cases of home workers visited and documented by the Women's Industrial Council, so the workers whose situations are described necessarily fulfil the same representative function as the participating workers in the exhibition. Their stories are not their own but have been collected and arranged by others as examples of a record of 'much the same features [of] unremitting toil'.[67]

The strategies behind Black's writing in *Sweated Industry* also show significant parallels with her early writings in favour of a consumers' league. As in articles like 'Caveat Emptor', she followed a line of reasoning that she ascribed to her reader, and then proceeded to mediate it with her own socio-economic analysis. This is particularly evident in the chapter entitled 'Supposed

Remedies', in an echo of her article 'Suggested Remedies' in the handbook, in which she explored a range of solutions to the problem of sweating that had proven to be inadequate. Among them, she revisited the idea of a consumers' league as an activist response prompted by the confrontation between the consumer and the exploited producer of consumer goods, such as in the context of the 'Sweated Industries Exhibition'. Acknowledging the feelings of guilt produced in the consumer by this confrontation, she proceeded to explain:

> When men and women who are not themselves underpaid come face to face with the evil of underpayment, it is natural enough for them to resolve that henceforth the articles purchased by themselves shall be articles the makers of which have been adequately paid. From this individual resolve it is but one step to an association of persons all thus resolved, and banded together for the purposes of investigation and exclusive dealing. Such an association is a 'Consumers' League,' the aim of which is to 'check unlimited competition not at the point of manufacture but at the point of sale.' Such associations [. . .] are likely to reappear at times like the present when many consciences are disturbed by recognition of the fact that a considerable proportion of British workers are scandalously underpaid.[68]

The construction of this paragraph is very similar to the descriptions in 'Caveat Emptor' or 'The Ethics of Shopping' of potential activists who resolve to avoid market dealing by setting their own rates of pay for the people they employ directly or by determining to produce for themselves. In those articles Black sought to illustrate that the market economy was too complex to allow for this as a viable solution and advocated a consumers' league as a structured response. In *Sweated Industry*, however, she immediately forestalled interest in a consumers' league as a suitable channel for consumer activism by proceeding to explain 'how and why a Consumers' League must inevitably fail in its aims'.[69] Her reasons for dismissing the well-intentioned scheme centred, once again, on the contemporary production process, the scale of which, she explained, was beyond the influence of individual consumers.

The key point she sought to make in *Sweated Industry* was that even the investigative potential of a consumers' league could not sufficiently explore and evaluate contemporary production processes and trade systems. These processes had become so dispersed that '[i]n regard to every single article it becomes necessary to trace every step of production and transmission', making it impossible to determine whether a particular shop would meet any standards of ethical employment.[70] She illustrated this with the example of the amount and range of labour involved in the production and sale of a single pair of shoes. She wrote:

> A pair of shoes cannot be satisfactorily guaranteed until we have discovered the wages and conditions of employment not only of every person who has worked upon the actual shoe, but also of the tanner, the thread weaver and winder, the maker of eyelets, the spinner and weaver of the shoe-lace and the various operatives engaged upon the little metal tag at the shoe-lace's end. Nor is the matter finished even then. At every stage of its evolution, a shoe requires the services of clerks, book-keepers, office-boys, warehousemen, packers, boxmakers, carmen, railway servants &c., and each new service introduces other material and other service – paper, ink, ledgers, harness, stable fittings, cardboard, string, glue, iron, coal – the series is endless.[71]

It would be impossible, she stated, to verify the conditions of each of these workers. Global trade confused the matter yet further. She concluded:

> The fact is that even the most apparently simple of commercial acts is but one link in a network that spreads over the whole field of life and labour; and the fabric of that network is not woven once and for ever, but is in continual process of change.[72]

In the simplified version of market relations Black had put forward in 'Caveat Emptor', she suggested that the distance between producer and consumer of specific goods was small enough for the consumer to be able to trace the provenance of their purchases. The circumstances reflected in the 'Sweated Industries Exhibition', however, gave a sense of complex production processes that required a national, legal solution. The idea that consumers could, as she had suggested in 'The Morality of Buying in the Cheapest Market', simply imagine themselves into the position of sweated workers was no longer applicable. Instead, the exhibition's promise to show to consumers the working conditions that were rendered invisible by the production process seemed a more accurate reflection of the growing distance between the experience of worker and consumer.

Blackburn refers to the same reality of worker and consumer alienation to argue the effectiveness of the 'Sweated Industries Exhibition', as she points out that seeing the workers at their trades revealed to '[t]hose who had advocated consumers' leagues as a possible solution' that 'clothing made in clean and healthy workshops and by well-paid labor might, nevertheless, be trimmed with braid, buttons, hooks and eyes carded in sweating dens'.[73] Writing in the *Labour Elector*, late-nineteenth-century socialist and labour activist Margaret Harkness cited the example of 'the poor wretch who made the trimming for the Queen's Jubilee carriages' which showed that the lavishness of the festivities marking Queen Victoria's Golden Jubilee in 1887 did not mean that all the workers involved in them were generously or even adequately paid.[74] In contrast to the consumer guilt argument that blamed consumers who paid low prices for the underpayment of workers, facts like these made clear that the idea that there was a direct link between the prices paid for goods and the wages paid to workers was by no means necessarily true. As these realities became increasingly understood, Black argued that a consumers' league 'may be a valuable social agency' – as the example of the NCL in the United States clearly showed – 'but can never hope to be an economic remedy for underpayment' in itself.[75] Instead, she argued, the 'cure of underpayment needs to be applied at the point of payment; and the establishment of a legal minimum wage is the most direct method of application'.[76]

Although its strategies to engage potential activists echoed those of the investigative tradition of which Black had so long been an important part, as well as the emotional appeal of the 'Sweated Industries Exhibition', *Sweated Industry* completely refuted the idea that sweating could be combated in any impactful way by individual or collective voluntary action, whether it be charity or ethical consumption. This realisation had gone hand in hand with the change of strategy among anti-sweating activists. Building on their observations of legislative measures in other countries, such as the Australian Trade Boards, they began to devise solutions that would be enforceable on a national scale. To enact these, however, it was no longer enough to reach individual consumers and potential activists through targeted publications in popular periodicals, for example. Instead, a broad base of support headed by voices of socio-economic influence was required to give momentum to their new proposal for minimum wage legislation. As in much of her earlier work, Black combined economic analysis with human interest to demonstrate that the problem had a severe impact on individuals but was also widespread and entrenched despite its relative invisibility. This strategy was intended to open her readers' eyes to the problem and provide them with a channel for their sympathy and concern. The difference was that now she invited them to put their influence behind a scheme for national change rather than a form of voluntary activism.

Conclusions: The sweated body in the sweating system

Black's engagement with narratives of consumer activism illustrates a central problem in her representations of sweated workers: the search for a balance in representing a social problem in such a way as would be likely to engage an audience of middle-class consumer-readers in activism, while still allowing that the workers portrayed as victims of the problem had individual identities. Black's arguments both for and against a consumers' league, and her support for the 'Sweated Industries Exhibition' in spite of her emphasis elsewhere on the personhood of sweated workers, all reflect a pull between attempts to enlighten the ignorance of her readers through argument but also to spur them to action through emotive appeals. Her writing always mediated the evidence she presented to guide her readers' understanding and response into the channels she pursued. The sweated workers, whether they were active participants or symbolic characters, were part of a narrative told about them, not one they told about themselves. The lack of individuality given to sweated workers in these narratives helped to build up a sense of the size of the problem: however different their characters might be, each of these workers had the same experience and underwent the same suffering. This also meant, however, that actions to help individual workers, whether they involved charitable donation or direct employment, could not solve the problem of sweating. This understanding reinforced the point that sweating constituted a 'national wrong'.

In *Sweated Industry* Black sought to demonstrate that this 'national wrong' also had a national impact that extended well beyond the large numbers of sweated workers: she warned that, in the long run, the harm done by sweating would spread through the population as well as the economy. The two-part structure of the book, with its economic arguments alongside the personal sympathy of human examples, worked to prove that underpayment could not be conducive to the development either of the national or global economy or of humanity itself. Black summed up this argument in her remark that '[f]rom a national point of view it would pay better to save the human machine from falling into that state of disrepair wherein it ceases to be profitable'.[77] Without articulating them outright, this spoke to contemporary fears about the degeneration of working people, as reflected for instance in the evident poor health of the adults and children depicted on the cover of the exhibition handbook. Essentially, the fear was that if the collective health and well-being of the working classes was consistently undermined, these people would lose the ability to do the work on which the economy relied.

This argument objectified the bodies of working people in a comparable way to the use of them as exhibits in the Queen's Hall. It would go on to underpin the cases made for many progressive changes to labour legislation in the early twentieth century in the USA as well as in the UK. Working women's bodies were particularly relevant in this context because of what was viewed as their biologically inherent ability to bear children. Campaigners argued that overwork could harm women's capacity for healthy childbearing. Damage to their own health would impact on that of their children, leading to future generations unable to work effectively due to physical impairment. Legislation based on these arguments was often used as an entering wedge to improve labour laws: concern for future generations was the prompt to broad acceptance that women required decent working conditions for their health and well-being, and this could in turn be used to prove that men would benefit from them too. We have seen how working women's bodies became a tool in the hands of anti-sweating activists from the mid-nineteenth century onwards as the helpless and vulnerable victims of sweating; now their objectification as childbearing bodies provided leverage for legal change. While the legislation this produced certainly did achieve the effect of improving these women's working conditions in material ways, the narrative on which these improvements were built disregarded the women's own humanity.

Black's campaign writing throughout her career stands out precisely because of its emphasis on the humanity and experience of working women, from 'Something about Needlewomen' to her comment in *Sweated Industry* regarding the pressures to which sweated workers who were parents or carers were particularly subject. Her focus, furthermore, is consistently on women's domestic and caring responsibilities rather than a childbearing role. Nevertheless, in order to make her argument for the minimum wage that she saw as the only reliable way to improve these women's conditions, she still had to present them as part of 'the human machine'. The next chapter will show how comparable arguments made by the NCL in order to help women workers relied on objectifying their bodies for an audience of judges and legislators.

Notes

1. Clementina Black, 'Suggested Remedies', in *Handbook of the 'Daily News' Sweated Industries' Exhibition*, compiled by Richard Mudie-Smith (London: Burt, 1906), pp. 22–6 (p. 26) <https://archive.org/stream/handbookofdailyn00mudi_0#page/n17/mode/1up> [accessed 24 July 2016].
2. Sheila C. Blackburn, '"Princesses and Sweated-Wage Slaves Go Well Together": Images of British Sweated Workers, 1843–1914', *International Labor and Working-Class History*, 61 (2002), 24–44 (p. 25).
3. *Handbook*, compiled by Mudie-Smith, p. 4.
4. Gerard Noel, 'Ena, princess of Battenberg (1887–1969)', *Oxford Dictionary of National Biography* (Oxford: Oxford University Press, 2004) <http://www.oxforddnb.com/view/article/36656> [accessed 27 February 2017].
5. *Handbook*, compiled by Mudie-Smith, p. 8.
6. 'Catalogue of Exhibits', in *Handbook*, compiled by Mudie-Smith, pp. 145–59.
7. Gertrude Tuckwell, 'Preface', in *Handbook*, compiled by Mudie-Smith, pp. 12–19 (p. 12).
8. On Mrs Biddell being forced to pawn her work, see *The Times*, 27 October 1843, p. 4.
9. 'Sweating Exhibition', *Daily News*, 4 May 1906, p. 7.
10. 'Facts at the Sweated Industries Exhibition', *Daily News*, 4 June 1906, p. 2.

11. H. W. Smith, 'The German Home-Work Exhibition, Berlin, 1906', in *Handbook*, compiled by Mudie-Smith, pp. 19–22 (p. 19).

12. Amsterdam, International Institute of Social History, Bro D 2970/125, *Die Heimarbeitausstellung in Berlin* (n.p. [Nuremberg]: n.pub. [Simon], n.d. [1906]), p. 1.

13. 'The Berlin Exhibition of Home-Industries', *Women's Industrial News*, March 1906, pp. 543–4 (p. 543).

14. Smith, 'The German Home-Work Exhibition', in *Handbook*, compiled by Mudie-Smith, p. 19.

15. Amsterdam, International Institute of Social History, Zw1960/356, Jakob Lorenz, *Heimarbeit und Heimarbeitausstellung in der Schweiz* (Zurich: Verlag der Buchhandlung des Schweiz. Grütlivereins, 1909), p. 3, and EHB Cat/2/F/95, *Gids voor de Nederlandsche Tentoonstelling van Huisindustrie* (n.p. [Amsterdam]: n.pub., n.d. [1909]), p. 29.

16. Judith G. Coffin, *The Politics of Women's Work: The Paris Garment Trades 1750–1915* (Princeton: Princeton University Press, 1996), p. 217.

17. Louis L. Athey, 'From Social Conscience to Social Action: The Consumers' Leagues in Europe, 1900–1914', *Social Service Review*, 52.3 (1978), 362–82 (pp. 362–3) <https://www.jstor.org/stable/30015641> [accessed 30 March 2020].

18. Maud Nathan, *The Story of an Epoch-Making Movement* (London: Heinemann, 1926), p. 100.

19. Kristina Huneault, *Difficult Subjects: Working Women and Visual Culture, Britain 1880–1914* (Aldershot: Ashgate, 2002), p. 135.

20. Ian Mitchell, 'Ethical Shopping in Late Victorian and Edwardian Britain', *Journal of Historical Research in Marketing*, 7.3 (2015), 310–29 (p. 324) <https://doi.org/10.1108/JHRM-08-2014-0021>.

21. See Berlin, Staatsbibliothek zu Berlin, Ff4281/55-9, Frieda Wunderlich, *Die Deutsche Heimarbeitausstellung, 1925* (Jena: Gustav Fischer, 1927), pp. 1, 2.

22. 'The Berlin Exhibition of Home-Industries', p. 544.

23. Ibid. p. 544.

24. Margaret MacDonald, 'The "Daily News" Sweated Home Industries Exhibition', *Women's Industrial News*, June 1906, p. 558.

25. Sheila Blackburn, '"To Be Poor and To Be Honest . . . Is the Hardest Struggle of All": Sweated Needlewomen and Campaigns for Protective Legislation, 1840–1914', in *Famine and Fashion: Needlewomen in the Nineteenth Century*, ed. Beth Harris (Aldershot: Ashgate, 2005), pp. 243–57 (p. 249).

26. Smith, 'The German Home-Work Exhibition', in *Handbook*, compiled by Mudie-Smith, p. 21, emphasis in original.
27. A German Mark was about equivalent to a British shilling in 1906. Source for currency conversion: *Historicalstatistics.org: Portal for Historical Statistics* <http://historicalstatistics.org/> [accessed 12 July 2022].
28. 'Ist der Wochenverdients einer fleissigen Durchschnittarbeiterin an sich schon gering, würde man doch sehr irren, wenn man diese Ziffer mit 52 multiplizieren und so einen Jahresverdienst von 468 Mk. herausrechnen wollte. Das währe falsch, den in der Handschuhbranche ist jährlich "tote Saison", in der wenig Bedarf ist, wochen- oder monatelang wird nur wening Arbeit ausgegeben, und der Verdienst sinkt ganz beträchtlich.' Berlin, Staatsbibliothek zu Berlin, Fd2381/5, 'Die Heimarbeit in der Handschuhindustrie', in *Heimarbeit-Ausstellung Berlin 1906* (Berlin: Vorwärts, 1906), pp. 1–5 (pp. 4–5). My translation.
29. Amsterdam, International Institute of Social History, EHB Cat/2/F/95, 'Algemene Vragenlijst', in *Gids voor de Nederlandsche Tentoonstelling van Huisindustrie*, pp. 60–4.
30. Black, 'Suggested Remedies', in *Handbook*, compiled by Mudie-Smith, p. 22.
31. Ibid. p. 23.
32. See for instance 'Cardboard-Box Making' and 'Hook and Eye Carding', in *Handbook*, compiled by Mudie-Smith, pp. 35, 38.
33. Black, 'Suggested Remedies', in *Handbook*, compiled by Mudie-Smith, p. 26.
34. Ibid. pp. 23–4.
35. Clementina Black, 'A Living-Wage League', *Daily News*, 13 June 1906, p. 6.
36. Black, 'Suggested Remedies', in *Handbook*, compiled by Mudie-Smith, p. 25.
37. Black, 'A Living-Wage League', p. 6.
38. 'The Anti-Sweating League', *Women's Industrial News*, September 1906, pp. 567–8 (pp. 567, 568).
39. MacDonald, p. 558.
40. '"Sweated Industries" and High-Placed Hypocrisy', *Justice*, 5 May 1906, p. 1.
41. T. Gavan-Duffy, 'Two May-Day Exhibitions', *Labour Leader*, 11 May 1906, p. 744. I arrived at the articles from *Justice* and the *Labour Leader* via citations in Blackburn's accounts of the exhibition.

42. Ibid. p. 744.
43. Ibid. p. 744.
44. L. G. Chiozza Money, 'Match Box Making', in *Handbook*, compiled by Mudie-Smith, pp. 95–8.
45. *Handbook*, compiled by Mudie-Smith, pp. 58, 66.
46. Ibid. p. 7.
47. Ibid. pp. 118–19.
48. Smith, 'The German Home-Work Exhibition', in *Handbook*, compiled by Mudie-Smith, p. 20.
49. MacDonald, p. 558.
50. *Handbook*, compiled by Mudie-Smith, p. 120.
51. Gavan-Duffy, p. 744.
52. I am grateful to Anna Poletti for suggesting the concept and vocabulary of testimony as a lens for the participation of workers in the exhibition.
53. Blackburn, 'To Be Poor', in *Famine and Fashion*, ed. Harris, p. 249.
54. Ibid. p. 249.
55. Ibid. p. 249.
56. Huneault, p. 144, emphasis in original.
57. Ibid. p. 155.
58. Blackburn, 'To Be Poor', in *Famine and Fashion*, ed. Harris, p. 249.
59. MacDonald, p. 558.
60. Blackburn, 'To Be Poor', in *Famine and Fashion*, ed. Harris, p. 244.
61. Ibid. p. 249.
62. Ibid. p. 251.
63. Maria Grever and Berteke Waaldijk, *Transforming the Public Sphere: The Dutch National Exhibition of Women's Labor in 1898*, trans. Mischa F. C. Hoyinck and Robert E. Chesal (Durham, NC: Duke University Press, 2004), p. 125.
64. 'The Anti-Sweating League', pp. 567–8.
65. A. G. Gardiner, 'Introduction', in Clementina Black, *Sweated Industry and the Minimum Wage* (London: Duckworth, 1907), pp. ix–xxiv (p. ix).
66. Black, *Sweated Industry*, p. 3.
67. Ibid. p. 3.
68. Ibid. pp. 205–6.
69. Ibid. p. 206.
70. Ibid. p. 208.
71. Ibid. pp. 208–9.
72. Ibid. p. 209.
73. Blackburn, 'To Be Poor', in *Famine and Fashion*, ed. Harris, p. 250.

74. Margaret E. Harkness, 'To the Editor of the *Labour Elector*', *Labour Elector*, October 1888, p. 8.
75. Black, *Sweated Industry*, p. 211.
76. Ibid. p. 210.
77. Ibid. p. 18.

4

'The Health and Welfare of the Republic': The National Consumers' League and the Question of Gender in US Protective Labour Legislation, 1895–1920

The implication reflected in notions such as Clementina Black's of the 'human machine', that the welfare of the individual should be guarded to achieve the long-term effective functioning of an economic system, is also conspicuous in the legal discourse around protective measures for workers in the United States around the turn of the twentieth century.[1] So too was the idea that it was up to more prominent and powerful social groups – not themselves likely to be part of the 'machine' of labouring people – to safeguard it. It surfaces, for example, in the foreword to Maud Nathan's *Story of an Epoch-Making Movement* by the prominent progressive Democrat Newton D. Baker. Baker's career moved between state appointments and campaign roles: he had been president of the National Consumers' League as well as mayor of Cleveland, Ohio, and Secretary of State under Woodrow Wilson. This experience of both official government and unofficial influences on it lent weight to his assessment of the impact of the NCL. For example, he states:

> The idea upon which the League is based is now an accepted part of our industrial philosophy while the League itself is relied upon by legislatures for accurate information as to industrial conditions and by executives for sympathy and support in the enforcement of regulations profoundly affecting the health and welfare of the republic.[2]

Baker's language here reads as gendered, with the notion of the NCL as a helpmeet to the state that supplied both information and 'sympathy and support' to protect the national 'health and welfare'. There is a sense of motherliness in this caring role for the NCL as well as of motherhood in the idea of protecting the national health.

This framing readily lends itself to be understood in a context of the NCL's own engagement with such ideas around gendered protection, which had shaped its landmark legal intervention for protective labour laws for women. The United States Supreme Court case of *Muller* v. *Oregon* (1908), a legal dispute in which the NCL interceded to defend a state-level maximum working hours law for women, forms the focus of this chapter. I begin by sketching the context of the NCL's engagement with *Muller* v. *Oregon* and the legal history leading up to it. The central text is the so-called Brandeis Brief presented at the trial, as published by the NCL with the appended text of the verdict handed down by Justice David J. Brewer. My analysis of the rhetoric and arguments presented in the brief specifically interrogates the representation of gender from an intersectional feminist perspective, noting also the implicit assumptions made about health and welfare in a context of the state, the nation and the economy as powered by a 'human machine'. This will contribute to a fuller evaluation of the relationship of the original text in its published form to its consequences in a social and legislative sense and its subsequent contextualised interpretations.

Muller v. *Oregon,* the NCL and gendered labour legislation

The case that became *Muller* v. *Oregon* originated in 1905 when Curt Muller, owner of the Grand Laundry in Portland, Oregon, was charged with violating a state law, introduced in 1903, that limited the working day for women in 'any mechanical establishment or factory or laundry' to ten hours in any twenty-four.[3] Muller had allowed his overseer at the Grand Laundry to 'require' one of his workers, trade unionist Emma Gotcher, to work beyond the legally stipulated maximum.[4] Aware of the 1903 law, Gotcher brought the case to court and Muller was fined $10. He appealed to the Supreme Court of Oregon which upheld the original judgment in 1906. He then proceeded in 1907 to appeal to the federal Supreme Court in Washington, DC, with a case based on the freedom of the individual to contract labour under the Fourteenth Amendment to the Constitution of the United States. The NCL saw an opportunity to enter the legislative debate on a point that spoke directly to its interest in working women's conditions. It engaged Louis D. Brandeis, a prominent lawyer with a reputation for working for progressive causes, as counsel for Oregon, to argue for the state law to be upheld. The groundbreaking Brandeis Brief presented at the trial had been compiled, however, by Brandeis's sister-in-law Josephine Goldmark, the publication secretary of the NCL and head of its labour law committee, with other NCL activists.

The fact that *Muller* concerned a maximum hours law specifically for women workers is highly relevant to the NCL's involvement and its chosen strategy. In her detailed analysis of US protective labour legislation for women, published in 1992, sociologist and political scientist Theda Skocpol explores campaigns for both minimum wage and maximum hours laws. Legislation for a minimum wage had become a matter of interest for consumers' leagues internationally, as it had for Black and other anti-sweating campaigners in the UK: it was raised at the first International Conference of Consumers' Leagues in 1908. The NCL pursued it specifically as another form of protective labour legislation for women workers, alongside maximum hours laws, and made the minimum wage part of its ten-year programme in 1910. The success and impact of minimum wage laws enacted in individual states remained limited, however.[5] Instead, maximum hours laws were quickly identified in the early twentieth century as the place where legislative gains could be made, especially to protect women workers; I suggest that this may have been in significant part due to the fact that maximum hours regulation fitted more easily into a narrative of protecting women to uphold socially assigned gender roles.

The gendered focus in protective labour legislation engaged support from two different camps: those who advocated the protection of women on the basis of an idea of binary gender difference as biologically and socially determined, and those who perceived gains for more vulnerable workers such as women and children as an entering wedge that would subsequently allow protective legislation to be enacted for all workers. Historian of gender and law Nancy Woloch connects this idea to the gendered self-representation of the NCL, showing that entering wedge arguments belonged to a 'sphere of influence for activist women, who in turn appealed to a women's constituency'.[6] In other words, it was easier for women activists to represent other women's interests, and once specific rights had been won for women they could be extended. As she points out, however, there was an unavoidable tension between the gender difference and entering wedge arguments. Woloch's study of gendered labour legislation, published in 2015, acknowledges its debt to Skocpol's meticulous research, but is on the whole more ready to identify difficult questions and conflicts in the narrative of Progressive Era developments in protective labour laws. Thus she notes that, while the gendered protection strategy achieved short-term victories, it promised to be difficult to unite over time the position that certain workers deserved special protections for specific and inherent biological reasons with that which held that all workers deserved these same protections regardless of the personal and physical characteristics on the basis of which they had been granted in the first place.[7] The question of whether gender difference was relevant in a constitutional sense also repeatedly resurfaced in the legal debates over hours laws, as the constitution should apply to all US citizens equally. The Brandeis Brief circumvented these theoretical questions by focusing exclusively on the difference argument, deliberately putting the matter squarely in an area of essentialist conceptions of biological gender based on childbearing.

The Brandeis Brief is widely remembered in both legal and historical discourse for its departure from the established notion of legal precedent. In essence, the question of precedent means the deciding of court cases on the basis of legal principles, often established by previous verdicts. Woloch places the understanding of precedent in the turn-of-the-twentieth-century US legal system in the context of a 'conservative swing of the judiciary [which] derived authority from formalism'. She explains this 'legal philosophy' as follows:

> To formalists, the law was logical, coherent, and harmonious. Judges discovered law, based on preexistent law; they did not create law. Formalism was based on deduction from general principles and analogies, or comparisons, among cases. Formalists expected law to play a neutral role in disputes, to sever the legal and political; cases could be decided apart from the political and social context in which they arose.[8]

The NCL was strongly aware of the recent legal context in which *Muller* v. *Oregon* occurred; previous cases on a comparable foundation had led to differing verdicts, making the question of precedent less than straightforward. The reason that *Muller* v. *Oregon* made legal history and ended previous legal wrangling over maximum hours laws was the NCL's decision to diverge from the idea of precedent as based solely on preceding court judgments. Instead it proffered an international selection of evidence that included both medical texts attesting to the detrimental physical impact of over-work on women, and economic analyses showing that countries where maximum hours laws had been instated had not suffered financially.

On the one hand, the NCL's involvement in the *Muller* case fits well into the trajectory rooted in the Consumers' League of New York's campaign for retail workers' conditions that culmi-nated in the Albany Mercantile Act. Both showed the Consumers' League mobilising on behalf of working women to prevent their being overworked and exploited. In both, the Consumers' League exercised influence in the legal system that led to protections for women workers being enshrined in law. Despite the fact that both were explicitly Consumers' League campaigns, however, the NCL's intervention in *Muller* v. *Oregon* was in reality far removed from the original narrative of concerned consumers weaponising their purchasing power. Skocpol gives a relatively modest assessment of the tools the NCL was working with, stating:

> The main resources the NCL national staff could bring to bear on any problem were social connections, small flows of money, and capacities for investigation and publicity – in short, resources ideally suited to the preparation and coordination of arguments before the courts.[9]

Nevertheless, the participation of NCL members, and their under-standing of the legal, social and economic contexts of the *Muller* case, highlight that this was a campaign by professional women using their own training and knowledge as well as their connec-tions to operate within the official channels of the legal system. The involvement of socially and economically influential women, which Black saw as the secret to the US consumers' leagues' success, here takes on a different form. The position of the women leaders of the NCL in the *Muller* case shows the relevance of their wealth and position in that these things had allowed them to pursue an academic education and participate on a professional level in conversations about the national interest. This meant that in framing their arguments about what workers needed and what was considered to be good for them, they could move away from the motherly or sisterly fellow feeling or gendered sense of compassion which had been central in the early days of the consumers' leagues. Instead they adopted a (quasi-)scientific perspective on 'the health and welfare of the republic'. In my opinion, however, this turned out to be an even more problematic strategy as it connected to unpalatable ideas related to eugenics, gender essentialism and social control.

US protective labour legislation up to 1908

The legal landscape into which *Muller* v. *Oregon* emerged was both a specific and a fraught one, in which state-level protective legislation had been repeatedly pitted against the US Constitution. Woloch describes the situation by the end of the nineteenth century as follows:

> seventeen states had passed [maximum hours] laws, all weak; they reached mainly employees in public works (men), curbed hours only 'in the absence of agreement to the contrary,' and lacked enforcement provisions. Laws to limit hours for women and children arose after 1870, mainly in states with textile mills; legislators typically dealt with women and children together.

Most of these existing laws, Woloch makes clear, 'lacked impact'.[10] In addition, the NCL knew from experience that 'after years of political struggle, progressive legislative enactments could be undone in the courts by the stroke of a judicial pen', as Skocpol puts it.[11] The situation in a nutshell was that wherever protective labour legislation was introduced by state governments, it remained uncertain whether it might still be challenged in the courts and, if it were, whether it would survive such a challenge. There was also the question of whether such laws as were implemented could be effectively enforced. Often they might be phrased vaguely or leave loopholes, for instance by allowing for changing shift patterns or extra hours at busy times, making it impossible for inspectors to check the actual length of workers' shifts. This dynamic marked the first decade of the Progressive Era.

Both Florence Kelley in *Some Ethical Gains through Legislation*, her 1905 text on the positive effects of legal intervention for worker protections, and Josephine Goldmark in *Fatigue and Efficiency*, a 1912 study of the physical and economic effects of overwork, would trace back this history to the 1895 case of *Ritchie* v. *Illinois*. Historically placed at the very beginning of the Progressive Era, this was a case in which Kelley had been directly involved as a factory inspector for Illinois, four years before she joined the newly founded NCL. It was brought before the state Supreme Court as a challenge to a section of the Illinois Factory and Workshop Inspection Statute, passed in 1893, that limited the working day for women in factories to eight hours. The statute was held to be unconstitutional on the basis of the Fourteenth Amendment. Surprisingly, this amendment, one of the so-called 'Reconstruction Amendments' made in 1868 following the US Civil War, had in fact been introduced to confirm the abolition of slavery by formalising the right of all citizens to equal freedoms and protections under US law. The first section pertains specifically to citizenship rights. It states:

> No State shall make or enforce any law which shall abridge the privileges or immunities of citizens of the United States; nor shall any State deprive any person of life, liberty, or property, without due process of law; nor deny to any person within its jurisdiction the equal protection of the laws.[12]

This clause was used to invoke the right to freedom of contract as a challenge to protective labour laws. It is worth noting that this argument was ostensibly made not on behalf of employers to contract labour without state interference, but on behalf of workers. It ran as follows: as a worker's labour was equated to their 'property', which they should be free to contract, any attempt on the part of the state to limit this was thus an infringement of the citizen's liberty and property as safeguarded by the constitution. In the *Ritchie* case, the Illinois court agreed with this assessment of the eight hours law as in contravention to the workers' right to labour under their own terms. As Goldmark puts it, the judges in the case

> declared that the police power of the state did not sanction such an interference with the working hours of adult women. There was no 'fair, just, and reasonable connection between such limitation and the public health, safety, or welfare proposed to be secured by it.'[13]

It is of interest that the point of 'public health, safety, [and] welfare' was already cited even in this adverse judgment: it sets the tone for this weighing of both the freedom and the welfare of the individual against the protection of a supposed greater public and national good, also measured in terms of health, safety and welfare.

While the judgment was a blow to campaigners like Kelley, it was also immediately relevant to them that the argument remained open for legal dispute. Lawyer Kelley noted already in her annual Illinois factory inspection report of 1895: 'Happily the weight of the precedent is not on the side of the Illinois court; the precedents are in the other direction.'[14] She proceeded to cite the example of twenty years of undisputed state regulation of women's and children's labour in Massachusetts. That Kelley continued to believe in this point is reflected in the fact that she chose to quote it verbatim from her own report ten years later in *Some Ethical Gains*; it also continued to inform the NCL's stance on comparable cases that arose in other states, up to and including *Muller* v. *Oregon*.

The *Ritchie* judgment was followed by a decade of cases brought on the same constitutional basis to challenge state maximum hours laws, with court judgments at local, state and federal level either agreeing or disagreeing with this interpretation of the Fourteenth Amendment. A clear contrast to the *Ritchie* case emerged in *Holden* v. *Hardy*, which came before the federal Supreme Court three years later in 1898. This case pertained to an eight hours law in Utah for men employed in mines and smelters. Because these working environments were acknowledged to pose a health hazard to the workers due to the toxic substances involved, the Supreme Court upheld the Utah law. Writing with hindsight in 1912, Goldmark identified this judgment as an important precursor to the outcome of *Muller* v. *Oregon*, not least because the judges were prepared to look beyond the specifics of this health, safety and welfare question to a broader context that also critically analysed the wider application of the Fourteenth Amendment. She describes the judgment at some length, explaining:

But the judges [. . .] struck a loftier note which rises clear and strong above the technical argument. They were preoccupied with something larger than the single law in dispute. It was the state which figured before them – a congregate whole which was only as great as 'the sum of all its parts.' These parts, they said in stirring words, did not stand upon an equality with one another in the economic scale, and therein lay both the need and the justification of the state's intervention.[15]

In other words, the freedom to contract labour as assigned to working people had little meaning when an imbalance of power between the two parties to the contract, as a result of economic inequality, meant that the contract could not in fact be entered into freely by the worker. Goldmark quotes the judges further:

> But the fact that both parties are of full age, and competent to contract, does not necessarily deprive the state of the power to interfere, where the parties do not stand upon an equality, or where the public health demands that one party to the contract shall be protected against himself. The state still retains an interest in his welfare, however reckless he may be. The whole is no greater than the sum of all the parts, and when the individual health, safety, and welfare are sacrificed or neglected, the state must suffer.[16]

The court here was evidently referring to the welfare of individual workers, arguing that their health and safety should be protected even if they themselves, for whatever reason, chose to be careless of it. In the health and welfare of the individual lay the wider health and welfare of the state as the 'sum of its parts'. Lastly, Goldmark noted a pointed addition by the court related to the peculiarity of a challenge being brought by employers if the matter at stake was the workers' freedom. She relates:

> It is significant, as the court pointed out also in this decision, that such cases as the one at bar have not been brought by working people eager to secure their 'right' to labor any number of hours, but by the employers to whose advantage it is for them so to labor. 'The argument,' said the court, 'would certainly come with better grace and better cogency from the other class.'[17]

This judgment suggests that the invocation of the Fourteenth Amendment had become something of an automated response, as an experiment with a reasonable expectation of success for employers who chafed at the introduction of maximum hours laws. The mere fact it had been used successfully, however, these judges suggested, did not mean that it was therefore inherently correct as an argument.

The key points in this judgment as recounted by Goldmark, then, are the following: inequality of power detracts from the significance of individual liberty; health, safety and welfare deserve protection for their own sake and the state has a responsibility to safeguard them for the individual in the interest of the community; and notions of individual freedoms and rights can be distorted for specific agendas. As this judgment pertained to a law for working men, it was read as encouraging by Goldmark and the NCL because of its generalised arguments relating to individual workers as part of the public health and safety and about wider questions of inequality. In Goldmark's representation, it is deemed praiseworthy on the part of the judges that they were prepared to think beyond the 'technical argument' of legal precedent. Using emotive language, probably to show general readers that the relevance of the question was more than a dry piece of legal history, she describes the judges' consideration of a wider social context as 'loft[y]', 'stirring', 'clear and strong', and 'rising above' legal discourse to a recognition of a greater good and their own role as guardians of the spirit as well as the letter of the law.

Goldmark includes one further court case in her potted history of the battle over protective legislation: *Lochner* v. *New York* (1901). In this case, the federal Supreme Court did not uphold New York's state law limiting the working day of bakers to ten hours because it did not see any danger arising from the work of bakers that would justify specific protections for their trade. As Goldmark puts it, '[b]akeries, unlike mines and smelters, did not seem to them [the judges] dangerous *enough* to regulate'. The knowledge of the subsequent outcome of *Muller* v. *Oregon* allows her to address this setback fairly dismissively. She notes that, legally speaking:

> In substance the Lochner decision does not over-rule the court's previous sanction of the Utah law [in *Holden* v. *Hardy*]. The way was still left open for the justification of other laws limiting the workday, if the judges could be shown 'that there is material danger to the public health, or to the health of the employe [*sic*], if the hours of labor are not curtailed.'[18]

This, along with Kelley's conviction that legal precedent was on the side of protective laws, explains why the NCL was not discouraged about future legislation, but felt spurred to interfere in the *Muller* case to bring about, if possible, a judgment closer to that in *Holden* v. *Hardy*. Indeed, the Brandeis Brief itself stated explicitly that '[t]he decision in this case will, in effect, determine the constitutionality of nearly all the statutes in force in the United States, limiting the hours of labor of adult women', and this was the objective with which the case for Oregon was conceived.[19]

It is striking that, in the preceding catalogue, the question of gender was really only relevant in the *Ritchie* case, and merely because the law under dispute happened to be one pertaining to women workers. *Holden* v. *Hardy* and *Lochner* both related to the working conditions of men: in the former, the judgment was generalised to refer to the vulnerability of all workers; in the latter the specificity of the judgment related not to gender but to the nature of the work. Like *Ritchie*, *Muller* concerned a maximum hours law for women, and evidently a clear decision was made in the Brandeis Brief to focus exclusively on the plight of women workers and their perceived physical vulnerability rather than to argue for protective labour laws in general on the precedent of *Holden* v. *Hardy*. Skocpol holds that it was in order to 'persuade the Supreme Court to differentiate between Muller and Lochner' that Brandeis and the NCL 'argued before the Court that industrial overwork was especially damaging for women workers as actual or potential mothers, thus justifying the use of police powers by the state to modify market contracts'.[20] In other words, if bakers did not deserve hours regulations because their work posed no clear risk to their health, it had to be proven that risks to women's health were clear and present across the different types of work covered in the Oregon law.

As we have already seen, women's position as workers was vulnerable for a number of reasons, from physical danger to the fact that their social position gave them less economic bargaining power. It is of course probable that this vulnerability, actual and perceived, was the reason for the existence of gender-specific protective laws in the first place. There is, however, nothing inherent in the *Holden* v. *Hardy* judgment that would make this an obvious conclusion. The emphasis on childbirth, furthermore, seems to put the argument firmly in the gender difference rather than the entering wedge camp. It is also obviously reductive, portraying women workers only as potential mothers rather than as individuals whose welfare mattered for its own sake, in a reinterpretation of the notion of the state as 'the sum of its parts' in the *Holden* v. *Hardy* judgment. Certainly the NCL felt that the argument based on an understanding of biological gender difference related to childbearing would sway the judges; and indeed this was borne out by the outcome of the *Muller* case, as the judgment appended to the published brief attested.

Louis D. Brandeis, assisted by Josephine Goldmark, *Women in Industry: Decision of the United States-Supreme Court in Curt Muller VS. State of Oregon* (1908)

The NCL published the text of the Brandeis Brief, including the court judgment, straightaway in 1908.[21] The title page lists Louis D. Brandeis as the author, 'assisted by Josephine Goldmark'. As mentioned, Goldmark was at this time the NCL's publication secretary. The organisation's swift publication of the successful judgment, showing how it had once again taken on the legal establishment and won its cause, was an effective piece of self-promotion. This transforms the brief into a public-facing campaign text in the same category as the others discussed in this book. As Goldmark and other NCL activists were the primary researchers and compilers of the brief, furthermore, it qualifies as a piece of women's campaign writing.

The brief made an accessible text for NCL supporters outside the legal sphere because, in many ways, it shows continuity with existing NCL strategies, arguments and publications. The decision to focus not on legal language and arguments of legal precedent but on medical evidence and international examples made the narrative of the brief more widely understandable, speaking to campaign language the NCL had used before. While it was a daring move in a legal sense, therefore, it was likely to be a popular one in the wider context of social influence within which the NCL operated. In Goldmark's recollection of the NCL's preparation for the case, cited by Woloch, she referred to Brandeis's stipulation of 'what he would need for a brief, namely, *facts*, published by anyone with expert knowledge of industry in its relation to women's hours of labor'. Accordingly, Goldmark and her team of researchers set out to collect the required data. 'Using the resources of Columbia University, the New York Public Library, and the Library of Congress', Woloch states, they 'found reports of British factory commissions and medical commissions, translated sources from western Europe, and collected information from states with maximum hours laws'.[22] The use of non-judicial authorities was a familiar strategy from earlier Consumers' League campaigns; for example, Alice L. Woodbridge had referred to the testimony of medical authorities in her 1890 report, while Kelley regularly cited factory inspectors' reports as official evidence on labour and public health. It also reflected the skills of NCL members in converting different forms and levels of information into campaign narratives for specific audiences: Kelley, for instance, referred to such evidence as state reports on food adulteration as sources containing information that needed to be converted into an accessible format for an average consumer. The research team's use of academic libraries and multilingual sources – they collected examples from England, France, Germany, Austria, Switzerland and Italy – also shows their education. Kelley had made academic connections on the NCL's behalf from the beginning, as demonstrated in Chapter 2, and, like Black, she had adapted her arguments to her target audience. All of this made it a logical step to redefine the idea of precedent by bringing different discourses into the brief's narrative for the courtroom. As even the federal Supreme Court had shown itself fickle in judging the legal arguments in previous outings, as shown in the different judgments between *Holden* v. *Hardy* and *Lochner* v. *New York* within three years of each other, it was decided instead to draw precedents from the legislation of other countries, demonstrating that workers had gained and economies had not suffered by protection.

The opening of the brief itself was cursorily framed in the legal context of Muller's constitutional appeal. It quickly, however, also brought in the language of previous court judgments by pointing out that the personal liberties and privileges stipulated in the Fourteenth Amendment were 'subject to such reasonable restraint of action as the State may impose in the exercise of the police power for the protection of health, safety, morals, and the general welfare'.[23] This made the point that, just as the constitution was beyond question, so too was the right of the state to intervene in the public interest. Alongside health and safety, which had been explicitly mentioned in *Holden* v. *Hardy*, the brief noticeably included 'morals' as well as 'the general welfare'. Intertextual readings of NCL campaign texts highlight the implicit meanings of these terms. For example, the language of morality is familiar from the Woodbridge report and already introduces a sense of gender and the specific risks women faced, as well as the social roles and duties ascribed to them.

Having thus established the right of the state of Oregon to institute and enforce laws such as that under which Muller was charged, the brief goes on to argue that

> when the validity of a [state-level] statute is questioned, the burden of proof, so to speak, is upon those who assail it. [. . .] The validity of the Oregon statute must therefore be sustained unless the Court can find that there is no 'fair ground, reasonable in and of itself, to say that there is material danger to the public health (or safety), or to the health (or safety) of the employees (or to the general welfare), if the hours of labor are not curtailed.'[24]

In short, this passage argues that it is obvious that the Oregon statute was created to protect women workers' health and safety, and that it is up to Muller and his counsel to disprove this for their claim of freedom to contract to be legally viable. The NCL's determination to differentiate the case from *Lochner* becomes evident here, as the brief tries to anticipate the argument that overwork is not in itself harmful enough to regulate. Instead it invites the judges to come to a different conclusion than that which related specifically to the baking trade, where it was found to be proven that there was 'no fair ground' for restrictions. In spite of this attempt to put the burden of proof on Muller's legal team, however, it was clear that the brief had set itself the task of positively proving the negative effects on women's health and the public welfare of working days that exceeded ten hours. While it noted that '[t]he legal rules applicable to this case are few and are well established', and listed these concisely in its opening pages, it held that this very fact justified the use of precedent that extended beyond US law, providing new evidence to bolster the arguments that had been known to succeed as well as to fail in the past.[25]

'Part First' of the brief gives an overview of 'legislation restricting the hours of labor for women' abroad and in the US.[26] As Kelley had done before and Goldmark subsequently went on to do again, the brief thus explores a historicised view of legal and economic discourse addressing the success of labour legislation in other countries. Like Woodbridge and Nathan, this approach speaks to the ongoing debate between notions of an old and a new world that featured the US as a leading force in progressive economic and social developments globally. In this case, it is suggested, legal squabbling in the US led to the nation getting left behind in developments that were already fully accepted in Europe. Europe here thus works as an authority based on its historical economic experience of experiments in labour legislation that had been found to be successful in the long term. The brief claims unequivocally that

> [a]bout two generations have elapsed since the enactment of the first law [to limit women's working hours in Europe]. In no country in which the legal limitation upon the hours of labor of adult women was introduced has the law been repealed. Practically without exception every amendment of the law has been in the line of strengthening the law or further reducing the working time.[27]

A similar case is then made for the existing legislation cited in the brief as enacted over preceding decades in twenty separate US states. It makes the point that this 'has not been the result of sudden impulse or passing humor, – it has followed deliberate consideration, and been adopted in the face of much opposition'. It goes on to say that '[m]ore than a generation has elapsed between the earliest and the latest of these acts' during which time the legislation was applied, tested and enforced and the effects were found to be beneficial and worth maintaining and extending.[28] In fact, it states that, '[i]n the United States, as in foreign countries, there has been a general movement to strengthen and to extend the operation of these laws'.[29] It does acknowledge that the *Ritchie* case was held to be unconstitutional, but presents this simply as a bit of a blip in an otherwise straightforward narrative of progress – contrary to the historical analyses of Skocpol and Woloch, but in keeping with Kelley's repeatedly expressed faith that legal precedent was not on the side of the *Ritchie* judgment.

'Part Second', the larger section of the brief, consists of medicalised arguments specifically against overwork for women, underpinned by an explicit assumption of inherent physical differences between men and women. It states:

> In structure and function women are differentiated from men. Beside these anatomical differences, physicians are agreed that women are fundamentally weaker than men in all that makes for endurance: in muscular strength, in nervous energy, in the powers of persistent attention and application. Overwork, therefore, which strains endurance to the utmost, is more disastrous to the health of women than of men, and entails upon them more lasting injury.[30]

While this argument is clearly in the gender difference camp, it should be noted that it still holds a door open for an entering wedge: overwork 'strains endurance to the utmost' for all workers but is particularly damaging for women. In this line of reasoning, it would thus make sense to argue that maximum hours laws were required for women first. While the benefit was less urgent for men, however, it could and should be extended to all workers subsequently.

It soon becomes evident nonetheless that the primary concern is not for women workers as individuals, but for women workers as potential mothers. The arguments about women's health are almost exclusively related to the knock-on effects they have for childbirth and childcare: matters associated with both biological and social conceptions of womanhood. The brief refers to the 'effect of labor on the reproductive organs' and the consequent 'effects on the offspring'. Physical work is associated with 'narrow pelves' which make childbirth difficult; a difficult birth may cause problems for subsequent pregnancies as well as disabilities for the baby.[31] The brief states: 'The long hours of standing, which are required in many industries, are universally denounced by physicians as the cause of pelvic disorders.'[32] In a section entitled 'Specific Evil Effects on Childbirth and Female Functions' it is stated that '[t]he evil effect of overwork before as well as after marriage upon childbirth is marked and disastrous'.[33] Concerns include physical questions, such as a loss of quality in breast milk, as well as social ones, such as work keeping breastfeeding mothers away from children at feeding times, thus requiring the children to be fed on other substances to their assumed detriment.[34] Alongside the essentialising of the gender identity of women workers, then, there is also an obvious element of social control here. Not only is it assumed to be women workers' inescapable fate to be biological mothers and suggested that this should be taken into account whether or not they are married (a euphemism for having reproductive sex); once they have become mothers, they must also be personally and physically available to their child for regular feeding. Needless to say, this would not be plausible even under a stipulated legal maximum of ten (or even eight) hours a day unless the employer allowed the child to be nearby and the mother to take feeding breaks – something that is still generally not legislated for. The fact that a mother may be the breadwinner on whom the child is also financially dependent is not considered.

The argument that begins to evolve in the subsection entitled 'Bad Effect of Long Hours on Morals' is unmistakably rooted in anxiety about degeneration. It opens by equating a conception of morality to physical health, arguing:

> The effect of overwork on morals is closely related to the injury to health. Laxity of moral fibre follows physical debility. When the working day is so long that no time whatever is left for a minimum of leisure or home-life, relief from the strain of work is sought in alcoholic stimulants and other excesses.[35]

Such excesses, it is claimed as understood, will have a bad effect not only on the 'home-life' that would foster good morals in the present and subsequent generations but also on the physical prowess of the debauched worker. This would not only make them a less effective worker but also risked passing poor health on to new children. Children who were disabled or physically and morally weak would in turn grow up to be worse workers, perhaps with their own tendencies to alcoholism. In a peculiar revision of the court's argument of the state as the 'sum of its parts' in *Holden* v. *Hardy*, this understanding of individual deterioration leading to class degeneration is argued as follows:

> Deterioration of any large portion of the population inevitably lowers the entire community physically, mentally, and morally. When the health of women has been injured by long hours, not only is the working efficiency of the community impaired, but the deterioration is handed down to succeeding generations. Infant mortality rises, while the children of married working-women, who survive, are injured by inevitable neglect. The overwork of future mothers thus directly attacks the welfare of the nation.[36]

The 'welfare of the nation', then, is understood to consist in the personal, physical and moral health of individual workers. If they keep healthy, avoid 'excesses' such as alcohol, and are available to care for their children, they will raise healthy offspring to become strong and effective workers; such healthy working families together will make up the tissue of a healthy working class, the 'human machine' which supports the nation economically.

The brief further emphasises that '[t]his needed protection to women can be afforded only through shortening the hours of labor. A decrease of the intensity of exertion is not feasible.'[37] In other words, it is not achievable that women should work a bit less hard while at work in order to save their energies for home; placing a legal curb on the length of their working day is the only way to preserve their health and energy for their role as mothers as well as workers. Furthermore, it is argued that working women themselves want this too, as do other authorities who can be relied on to know what is good for working women based on long experience: 'Factory inspectors, physicians, and working women are unanimous in advocating the ten-hour day, wherever it has not yet been established.'[38] Having thus confirmed that this is the only way forward, the brief goes on to urge that such legislation should be universally applied, without exceptions for specific industries or busy periods. Such loopholes would only make the rules less clear for workers, employers and customers, and would thus encourage evasion of the laws, whether deliberately or out of ignorance; it would also cause difficulties for inspection and enforcement. The brief argues, furthermore, that it is demonstrably fairer to employers if the same laws apply across the board, so that no employer or industry is disadvantaged – again differentiating the case from the trade-specific *Lochner* judgment.[39] The brief proceeds to pre-empt a range of economic arguments that might be made for a longer working day. It states that shorter hours actually increase output as well as raise its quality.[40] To the potential matter of customer discontent, it argues that customers readily adjust to changes brought about by new legislation – a statement the NCL could back up from its own campaign experience.[41]

That this approach was successful is evident from the judges' verdict appended to the published version of the brief. Its conclusion reads:

> That women's physical structure and the performance of maternal functions place her at a disadvantage in the struggle for subsistence is obvious. This is especially true when the burdens of motherhood are upon her. Even when they are not, by abundant testimony of the medical fraternity continuance for a long time on her feet at work, repeating this from day to day, tends to injurious effects upon the body, and as healthy mothers are essential to vigorous offspring, the physical well-being of woman becomes an object of public interest and care in order to preserve the strength and vigor of the race.[42]

The difference between this judgment and that in *Holden* v. *Hardy* is noticeable. The question of worker rights for their own sake barely comes into it: the focus is purely on women's physicality. The gendered disparity in 'the struggle for subsistence' here does not refer to social constructs that placed women at a disadvantage in, for example, collective bargaining or wage negotiations; it is read as related to physical weakness and maternity. The final note of concern is not for the individual woman worker but for healthy offspring and 'the strength and vigor of the race'. The 'health and welfare of the republic' is here interpreted in a purely eugenicist sense, with a healthy, non-disabled working population seen as a requirement for economic progress. While the brief itself left a small opening for entering wedge arguments, the conclusion of the verdict does not: the focus on gender difference, presented in a binary biological way, is absolute. In this way the NCL won a victory for the state of Oregon which was permitted to uphold its maximum hours law; and a legal precedent was set for such laws in other states too, as further challenges under the Fourteenth Amendment were forestalled.

The verdict thus paved the way for other protective legislation for women on a more solid foundation than had previously been available. Skocpol notes that the judgment was rapidly followed by a 'veritable flood of new legislation' establishing maximum working hours for women.[43] The success of its experimental strategy also emboldened the NCL in its trajectory of legal intervention as '[o]ver succeeding years into the mid-1930s, the NCL sponsored some fifteen legal briefs in support of labor laws challenged before the courts'.[44] Writing in the Florida daily *Pensacola Journal* in April 1908, some two months after the verdict had been made public, Kelley already affirmed this intention. Again placing the court decision in its existing legal context, which she describes as being 'in a singularly chaotic state', she states that the judgment 'is more far-reaching than at first appeared'. She goes on to explain:

Nominally it applied only to laundries, mechanical establishments and factories in Oregon. In fact, however, it establishes for the whole country the principle that a statute limiting women's working hours is, in general, to be regarded as a measure in the interests of the public health. The right of the states thus to legislate is not confined to the working day of ten hours, or to any group of industries.

As such, she announced that

> [t]he circulation of Mr. Brandeis' brief is the initial step in a campaign
> for re-enacting in Illinois and any other states in which such legislation
> may have been repealed or annulled, eight, nine or ten hours laws for
> working women.[45]

The publication, then, was intended not only as a persuasive piece
to win support for the NCL, as other campaign texts considered in
this book had been; it was in fact a practical blueprint for further
action on a national level. The NCL, furthermore, had already
begun to take active steps with this end in view. Kelley closes her
article on this invigorating point, writing that

> [t]he decision [. . .] opens the way for the National Consumers' League,
> through its sixty-five branches in twenty-two states, to begin a cam-
> paign for legal protection of working women. The decision having
> been made public on February 24, the League at its ninth annual
> meeting on March 3, unanimously voted to change the name of its
> committee on legislation by adding the words, 'and defense of labor
> laws.' By this way of undertaking the double task of obtaining a legal
> working day for women, and defending in the courts the statutes
> which it is so laborious to obtain and has hitherto, been so difficult to
> enforce and sustain after enactment.[46]

While Kelley's article does not explain why women workers need
special protection, it is noteworthy that, while her summary of
the NCL meeting's decision does not appear to gender labour
laws, the way she explains the task it has set itself does pertain
to 'a legal working day for women'. While it is clear, then, that
Kelley and the NCL were keen to capitalise on the success of the
Muller decision, and that Kelley in any case still perceived it as a
way to redress the Illinois decision of 1895, this article does not
take an explicit stance on the question of gender difference or the
entering wedge as underpinning the strategy. While this appears to
have left opportunities to continue the campaign in either or both
directions, the influence of the understanding of gender reflected
here, as a culmination of the development of the gendered rhetoric
that the US consumers' leagues had engaged in from the beginning, sets a particular agenda that is carried forward by prominent
voices including Kelley and Goldmark. As well as medical and

other non-judicial testimony, the brief had mobilised emotional arguments playing into socially conservative and eugenicist concerns. While it was intended to protect women workers, it was also designed to keep them in their social place.

Gendered notions of regeneration and degeneration in the NCL's Progressive Era rhetoric

In his foreword to *The Story of an Epoch-Making Movement*, Baker summed up the NCL's ambitions and achievements in directly influencing legislation and policy as follows:

> Before local and general legislatures of every state, and committees of Congress, in the offices of mayors, governors, cabinet officers, and Presidents, the voice of the League has been lifted in the interest of better conditions of life and work, notably for women and children.[47]

Again, however, even as he lionised its impact, he also reduced this once again to a context of benign gendered influence that represented the NCL as non-threatening because it remained an independent and unofficial body acting in an advisory capacity. He wrote:

> In a peculiar sense the Consumers' League is an ideal voluntary agency involved in an industrial democracy. For the most part, laws are needed only for recalcitrants. Spontaneous good behaviour, dictated by good will and enforced by common consent, makes up the larger part of the sanction of civilised life. Such spontaneous good behaviour can rest only upon knowledge of the implications of conduct, and knowledge can only be acquired, under modern conditions, when high-minded and disinterested inquirers investigate and tell us what they find. This sort of work the Consumers' League has done supremely well in a field in which it was a pioneer.[48]

Although it mentions laws in passing, this passage in fact makes relatively light of the organisation's legal impact, even though this was a point of pride for Nathan in the main body of the book. The image thus invoked here of the Consumers' League campaigners is again in keeping with the idea of the interest and influence of women from higher social classes being linked with care in a maternal and educational as well as a protective sense. By guiding the state, as well as individuals, into good behaviour, they are helping to protect the welfare of weaker individuals and thus the greater good for all. This representation of the organisation's work further adds to the idea of offering social regeneration to a specific social group of women. Reading through the lens of the Brandeis Brief, this regeneration is counterbalanced with the threat of degeneration in another class. It is implied that, by keeping both the workers and the employers and politicians on the right track, the Consumers' League contributed to the Progressive Era's reaction against the degeneration of the state. It also, however, gave itself the task of halting a perceived degeneration in the workers it set out to protect. In this way, it is suggested, the Consumers' League could preside over a collective national regeneration based on established values.

Baker's passing reference to legal intervention as 'needed only for recalcitrants' gives a conciliatory impression that is linked to the notion of the Consumers' League as understanding both parties and thus being able to mediate successfully between them. This sense of rapprochement between classes appears in many consumer campaigns, going back to Black's remark that employers are not 'ogres'.[49] The same stance is also evident from testimony that Brandeis gave to the Commission on Industrial Relations, a commission for Congress on the state and impact of labour legislation which ran from 1912 until 1915. In his testimony, Brandeis revisited both subject matter and arguments that had also arisen in the *Muller* case, including the invocation of the liberty of contract. Speaking specifically to the question of employers' refusal to negotiate with trade unions, Brandeis claimed that this was 'ordinarily due to erroneous reasoning or false sentiment'. He stated:

> He [an employer] is apt to think 'this is my business and the American has the right of liberty of contract.' He honestly believes that he is standing up for a high principle and is willing often to run the risk of having his business ruined rather than abandon that principle. They have not thought out clearly enough that liberty means exercising one's rights consistently with a like exercise of rights by other people; that liberty is distinguished from license in that it is subject to certain restrictions, and that no one can expect to secure liberty in the sense in which we recognize it in America without having his rights curtailed in those respects in which it is necessary to limit them in the general public interest.

Having thus situated the question of individual liberty in the now familiar context of a common good and collective welfare, he went on to excuse the stance of employers as caused by their honest ignorance. He told the commission:

> I think our employers, as a rule, are kind-hearted; they mean to do right; they mean to be just; and there is no difference between the men who have fought the hardest against labor unions and those who have yielded to and dealt with labor unions in that respect, except that the former have not had that education which comes from actual active co-operation with unions in the solution of these problems.[50]

Framing the conclusion in this way transforms plaintiffs like Muller from 'recalcitrants', in Baker's phrase, into principled people whose minds may be changed if the matter is put to them as a common-sense point of a shared interest. In each of these examples, however, the question of mediation is key and the employer class is to be placated. This approach clearly shows the role of organisations such as the NCL who can wield their gendered identity as consumers to access both the employer class and policy makers with arguments of sympathy and the national interest. Lines of reasoning such as that of Brandeis above would have helped to make the *Muller* judgment more widely acceptable, facilitating the increase in protective legislation that marked the Progressive Era.

The persistence of this classed and gendered framing of the NCL's mediating role is particularly interesting when we consider that the NCL's intervention in the *Muller* case was no longer a consumer campaign, but rather a campaign run by professionals belonging to an organisation with a supporter base for which the consumer identity was the unifying factor. A lot of its strategies nevertheless remain recognisably rooted in the well-established approaches of the US Consumers' Leagues. It employed the idea of collapsing distance between workers and non-workers, applying global examples to a state-level question. Firstly, it drew parallels of common humanity, albeit in a context of talking about a working class who were equated with their counterparts in western Europe on the basis of physicality: the brief worked on the logical assumption that the bodies of US women workers would suffer in the same ways as those of working women in European countries. Secondly, it offered proof of how the NCL was prepared to scale its own activities both up and down: in following a local dispute to the federal Supreme Court, they showed that state- (and even single workplace-)level problems were not too small to warrant its attention. Similarly, however, the opening to the Brandeis Brief made clear that their interest in this local case was motivated by the potential they saw for it to provide a type of entering wedge for national improvement too, by establishing a new legal precedent and using this to pursue the matter in different states to achieve protective parity – at least for women workers.

By the twentieth century, then, the precise application of the question of gender in Consumers' League rhetoric and practice had evolved. While they depended on a man to present their case as their counsel, the NCL's approach to the *Muller* case was strongly informed by the professional knowledge of its legally schooled women leaders. On the other hand, their long-established tactic of speaking on behalf of other women citing health and welfare concerns also allowed them in part to bypass legal and economic reasoning. Arguably, this bias was what caused the NCL in many ways to fall short in achieving better conditions for women workers. Woloch's summary of *Muller* v. *Oregon* highlights the fact that it was the arguments regarding the 'welfare of the nation', rather than the welfare of individual workers, that swayed the judges in the case.[51] Landon R. Y. Storrs complicates this analysis somewhat, noting that, while women's ability to bear children was brought forward in Goldmark's research for the brief, differences between the social positions of men and women were also pointed out as factors in women's greater vulnerability in the workplace. He observes that Goldmark addressed 'women's lesser bargaining power with employers (due to their exclusion from unions)' and acknowledged that the effects of overwork on women were related to the fact that 'women's unpaid domestic labor left them less time to sleep and relax than men'. According to Storrs, it was the verdict, not the brief itself, that 'emphasized biological differences between the sexes [rather than] the differences that flowed from social inequality', as these were the arguments that swayed the court's decision against Muller.[52] My close reading in this chapter, however, makes clear the large extent to which the Brandeis Brief did participate in and deliberately mobilise emotional and exclusionary concerns about what the judges called 'the vigor of the race'.

Skocpol argues that in fact the brief's focus on women and specifically the gender essentialist conception of women as potential biological mothers was a purely opportunistic approach that was viewed as a better guarantee of persuading the judges. She states:

> Ideally, Kelley, Goldmark, and Brandeis would have preferred to argue on behalf of legally limited hours for all workers regardless of gender; we know this because in 1916–17 the National Consumers' League actually made such an argument in Bunting v. Oregon. But in 1908, the only available opportunity seemed to be to persuade the Supreme Court that women workers were unusually vulnerable employees rather than regular workers, like bakers, who should take their chances in unfettered labor markets as freely contracting individuals. Thus women's biological vulnerabilities were highlighted in the 'facts' and expert opinions that Goldmark mobilized for Brandeis, even though most of them were gleaned from European sources that had often advocated protection for workers in general.[53]

In other places, however, both Goldmark and Kelley revealed that they shared the ideas about women's social position that were expounded in the brief. Woloch observes that Kelley, herself a working mother of three who was separated from her abusive husband, opposed the employment of married women and objected to childcare provision to facilitate the participation of mothers in the workforce. In 1910 she argued that the 'industrial employment of married women' did 'harm and only harm'; according to Woloch, she thought that it 'depressed the birth rate, demoralized husbands, reduced men's wages, injured children, encouraged industrial homework, increased urban congestion, hurt employers, damaged public health, and harmed the whole community'.[54] In addition, Woloch also shows that Kelley took a contrasting view to fellow labour campaigners over the question of paid maternity benefits for women workers. She

> charged that maternity insurance would encourage shiftless immigrant men to send pregnant wives to work, unfairly burden unmarried working women, and serve as 'an actual bribe to increased immigration of the kind of men who make their wives and children work.'[55]

The perceived threat to the greater good as represented by social stability and separate gendered spheres, then, was here also cast in racist and anti-immigrant terms.

Comparable conceptions of gendered social roles as underpinning social stability are also evident in Goldmark's representations of women's work. In a discussion in *Fatigue and Efficiency* of the effects of nightwork, particularly for women, she argues that

[i]n [. . .] destroying home life, night work militates against morals as well as against health. Clearly, no form of women's work so interferes with their domestic relations as enforced absence from home in the evenings, the only time when wage-earning families are together. Young women who work at night are deprived of all the restraining influences of home life. When the mother of a family spends the night or evening in work, disorder is almost unavoidable, and the comfort of the men as well as of the children dependent upon her ministrations, is lost.[56]

Goldmark extensively unpacks her ideas about the relationship between overwork and working-class degeneration and regeneration across genders. In doing so she mobilises a range of popular discourses from that of the Brandeis Brief and the *Muller* verdict to the Ruskinian argument we also saw Black adapting in Chapter 1. Describing developments in factory legislation in England, she claims that

wherever sufficient time has elapsed since the establishment of a more humane workday, allowing a wider margin of leisure, the workers have made extraordinary advance in physique and morals. The gradual emergence of the English mill operatives from the physical and moral degradation into which they had sunk in the thirties of the last century, is not exceptional but typical. It is a humble chronicle, but full of meaning to any reader who loves the fullness of human nature. Gardening, sewing, the out-of-doors on summer evenings, evening schools in winter, time for the 'endearing trivialities of home life,' – these were some of the simple, yet enduring things at which mill workers learned to spend their leisure.[57]

Her argument is that this kind of leisure for individual and creative expression is necessary in the face of the development of work into 'monotonous and subdivided labor'. Echoing Ruskin, she states that the nature of most workers' jobs 'destroys what we inadequately call pleasure in work, – the ever-so-slight satisfaction of man's creative sense, his dimmest feelings of mastery of self-expression in work'.[58] In other words, if there can be no 'pleasure in work', it is necessary to free up some of the workers' time from work to allow them to find pleasure elsewhere – and to ensure that they did not leave work so exhausted that the only pleasure within reach would be intoxicants and transgressive sexual relations.

While this argument is cast with reference to 'man's creative sense', the examples given of the forms that workers' regeneration could take – '[g]ardening, sewing, the out-of-doors [. . .], evening schools [. . .] the "endearing trivialities of home life"' – are not necessarily gendered. 'Home life' here suggests that it could be applied to all family members and have a beneficial effect for any and all of them. It is connected to the conception of 'moral' behaviour linked to regeneration as opposed to the 'immoral' behaviour – such as sexual promiscuity, intercourse with sex workers, sex for pleasure without a procreative goal – that is presented as both the cause and effect of working-class degeneration. The sense of social control in safeguarding a specific understanding of 'home life' is still very present, however, and remains linked to physical health and ability across generations. Returning again to the wording of the *Holden* v. *Hardy* verdict, Goldmark claimed that

> when overwork unfits man or woman for normal parenthood, it is in a deep sense, anti-physiological and anti-social. It touches not alone the welfare but the very fibre of human society, that congregate 'whole,' which it should be our passionate concern to recognize, in the stirring words of the Supreme Court, as 'no greater than the sum of all its parts,' for 'when the individual health, safety, and welfare are sacrificed or neglected, the state must suffer.'[59]

Like Kelley, Goldmark also situates the fear of moral and physical degeneration within racist and anti-immigrant discourse. She suggests that the pace of manufacture in the USA was not so much a sign of its industrial superiority as a risk to the national welfare as it ignored workers' health. She states:

> It is a truism that trade life in America has been shorter than in foreign countries, where the pace is slower. The race is to the swift in a sense never dreamt of before, and in our industries the swift are necessarily the young, even the very young.

The pace has indeed been kept so high in many great trades, partly because the steady flow of immigration keeps bearing to our shores at intervals of time, young laborers of new immigrant races, able to replace those workers who have broken under the strain. So long as immigration streams westward it may be expedient, from a narrow economic point of view, to press all workers to their physical limits, and to dismiss them so soon as efficiency shows signs of failing. What shall we say from the physiological or racial point of view?[60]

In other words, according to Goldmark the systematised degeneration and exhaustion of the US working class – already, it should be noted, made up in very large part of migrant labour – perpetrated harm by encouraging further immigration. The suggestion here is that the risks this poses also relate to a threat to national and ethnic unity. All of these arguments ultimately functioned to illustrate the need for labour legislation to contain and counteract what Goldmark wants to prove is the far-reaching impact of overwork. Thinking back to Baker's argument about the influence of the NCL, then, this may again be seen as justifying legal intervention as part of the wider protective drive in keeping with the social role appropriate to the social segment represented by the Consumers' Leagues.

The significance given to arguments for women's welfare as related to their ability to bear children evokes a reduction of the individuality of women workers similar to the 'Sweated Industries Exhibition' and other campaigns to change women's working conditions. Daniel E. Bender remarks how many turn-of-the-twentieth-century anti-sweatshop campaigns assigned to women 'the role of transients and future mothers' in the workplace; protective legislation focusing on women's health with an emphasis on their childbearing ability could and often did have the effect of divorcing the roles of woman and worker.[61] The international history of protective legislation is dogged by how it could be applied to separate women from the workplace, making work a temporary interlude in the lives of women who would go on to be mothers and ensuring that these spells of work caused the least damage possible to the woman in her role as (future) mother. There are manifold instances of protective legislation in European countries, including France and the Netherlands, being deliberately designed to return women to the domestic sphere through tactics such as discouraging married women's employment in communal workplaces like factories and basing the limitation of working hours on the need for women to be available for caring responsibilities.[62] In spite of their claim to represent the wishes of women workers, many of these arguments in fact relate to the long pre-existing conception of the woman worker as someone who could never stand up for her own social, economic or political position, and who was defined primarily in terms of her gender and was therefore not permitted full access to the rights of the workforce.

It is telling that this became the basis of the Brandeis Brief in spite of the fact that the case against Muller was originally brought by a woman trade unionist insisting on her legal working rights. Whether or not it was true that NCL campaigners had a preference for protective laws without a gender focus, as Skocpol argued, Woloch notes that '[i]nnate difference and potential motherhood gained potency after the *Muller* v. *Oregon* decision'. She goes on:

> 'Difference' arguments, especially any reference to helplessness, proved useful to raise support for protection among middle-class women [. . .]. 'Women of larger opportunities should stand for the toilers who cannot help themselves,' a GFWC [General Federation of Women's Clubs] resolution of 1897 declared, and the theme persisted. Women workers, declared the head of the GFWC industrial committee in 1910, were 'frequently almost as helpless as the children in obtaining redress from oppression.'[63]

Resolutions such as these had a further reductive effect on the identity of women workers and reinforced the idea that middle-class women campaigners had both the duty and the right to take action on their behalf, without the obligation to take the position and ideas of the affected women workers into account. This may be viewed as a culmination of the regeneration of non-wage-earning women through the activist potential of their identity as consumers: for this ideal to work, it required buoying up by narratives around the helplessness of another group of women in the face of potential degeneration.

The reasoning revealed in *Muller* v. *Oregon* had grown far apart from Black's legislative campaigns to improve working conditions and wages, as the primary concern was no longer with achieving acceptable conditions and fair wages for people who were identified as workers first and foremost, but with protecting working women to allow them to fulfil the role of mother prescribed by middle-class gender ideology. The campaigns were distanced from the problem of underpayment: as we have seen, a minimum wage was considered part of the drive for protective legislation, but it was decided that maximum hours laws were more readily achievable. The campaigners also distanced themselves from the workers, rather than communicating directly with them. The international research that went into the Brandeis Brief may be seen to suggest a willingness to reach for foreign evidence of what middle-class specialists felt women workers needed, rather than to enter into a dialogue with the workers themselves about their needs and wants within and outside the workplace. The wishes of working women are only mentioned once in the brief, and that is to suggest collective assent. Woloch explains the endpoint of this line of reasoning as follows:

> Commitment to difference, though effective, proved a risky maneuver long term; the reformers' rationale had liabilities not immediately visible, though clear in retrospect. Protective laws deprived women workers of agency; they empowered the state to make decisions on women's behalf; they treated women workers [. . .] as unwilling or unable to speak for themselves, or irrational. Difference rationales reinforced gender disparities in the labor market and in law. When Progressive Era reformers defended single-sex protective laws, they often subsumed women's interests in some greater and more important ultimate purpose – whether future achievement of 'general' laws or community welfare or the well-being of the unborn.[64]

This is reflected, for instance, in Goldmark's passing observation on the NCL's entering wedge ideal in *Fatigue and Efficiency*: she believed the situation in which she campaigned to be such that '[s]hortening the workday is something that legislation can effect for women and children today, for men doubtless in the future'.[65] No clear trajectory was given for how or when this advance for all workers would 'doubtless' be achieved, despite the fact that she cited UK labour legislation that had led to the 'regeneration' of men as well as women workers.

Conclusions: Assessing the impact of the US Consumers' Leagues in the Progressive Era and beyond

The story of the Consumers' Leagues' campaigns in the USA shows that they regularly smoothed the way for ultimately objectively progressive developments, but that they achieved this by sometimes engaging in narratives that could lead to short-term gain but also shored up issues for the future, laying their achievements open to attack through problematic reasoning. Lawrence B. Glickman gets at the heart of the contradiction within the US Consumers' Leagues as a consumer movement that moved away from consumer activism. He states that '[t]he NCL aimed to reconcile the view that consumers were both incompetent and all-powerful', explaining: 'Although it maintained a critical distance, the NCL identified itself with the great consuming public. NCL activists acted as if they were in a sibling relationship with ordinary consumers, teaching consumers things that they were fully capable of mastering.'[66] This sibling relationship is evident from the campaign texts considered here and comes across very strongly in the professionalisation of NCL activism as in the *Muller* case. Bender highlights the more sinister sides to this aim of enlightening consumers in reference to the CLNY's campaigns on the sweated garment trade. He describes how the CLNY declared the sweatshop, which primarily employed migrant workers whose financial needs tended to be urgent and who generally had less access to the established channels of labour representation, 'a "menace to the home"', explaining that this 'referred to the homes of middle-class consumers who might purchase infected clothing and to the homes and families of working-class immigrants'.[67] This line of reasoning connects to the narratives of risks to public health and social control. The sweated goods were considered dangerous to middle-class families as they might carry diseases from the worker's home. The 'homes and families' of the workers were also considered to be in danger, but on the basis that home work disrupted the 'morals' of family home-life, rather than because of the very real danger sweating posed to the health and wages of the workers. The sense of a greater good that the Consumers' Leagues claimed to participate in serving by influencing official policy became linked to control and exclusion, including with a racist and anti-immigration slant.

Skocpol shows, moreover, that the impressive impact with which writers like Nathan and Baker credit the Consumers' Leagues was not truly justified. She explains:

> Because the NCL's geographical reach was limited, and because its individual membership never exceeded several thousand people – mostly elite married women in major cities, plus some token male

university professors and scattered students in women's colleges and schools – the NCL could hardly equal the legislative lobbying potential of other contemporary women's federations. Other federations, and especially the GFWC, not only had many more members than the NCL but also included local units disproportionately more likely to be situated in rural states and in smaller cities and towns. Indeed, the Consumers' Leagues often promoted legislation primarily by working with and through other associations, including the Federations of Women's Clubs, with which the Consumers' Leagues had an intimate and symbiotic relationship in many areas.[68]

This narrative of necessary cooperation with other groups detracts from the sense of the Consumers' Leagues as an independent but widely supported pioneering force that is presented, for instance, in Nathan's retrospective. The progress they made also remained incremental: significant problems and exploitative conditions persisted for workers across the United States. The Consumers' Leagues, then, were by no means the sole answer to the USA's industrial problems.

In 1911, the infamous Triangle Shirtwaist Factory fire occurred in Manhattan, killing and injuring over one hundred workers, most of whom were women and girls, including a large proportion of mainly Italian and Jewish migrant workers. The tragedy garnered substantial media attention and the horror it provoked led to calls for practical action. Among a significant number of industrial disasters from the period, this is the event that remains widely remembered as a symbol for the potential catastrophic effects of poor working conditions and a lack of worker protections and health and safety standards. Dana Thomas includes it in her contemporary study of fast fashion as an example of the relatively recent existence within the United States of appalling labour conditions in the fashion industry, comparable to iniquities still regularly reported in the same industry abroad, such as the Rana Plaza clothing factory disaster in Bangladesh in 2013, in which the collapse of the building caused more than a thousand deaths.[69] According to Skocpol, the Triangle Factory fire prompted a significant increase in activity to address such conditions directly, and 'organized labor was able to work more closely with elite reformers, including the leaders of women's groups, to influence the state commission set up to investigate conditions and propose new laws'.[70] As before, Skocpol suggests that this progress relied on collaboration between different organisations.

As the concerns that the NCL had participated in raising became more commonly accepted as requiring official action, NCL campaigners also transitioned into more prominent roles in the ruling and policy-making establishment that Baker had previously credited them with influencing from the outside. Brandeis became an associate justice of the US Supreme Court in 1916, the same year the final report of the Commission on Industrial Relations was published. Meanwhile Frances Perkins, a Charity Organization Society worker and secretary of the CLNY, was on her way to becoming the 'NCL's most prominent alumna'.[71] Partly motivated by the Triangle Factory tragedy, Perkins joined New York State's Factory Investigating Commission. In the New Deal Era, which followed the Progressive Era and built on many of its developments, President Franklin D. Roosevelt appointed her Secretary of State for Labor. Thomas dedicates a lengthy description to Perkins's role in making labour legislation a priority for the US government, noting that she was 'the country's first female cabinet member' whose twelve years in post made her the longest-serving incumbent. During this time, Thomas writes,

> a multitude of landmark acts were passed and agencies created, including the Public Works Administration; the Social Security Act, which established unemployment, welfare, and retirement benefits; and the Fair Labor Standards Act (FLSA), which set forth the country's first minimum wage, guaranteed overtime payment, banned child labor, and instituted the forty-hour workweek. With the FLSA, American manufacturing cleaned up and moved into its golden age.[72]

While Thomas sees Perkins's work as legitimately groundbreaking in the progressive innovations it brought about in US manufacturing, Woloch notes how Perkins remained loyal to NCL principles in her achievements in government. She quotes Perkins as declaring: 'Legislation is the most important thing' and 'I'd much rather get a law than organize a union'.[73] This position again echoes the notion of protection for workers over dialogue with them. Skocpol also points to another development that solidified action on behalf of women workers as official policy. She notes how,

> in 1920, Congress passed legislation to establish a federal Women's Bureau, making permanent what had earlier been an emergency wartime agency. From its beginnings in 1918, the Women's Bureau

gathered data on the conditions faced by female wage earners and generally promoted the cause of protective labor legislation for women.[74]

In this way, the investigative strategies that organisations such as the NCL had popularised became a mainstream administrative tool. As the developments of the Progressive Era were consolidated as national policy, the NCL's attitudes and priorities moved into official executive hands where they naturally proved more effective and impactful.

While we should not be tempted, then, to follow Nathan's lead in overestimating the influence of the Consumers' Leagues, we should acknowledge that they did help to pave the way for developments that gradually came to be accepted as official policy. Their role was indeed a pioneering one and, whether in consequence of this or for other reasons such as private agendas, often meshed with and consciously mobilised problematic positions to begin these processes. As Skocpol puts it,

> the efforts of women's organizations were extensive and sustained. It is hard to imagine these laws spreading so quickly across the United States without the victories of the National Consumers' League in the courts and the efforts at public education and legislative lobbying mounted by alliances of womens' [sic] groups before and after the watershed judicial decisions.[75]

The Consumers' Leagues were not, of course, by any means the only force at work to defend the rights of workers. As the CLNY's original connections to working women's associations show, workers themselves also pursued better conditions, and the directions taken by the Consumers' Leagues did not always heed or chime with worker representation. Especially at a time like the present, when many protections for worker rights are at risk once more, it is important to recognise the history of where these protections have come from. This should include the more problematic influences that were brought to bear on these developments, alliances that were or were not made and the reasons behind this, and how and why these initiatives succeeded or failed. Unpicking these details critically can help build understanding of where workers and their rights may be vulnerable, and whose agendas are at stake in specific developments. The examples of the US consumers' league movement, as well as that of the 'Sweated

Industries Exhibition', highlight the importance of collaboration, but also demonstrate that this should consist in allyship rather than in allowing any one group to speak on behalf of another.

Notes

1. Clementina Black, *Sweated Industry and the Minimum Wage* (London: Duckworth, 1907), p. 18.
2. Newton D. Baker, 'Foreword', in Maud Nathan, *The Story of an Epoch-Making Movement* (London: Heinemann, 1926), pp. xi–xiv (p. xi).
3. Law quoted in Louis D. Brandeis and Josephine Goldmark, *Women in Industry* (New York: National Consumers' League, 1908), p. 1. University Microfilms International.
4. 'Curt Muller, Plff. in Err., v. State of Oregon', *Legal Information Institute* (Cornell Law School) <www.law.cornell.edu/supreme court/text/208/412> [accessed 25 July 2022].
5. See Theda Skocpol, *Protecting Soldiers and Mothers* (Cambridge, MA: Harvard University Press, 1992), p. 405.
6. Nancy Woloch, *A Class by Herself: Protective Laws for Women Workers, 1890s–1990s* (Princeton: Princeton University Press, 2015), p. 31; see also Landon R. Y. Storrs, *Civilizing Capitalism: The National Consumers' League, Women's Activism, and Labor Standards in the New Deal Era* (Chapel Hill: University of North Carolina Press, 2000), p. 42.
7. Woloch, p. 21.
8. Ibid. p. 29.
9. Skocpol, p. 393.
10. Woloch, p. 7.
11. Skocpol, p. 393.
12. 'Fourteenth Amendment. Constitution of the United States', *Constitution Annotated* <https://constitution.congress.gov/constitu tion/amendment-14/> [accessed 4 September 2020].
13. Josephine Goldmark, *Fatigue and Efficiency* (New York: Russell Sage Foundation, 1917 [1912]), p. 245.
14. Florence Kelley, *Some Ethical Gains through Legislation* (New York: Macmillan, 1905), p. 141.
15. Goldmark, pp. 245–6.
16. Ibid. p. 246.
17. Ibid. p. 246.
18. Ibid. p. 247.

19. Brandeis and Goldmark, p. 1.
20. Skocpol, p. 394.
21. The verdict in the case is also available through less partisan sources, for example online through Cornell Law School's *Legal Information Institute* <www.law.cornell.edu/supremecourt/text/208/412> [accessed 25 July 2022].
22. Woloch, p. 64, emphasis in original.
23. Brandeis and Goldmark, p. 9.
24. Ibid. p. 10.
25. Ibid. p. 9.
26. Ibid. p. 11.
27. Ibid. p. 11.
28. Ibid. p. 16.
29. Ibid. p. 17.
30. Ibid. p. 18.
31. Ibid. pp. 22–3.
32. Ibid. p. 28.
33. Ibid. p. 36.
34. Ibid. p. 38.
35. Ibid. p. 44.
36. Ibid. p. 47.
37. Ibid. p. 56.
38. Ibid. p. 92.
39. See ibid. p. 89.
40. See ibid. p. 65.
41. See ibid. p. 79.
42. Verdict, appended to Brandeis and Goldmark, 6pp. (p. 6).
43. Skocpol, p. 377.
44. Ibid. p. 393.
45. Florence Kelley, 'The Ten Hours Law for Working Women', *Pensacola Journal*, 19 April 1908, p. 14.
46. Ibid. p. 14.
47. Baker, in Nathan, p. xiii.
48. Ibid. pp. xiii–xiv.
49. Clementina Black, 'Caveat Emptor', *Longman's Magazine*, August 1887, pp. 409–20 (p. 416).
50. Excerpts from the testimony of Louis D. Brandeis before the United States Commission on Industrial Relations, in *The Brandeis Reader*, ed. Ervin H. Pollack (New York: Oceana, 1956), pp. 207–8.
51. Woloch, p. 55.
52. Storrs, p. 45.

53. Skocpol, p. 394.
54. Woloch, p. 23.
55. Ibid. p. 23.
56. Goldmark, pp. 253–4.
57. Ibid. p. 279.
58. Ibid. p. 285.
59. Ibid. pp. 286–7.
60. Ibid. p. 286.
61. Daniel E. Bender, *Sweated Work, Weak Bodies: Sweatshop Campaigns and Languages of Labor* (New Brunswick and London: Rutgers University Press, 2004), p. 101.
62. On French legislation, see for instance Judith G. Coffin, *The Politics of Women's Work: The Paris Garment Trades 1750–1915* (Princeton: Princeton University Press, 1996); on legislation in the Netherlands, see for instance Selma Leydesdorff, *Verborgen Arbeid, Vergeten Arbeid: Een verkenning van de vrouwenarbeid rond negentienhonderd* (Assen and Amsterdam: Van Gorcum, 1977).
63. Woloch, p. 21.
64. Ibid. p. 24.
65. Goldmark, p. 283.
66. Lawrence B. Glickman, *Buying Power: A History of Consumer Activism in America* (Chicago: University of Chicago Press, 2009), p. 187.
67. Bender, p. 66.
68. Skocpol, p. 393.
69. Dana Thomas, *Fashionopolis: The Price of Fast Fashion and the Future of Clothes* (London: Head of Zeus, 2019), p. 46.
70. Skocpol, p. 382.
71. Woloch, p. 16.
72. Thomas, p. 47.
73. Woloch, p. 16.
74. Skocpol, p. 374.
75. Ibid. p. 401.

Conclusion

Afterlives: Citizen Consumers and the Continued Influence of Consumers' League Strategies

The consumers' league campaigns in the UK and the USA were both originally rooted in a form of ethical shopping that remains instantly recognisable in the present day, as it advocated common and accessible practices such as choosing goods with a guarantee of ethical production and treating workers in service industries with consideration. What is striking about the development of both of these campaigns, however, is that the strategy of ethical consumption was quickly superseded by other forms of action. In these, the consumer identity continued to matter as a unifying concept, but the essential point of shopping quickly lost much of its original relevance. I suggest here that this shift could be made due to the opportunities the consumer identity offered – especially to a specific cohort of non-wage-earning women – for transformation not only into an activist identity, but into proof of citizenship.

Introducing his edited collection *The Making of the Consumer* (2006), Frank Trentmann pointed to the development, roughly since 1980, of 'a dramatic turn to the "active" or "citizen" consumer – a creative, confident and rational being articulating personal identity and serving the public interest'.[1] This trend has also been embraced in historical readings of consumer movements; for example, it is a useful way of framing the reversal of the narrative of consumer guilt. As they generally did not have access to more usual identifiers of citizenship, such as a professional identity or voting rights, the non-wage-earning women who were the key subjects of consumer guilt mobilised the potential of their consumer power. When the movement was adopted by women who were accustomed to wielding social and economic influence based on their status, it also connected neatly to earlier perceptions of middle- and upper-class women's correct sphere of influence in charitable and philanthropic initiatives. This was particularly relevant to the idea of consumers acting on behalf of workers who were portrayed as unable to represent their own interests. This development belonged, once again, very strongly to the gendered perception of the consumers' league movement. This is the case especially for the movement as it emerged in the USA, but the same idea is also present, and becomes increasingly influential, in the UK campaigns led by Clementina Black. It spoke to notions of women's duties of care, specifically in a philanthropic context; it allowed the leagues to produce a campaign narrative based on gendered identification between women consumer activists and women workers, who were generally the most vulnerable to exploitation – reaching back to the roots of the consumer guilt narrative in the image of the exploited seamstress working herself to death to produce unnecessary clothing to feed wealthier women's vanity. It also, as we have seen, allowed for the dubious framing of protective legislation for women workers around a biological gender identity based on motherhood.

Situating consumer power

The example of *Muller* v. *Oregon* shows the continued usefulness of the consumer identity as a basis for campaigns, even when they were run by women such as Florence Kelley and Josephine Goldmark who drew at least as much on their professional identity as legal experts. It may be argued that this additional, gendered identity was what allowed this case to place the spin it did on the understanding of legal precedent. That the National Consumers' League retained its gendered identity is evident from examples such as Newton D. Baker's foreword to *The Story of an Epoch-Making Movement*, in which he echoed gendered language about responsibility of care and unofficial influence. The sense of gendered duty also applied to international iterations of the US consumers' league model such as, for instance, to the strong Catholic religious influences on women's prescribed social roles in the French context described by Louis Athey and Marie-Emmanuelle Chessel. As Chessel notes, '[b]y insisting on their duties (as consumers) they [the Ligue Sociale d'Acheteurs] posed, in fact, as citizens who had rights, in particular the right to intervene in capitalism'.[2] What we see here, then, is an interpretation of citizenship based on gender and class difference and the sense of a duty of community care expanded to include a national interest.

A comparable understanding of consumers' influence as citizens is central to the argument Naomi Klein made in *No Logo* in 2000. Discussing the garment industry and its outsourcing models that moved exploitative practices to other countries without protective labour laws, she is especially critical, as we have seen, of allowing these multinational corporations to draft their own codes of conduct on labour and human rights. She sees this as a privatisation of human rights that will allow corporations to keep up a pretence of ethics while infringing not only the human rights of workers abroad, but also those of consumers who believe they are making conscious choices in their purchases. Throughout the book, she repeatedly frames this in the language of citizenship, stating, for instance:

> Ever since key multinationals stopped denying the existence of any human-rights abuses in their global production operations, the struggle has not been over whether controls need to be put in place, but rather over who will get to place those controls. Will it be the people and their democratically elected representatives? Or will it be the global corporations themselves? It's clear from the privatized codes which direction the corporations want to go. The question is, What will citizens do in response?[3]

What Klein is calling for is, in effect, a more overtly political version of the influence exercised by the NCL on the legislature: her attitude is that consumers should elect, and then put pressure on, political representatives who can interfere in the tendency to allow corporations to dictate terms. She argues that '[w]hen we start looking to corporations to draft our collective labor and human rights codes for us, we have already lost the most basic principle of citizenship: that people should govern themselves'.[4] Again, this point of self-governance applies both to the consumers – generally assumed to be based in North America in the context of the book – and to workers, generally overseas: while the latter should be able to represent their own interests through labour organisations, the former should demand not to be presented with products of exploited labour. This perception of the role of the consumer activist is very close to Black's original conception of a consumers' league as working in parallel to the labour movement, although

Klein has been able to envisage the international expansion of this approach that Black struggled with in *Sweated Industry and the Minimum Wage*.

More than twenty years after the publication of *No Logo*, the questions and solutions Klein poses remain relevant, but have gained further complexity again. As I explained in the introduction, I started writing this book during the first year of the coronavirus pandemic in 2020, when citizens' responsibility for the general interest was widely invoked in the face of a global crisis. As I completed writing the book in the summer of 2022, the worldwide sense of crisis had developed further to comprise economic, political and environmental emergencies (a cost-of-living crisis, war and extremist political rhetoric, the noticeable impact of human-made climate change). So where does this leave concerned consumers and citizens? It seems a reasonable supposition, for example, that an awareness of financial precarity may prevent individuals from making the ethical consumer choices that tend to come at a financial mark-up. On the other hand, the same awareness may lead to a breaking down of the imagined barrier between the identities of worker and consumer as general understanding of the consumer identity has moved away from the idea that only those with wealth are able to exercise their spending power.

Consumer influence(r)s

The afterlives of the consumers' league initiatives, then, comprise the same recurring problems as well as many of the same impulses, arguments and strategies seen in this volume. We still have no choice but to be consumers, but we do have choices as consumers – a point of which many of us are highly conscious. The choices that we have are limited by different factors including our own knowledge or ignorance as well as our financial means. Often there are also other factors at play such as external pressures and influences. In addition, over the century since Black published *Sweated Industry*, the processes of sourcing, production and retail have become even more globalised, fragmented and opaque, as Klein already showed in 2000, making it harder to find out about the goods we buy. Information has become easier to access with the internet – there are plenty of helpful websites such as the Ethical Consumer – but this has also meant that the amount of information can become overwhelming and difficult to filter or verify.[5] Not dissimilarly from the issue Kelley raised in regard to state reports on food adulteration, then, the problem is not that the information does not exist or is not available, but that it may not always be readily accessible or comprehensible for consumers. Certainly there are now plenty of consumer organisations in operation, many of them – like the present-day incarnation of the NCL – representing consumer interests. In spite of this, however, it is likely that most consumers are still left trying to make the best decisions they can independently and are consequently left unsure of the effects their efforts are having.

As the problems faced by the would-be conscious or ethical consumer are still so similar to those of 100 or 150 years ago, therefore, it is not surprising that the ways in which campaigners try to influence consumers have also been fairly constant. It is noticeable that arguments are often made in such a way as to make it seem plausible that this is the first time the consumer has heard them. Fast fashion, the modern-day equivalent of the sweated garment trade at the heart of the original narrative of consumer guilt, is, of course, the case in point. In the early pages of *Fashionopolis*, Dana Thomas uses herself as an example of a consumer doing unconscious harm through her purchasing power. She opens with:

> As I sit here and write this, I'm wearing a black cotton jersey dress with a white pointed collar and shirt cuffs, made in Bangladesh. I spotted it on a Facebook ad, clicked through, and within days it was delivered to my home. It is flattering and fashionably on point. But did I think about where it came from when I ordered it? Did I consider why it only set me back thirty bucks? Did I need this dress?
> No. No. And nope.[6]

Here, Thomas is using a version of Black's approach of ranging herself with her readers as well-meaning but ignorant consumers, but hers is, if anything, a refinement of the original strategy. Instead of using Black's collective 'we', Thomas uses 'I': although insinuating that many of her readers are likely to have acquired clothing in the same thoughtless way, she is here taking the sole blame for a concrete instance of what is clearly, by the standards she herself sets out in her book, culpable behaviour. Writing this example of her own growing awareness into the introduction of her manifesto against fast fashion already makes the point, furthermore, that if she could become enlightened enough, as a fashion journalist, to research and write the book, her readers can similarly become more conscious consumers after reading it. With the sleight of hand of enlightened ignorance comes a sense of absolution from previous harmful acts: if you did not know, how could you do better – but it follows that now that you do know, there is no excuse not to do better. (Of course, the reader is welcome to think what they will about the symbolism of typing a book against fast fashion while wearing a fast-fashion-produced dress, the stylishness and fashionableness of which is still described for vicarious enjoyment.)

In a nutshell, the message of Thomas's book is that '[s]ubcontracting is endemic in the apparel industry, creating a fractured supply chain in which workers are easily in jeopardy' – a conclusion familiar from many of the campaign texts examined in this book.[7] Like Black, she proceeds in her book not only to expose some of these iniquities, such as the presence of sweatshops in California as well as overseas, but also to present a range of solutions, generally introduced as stand-alone chapters about encounters with individuals trialling different ways of producing non-exploitative fashion, from local workshops and ethically farmed indigo to renting outfits for special occasions. This structure is clearly intended to counteract a potential reaction of hopelessness and resignation in the reader by showing that alternatives are possible. Unlike Black, however, Thomas regularly falls into the trap of idealising localised production and a solid economic analysis is missing from her piecemeal journalistic approach. She can be inconsistent in the ideas she advocates, some of which seem to contradict one another – such as her changeable attitude to the potential of introducing more technology into the supply chain. The key point is, however, that books like hers contribute to a general awareness-raising and offer readers a range of alternatives.

Although they discuss essentially the same problems, Klein's approach is more explicitly political than Thomas's and offers more of a direct challenge, both for individual readers and for broader political and economic forces and their representatives in governments and boardrooms. In Klein's book, too, plenty of strategies are presented that are familiar from the consumers' league movement, including some examples of obvious parallels with NCL campaigns that demonstrate the tendency of consumer movements to keep reinventing the same wheel. Like Thomas's, Klein's book contains a large number of interviews with spokespeople for groups working to combat labour exploitation in the production of branded products sold in North America, although *No Logo* incorporates these into a sustained argument of its own. For example, she describes the work of the National Labor Committee (NLC), for which, she states, brand logos serve as both 'targets and props'. This is the reason, she goes on, that

> when [NLC director Charles] Kernaghan speaks to a crowd – at college campuses, labor rallies or international conferences – he is never without his signature shopping bag brimming with Disney clothes, Kathie Lee Gifford pants and other logo gear. During his presentations, he holds up the pay slips and price tags to illustrate the vast discrepancies between what workers are paid to make the items and what we pay to buy them. He also takes his shopping bag with him when he visits the export processing zones in Haiti and El Salvador, pulling out items from his bag of tricks to show workers the actual price tags of the goods they sew.[8]

There is an obvious parallel here with the international trend for exhibitions of sweated labour and its products used in the decades around the turn of the twentieth century by consumers' leagues across North America and Europe, as well as by a range of other organisations including the Women's Industrial Council for the 'Sweated Industries Exhibition'. The NLC's innovation is the systematic practice of also reporting back to the subcontracted workers overseas about the profits made on their labour. While this knowledge was undoubtedly conveyed to the sweated workers involved in initiatives such as the 'Sweated Industries Exhibition' if they did not know it already, it is not generally addressed in the written accounts of these earlier campaigns. Of course, a large part of Klein's argument is the need for workers to be able to represent themselves; her inclusion in the book of the words of a labour organiser in Cavite export processing zone in the Philippines challenges those ideas of exploited workers as inert victims that still do periodically surface in more superficial texts such as Thomas's.[9] In this sense Klein's text may be seen as writing back into consumer activist campaigns the role of the labour movement, which had been so important to Black's original proposals but was lost from both the US and international incarnations of the scheme and largely from the presentation of the 'Sweated Industries Exhibition'.

Perhaps unsurprisingly, the same line of reasoning leads Klein to object to another echo of an NCL campaign: the 'No Sweat' label designed to tell consumers that clothing had been produced without sweated labour, exactly as the NCL 'white label' had been. We have seen how the white label was a tactic originally adopted from trade unions – including with problematic aims such as the exclusion of Chinese migrant workers – but also that it was deliberately framed as a way of reassuring concerned consumers who, nevertheless, did not want to have anything to do with trade unions. Klein's objection to the 'No Sweat' label rests on this idea that the priority is to ensure guilt-free shopping, as the double meaning of the label's name also suggests. She explains:

> Tellingly, Bill Clinton's 'No Sweat' labeling initiative is modeled after the 'Dolphin Safe' stamp on cans of tuna, which reassures buyers that the much-loved dolphin was not killed in the canning of the fish. What the proposal fails to grasp is that the rights of garment workers, unlike dolphins, cannot be assured by a symbol on a label, the equivalent of a best-before date; and that trying to do so represents nothing less than a wholesale privatization of their (and our) political rights.[10]

In Klein's view, then, a label is a way of depoliticising the question of the rights of both the worker and the consumer. It is a distraction from the severity of the problem constituted by systematic exploitation by profit-making corporations on a global scale, offering would-be ethical consumers a sop to their conscience and allowing them to believe that by choosing labelled clothing they are doing enough to improve the situation: there need be 'no sweat' on their part.

Klein's analysis of the modern-day labelling campaign highlights the arguable downside to attempts to make the activist potential of the consumer identity more widely accessible. While it allows for the engagement of people who are prepared to do a little, so long as it does not interfere too much in the rest of their lives – which, it should be noted, may as often be due to the fact that they may themselves be overworked and/or struggling financially as it may be the result of a general unconcern or lack of sympathy – it may also give the erroneous suggestion that a little is sufficient to address an entrenched global problem. As Klein puts it:

There's no doubt that anticorporate activism walks a precarious line between self-satisfied consumer rights and engaged political action. Campaigners can exploit the profile that brand names bring to human-rights and environmental issues, but they have to be careful that their campaigns don't degenerate into glorified ethical shopping guides: how-to's on saving the world through boycotts and personal lifestyle choices. [. . .] Some of these initiatives have genuine merit, but the challenges of a global labor market are too vast to be defined – or limited – by our interests as consumers.[11]

She concludes that '[p]olitical solutions – accountable to people and enforceable by their elected representatives – deserve another shot before we throw in the towel and settle for corporate codes, independent monitors and the privatization of our collective rights as citizens'.[12] Ultimately, then, her argument brings together and reinforces a similar trajectory to Black's original idea. In essence, this is that consumers have a responsibility to address exploitation collectively, working alongside organised labour in a manner that follows and supports its lead and safeguards its interests. Particularly in a fragmented production system, however, this approach can only be effective if it has official support from political leaders and becomes a formal part of national policy. Black came to see this as enforceable through a legal minimum wage; but while she formulated this idea based on international examples, she was not herself concerned with labour conditions beyond the UK's borders; as *Sweated Industry* demonstrates, she did not feel the need to consider the plight of workers in non-'western' countries, even in parts of what was then the British Empire.[13] For Klein, conscious of the growth of a multinational economy able to take advantage of lower labour standards across borders, workers abroad are a key concern and she sees the role of governments in the global north as regulating the corporations that sell branded goods in their countries, to stop these from exploiting cheap and unprotected labour in the global south.

Imagined futures

As we have seen, the two consumers' league initiatives contrapuntally examined in this book came to very different ends. The UK movement subsided after Black gave up on it to pursue alternative strategies. The movement in the USA has survived and retains influence, but it now functions to represent and protect consumer interests. Comparable independent consumer interest bodies now exist in many countries, including for instance Which? in the UK.[14] Meanwhile other organisations have taken the place of the original consumers' league initiatives to guide consumers in making ethical choices; several were showcased in No Logo, and since then a range of online resources have been developed too. The continued need for such initiatives shows the continuity in the history of ethical consumerism. We are still grappling with many of the same problems, although they may have shapeshifted to fit present-day economic and political structures. Equally, large numbers of concerned consumers remain conscious of these problems and wish to direct their purchasing power towards good instead of harm, but for most it is not an option to step outside of the economic systems that have produced and that sustain the iniquities they seek to challenge. General awareness of different kinds of problems linked to the consumer economy has also grown: notably, environmental concerns are now recognised as critical, while they were absent from consumers' league campaigns. While online shopping may have increased consumers' access to more ethical and sustainable choices, it has also created more and larger problems in terms of both the environment and labour exploitation. As labour continues to be outsourced in ways that are often difficult to trace, potentially putting labour rights at risk, it also remains tricky for consumers to plan and direct their campaigns in dialogue with affected workers and communities.

Towards the end of The Story of an Epoch-Making Movement, a book wholly geared towards praising the achievements to date of the consumers' league movement and marking a jumping-off point for it to go on to greater things, Maud Nathan pitches a vision of the potential power still latent in the organisation. She claims: 'When consumers organize, as capital and labour have organized, their power will be greater than either of the other two forces. The consumer will then be in a position to dictate terms.'[15] It is worth noting that the consumer is here presented as a separate entity from both capital and labour, an in-between force untainted by the negative connotations of either of the others. By singling this identity out as unique, Nathan also sets it apart from the Marxist understanding of the conflict between the other two, again casting it as a form of mediator – except that it now becomes clear that she envisions this mediator, literally, as a benevolent dictator who knows better than either of the others and deserves to direct them. She goes on: 'This dictator need not be arbitrary, he [*sic*] can be fair-minded and beneficent, coöperating [*sic*] with labour and capital in such manner as to bring about the complete democratization of the economic world.'[16] Nathan here exaggerates the success and potential of the consumers' league movement to such an extent that it is difficult to believe that she can have taken it seriously herself. The inherent conflict within her use of the word 'dictator' for what she presents as a democratising force is remarkable. It is also interesting that she applies the idea of democratisation to the economy. What she means, of course, is that the economy will be directed by the demands of consumers; and that these demands promise to be considerate of the interests of both employers and employees.

The examples we have seen from the NCL's strategies demonstrate that a sense of benevolent despotism was already present in their engagement with the interests of workers, and particularly in a gendered context. The focus on the need to preserve the health of women workers in order to ensure the propagation of a healthy working class already makes workers' interests subservient to a particular perception of a greater good; the decision in *Muller* v. *Oregon* further determined that legislation could also subject employers to this idea of the public interest by banning them from overworking their employees to such an extent as to jeopardise the public health and the welfare of the nation. In addition, Nathan's representation of the power of the consumer identity appears completely to bypass legislative and political powers: the suggestion is that consumer interest will be able to direct these too – again, as the impact of the NCL on protective legislation already had done. The implication is that consumer interests represent the greater good, and that democratisation signifies the protection of this – without explicitly accepting, of course, that the representatives of both labour and capital are consumers too. The consumer identity, then, becomes at once all-encompassing and exclusionary, democratising and despotic. In short, Nathan's vision represents the ultimate regeneration of the non-political, non-wage-earning woman consumer, from a caricature whose influence was limited to ignorant harm proceeding from frivolous and uncontrolled desires, into a member of an all-powerful collective justly representing and guarding the general interest.

Needless to say, what Nathan predicted did not come to pass. Equally obvious, however, is that the original idea of consumer influence remains persistently powerful. In this book I have, on the whole, tended to express myself rather negatively about consumer activism and its achievements. This has partly been a result of the focus on the consumers' league movements, the practical and enduring successes of which have been limited. Other consumer initiatives, such as the Sugar Boycotts and the cooperative movement, have been more successful in achieving their immediate aims and have given us models for activism that still survive, although their rate of success in other incarnations has been inconsistent. The consumers' leagues and especially the NCL also achieved short-term successes, but these have in their turn often been situated in a context that has distinctly problematic elements, from both a present-day and a historical point of view. I have argued, however, that their strategies have potent echoes in the present, and that from examining the more and less problematic elements of their original application we can gain insights that we can continue to use in current and future campaigns.

My examination of the consumers' league movements has been prompted by my interest in their recognisability: it is evident that the problems they sought to address have not gone away, and the arguments and strategies they employed are still in regular circulation. Existing campaigns, the media and personal interactions suggest that many of us still do our best to be conscious and ethical consumers, whether or not we can see the results of our choices. We do this because both the narrative and the reality of consumer guilt also persist, telling us that if we do not at least try to make ethical choices, we will most likely be contributing to making things worse. It is precisely because of this general sense of goodwill combined with ignorance that it seemed worthwhile to shine a light on the consumers' leagues as a precursor to the present day. Highlighting the failures and the dubious nature of some of the successes of the movement may help us to remain alert to the pitfalls of our good impulses, the risks that may be involved in making certain alliances for short-term victories, and above all the importance of not believing that we can construct campaigns without including those directly affected by the problems we seek to resist.

Notes

1. Frank Trentmann, 'Knowing Consumers – Histories, Identities, Practices: An Introduction', in *The Making of the Consumer*, ed. Trentmann (Oxford: Berg, 2006), pp. 1–27 (p. 2).

2. Marie-Emmanuelle Chessel, 'Women and the Ethics of Consumption in France at the Turn of the Twentieth Century: The *Ligue Sociale d'Acheteurs*', in *The Making of the Consumer*, ed. Trentmann, pp. 81–98 (p. 94).

3. Naomi Klein, *No Logo* (London: Flamingo, 2001 [2000]), p. 435.

4. Ibid. p. 441.

5. See *Ethical Consumer* website <https://www.ethicalconsumer.org/> [accessed 12 January 2023].

6. Dana Thomas, *Fashionopolis: The Price of Fast Fashion and the Future of Clothes* (London: Head of Zeus, 2019), p. 3.

7. Ibid. p. 42.

8. Klein, p. 353.

9. See ibid. p. 440.

10. Ibid. p. 429.

11. Ibid. p. 428.

12. Ibid. p. 442.

13. Clementina Black, *Sweated Industry and the Minimum Wage* (London: Duckworth, 1907), p. 268.

14. See the *Which?* official website <https://www.which.co.uk/> [accessed 12 January 2023].

15. Maud Nathan, *The Story of an Epoch-Making Movement* (London: Heinemann, 1926), p. 125.

16. Ibid. p. 126.

Bibliography

Archival sources

Amsterdam, International Institute of Social History:

Bro D 2970/125, *Die Heimarbeitausstellung in Berlin* (n.p. [Nuremberg]: n.pub. [Simon], n.d. [1906]).

EHB Cat/2/F/95, *Gids voor de Nederlandsche Tentoonstelling van Huisindustrie* (n.p. [Amsterdam]: n.pub., n.d. [1909]).

Zw1960/356, Jakob Lorenz, *Heimarbeit und Heimarbeitausstellung in der Schweiz* (Zurich: Verlag der Buchhandlung des Schweiz. Grütlivereins, 1909).

Berlin, Staatsbibliothek zu Berlin:

Fd2381/5, 'Die Heimarbeit in der Handschuhindustrie', in *Heimarbeit-Ausstellung Berlin 1906* (Berlin: Vorwärts, 1906), pp. 1–5.

Ff4281/55-9, Frieda Wunderlich, *Die Deutsche Heimarbeitausstellung, 1925* (Jena: Gustav Fischer, 1927).

Works cited

'1892–3 Fourth Annual Report', in *Helping Women at Work: The Women's Industrial Council 1889–1914*, ed. Ellen Mappen (London: Hutchinson, 1985), pp. 45–9.

'The Anti-Sweating League', *Women's Industrial News*, September 1906, pp. 567–8.

Athey, Louis L., 'From Social Conscience to Social Action: The Consumers' Leagues in Europe, 1900–1914', *Social Service Review*, 52.3 (1978), 362–82 <https://www.jstor.org/stable/30015641> [accessed 30 March 2020].

August, Andrew, *Poor Women's Lives: Gender, Work, and Poverty in Late-Victorian London* (Madison: Fairleigh Dickinson University Press, 1999).

Baker, Newton D., 'Foreword', in Maud Nathan, *The Story of an Epoch-Making Movement* (London: Heinemann, 1926), pp. xi–xiv.

Bender, Daniel E., *Sweated Work, Weak Bodies: Sweatshop Campaigns and Languages of Labor* (New Brunswick and London: Rutgers University Press, 2004).

'The Berlin Exhibition of Home-Industries', *Women's Industrial News*, March 1906, pp. 543–4.

Black, Clementina, 'Caveat Emptor', *Longman's Magazine*, August 1887, pp. 409–20.

——, 'The Ethics of Shopping', *Seed-Time: The Organ of the New Fellowship*, October 1890, pp. 10–11.

——, 'The Grievances of Barmaids', in *The Woman's World* (London: Cassell, 1890), pp. 383–5.

——, 'A Living-Wage League', *Daily News*, 13 June 1906, p. 6.

——, 'The Morality of Buying in the Cheapest Market', in *The Woman's World* (London: Cassell, 1890), pp. 42–4.

——, 'Something about Needlewomen', in *The Woman's World*, ed. Oscar Wilde (London: Cassell, 1888), pp. 300–4.

——, 'Suggested Remedies', in *Handbook of the 'Daily News' Sweated Industries' Exhibition*, compiled by Richard Mudie-Smith (London: Burt, 1906), pp. 22–6 <https://archive.org/stream/handbookofdailynoo mudi_o#page/n17/mode/1up> [accessed 24 July 2016].

——, *A Sussex Idyl* (London: Tinsley, 1877).

——, *Sweated Industry and the Minimum Wage* (London: Duckworth, 1907).

Blackburn, Sheila, *A Fair Day's Wage for a Fair Day's Work? Sweated Labour and the Origins of Minimum Wage Legislation in Britain* (Aldershot: Ashgate, 2007).

——, '"Princesses and Sweated-Wage Slaves Go Well Together": Images of British Sweated Workers, 1843–1914', *International Labor and Working-Class History*, 61 (2002), 24–44.

——, '"To Be Poor and To Be Honest . . . Is the Hardest Struggle of All": Sweated Needlewomen and Campaigns for Protective Legislation, 1840–1914', in *Famine and Fashion: Needlewomen in the Nineteenth Century*, ed. Beth Harris (Aldershot: Ashgate, 2005), pp. 243–57.

Boris, Eileen, *A Coat of Many Colors: Immigration, Globalization, and Reform in New York City's Garment Industry* (New York: Fordham University Press, 2005).

Brake, Laurel, and Marysa Demoor, eds, *Dictionary of Nineteenth-Century Journalism in Great Britain and Ireland* (Ghent: Academia Press, 2009).

Brandeis, Louis D., and Josephine Goldmark, *Women in Industry: Decision of the United States-Supreme Court in Curt Muller VS. State of Oregon* (New York: National Consumers' League, 1908). University Microfilms International.

Bressey, Caroline, 'Invisible Presence: The Whitening of the Black Community in the Historical Imagination of British Archives', *Archivaria*, 61 (2006), 47–61.

Brooks, John Graham, 'The Label of the Consumers [*sic*] League', *Publications of the American Economic Association*, 1.1 (1900), 250–8 <https://www.jstor.org/stable/2485833> [accessed 30 March 2020].

Caine, Barbara, 'Feminism, Journalism and Public Debate', in *Women and Literature in Britain 1800–1900*, ed. Joanne Shattock (Cambridge: Cambridge University Press, 2001), pp. 99–118.

Chessel, Marie-Emmanuelle, 'Women and the Ethics of Consumption in France at the Turn of the Twentieth Century: The *Ligue Sociale d'Acheteurs*', in *The Making of the Consumer*, ed. Frank Trentmann (Oxford: Berg, 2006), pp. 81–98.

Clayworth, Anya, '*The Woman's World*: Oscar Wilde as Editor: 1996 Vanarsel Prize', *Victorian Periodicals Review*, 30.2 (1997), 84–101.

Coffin, Judith G., *The Politics of Women's Work: The Paris Garment Trades 1750–1915* (Princeton: Princeton University Press, 1996).

'Co-op Group History', *Co-op Legal Services* <https://www.co-oplegal services.co.uk/about-us/the-co-operative-group-history/> [accessed 10 September 2022].

'Curt Muller, Plff. in Err., v. State of Oregon', *Legal Information Institute* (Cornell Law School) <www.law.cornell.edu/supremecourt/text/208/412> [accessed 25 July 2022].

Edwards, Rebecca, *Angels in the Machinery: Gender in American Party Politics from the Civil War to the Progressive Era* (New York: Oxford University Press, 1997).

Ethical Consumer <https://www.ethicalconsumer.org/> [accessed 12 January 2023].

'Facts at the Sweated Industries Exhibition', *Daily News*, 4 June 1906, p. 2.

'Fourteenth Amendment. Constitution of the United States', *Constitution Annotated* <https://constitution.congress.gov/constitution/amend ment-14/> [accessed 4 September 2020].

Gardiner, A. G., 'Introduction', in Clementina Black, *Sweated Industry and the Minimum Wage* (London: Duckworth, 1907), pp. ix–xxiv.

Gavan-Duffy, T. [Thomas], 'Two May-Day Exhibitions', *Labour Leader*, 11 May 1906, p. 744.

Glickman, Lawrence B., *Buying Power: A History of Consumer Activism in America* (Chicago: University of Chicago Press, 2009).

——, 'Consumer Activism, Consumer Regimes, and the Consumer Movement: Rethinking the History of Consumer Politics in the United States', in *The Oxford Handbook of the History of Consumption*, ed. Frank Trentmann (Oxford: Oxford University Press, 2012), pp. 399–417.

Goldmark, Josephine, *Fatigue and Efficiency* (New York: Russell Sage Foundation, 1917 [1912]).

Green, Stephanie, 'Oscar Wilde's *The Woman's World*', *Victorian Periodicals Review*, 30.2 (1997), 102–20.

Grever, Maria, and Berteke Waaldijk, *Transforming the Public Sphere: The Dutch National Exhibition of Women's Labor in 1898*, trans. Mischa F. C. Hoyinck and Robert E. Chesal (Durham, NC: Duke University Press, 2004).

'Guide to the Consumers' League of New York City Records', Cornell University Library <http://rmc.library.cornell.edu/EAD/htmldocs/KCL05307.html> [accessed 12 July 2022].

Hannam, June, and Karen Hunt, *Socialist Women: Britain, 1880s to 1920s* (London: Routledge, 2002).

Harkness, Margaret E., 'To the Editor of the *Labour Elector*', *Labour Elector*, October 1888, p. 8.

Harris, Beth, 'All That Glitters Is Not Gold: The Show-Shop and the Victorian Seamstress', in *Famine and Fashion: Needlewomen in the Nineteenth Century*, ed. Harris (Aldershot: Ashgate, 2005), pp. 115–37.

——, 'Introduction', in *Famine and Fashion: Needlewomen in the Nineteenth Century*, ed. Harris (Aldershot: Ashgate, 2005), pp. 1–10.

Haydu, Jeffrey, 'Consumer Citizenship and Cross-Class Activism: The Case of the National Consumers' League, 1899–1918', *Sociological Forum*, 29.3 (2014), 628–49.

Hilton, Matthew, 'Consumer Movements', in *The Oxford Handbook of the History of Consumption*, ed. Frank Trentmann (Oxford: Oxford University Press, 2012), pp. 505–19.

——, *Consumerism in Twentieth-Century Britain: The Search for a Historical Movement* (Cambridge: Cambridge University Press, 2003).

Historicalstatistics.org: Portal for Historical Statistics <http://historical statistics.org/> [accessed 12 July 2022].

'History', *National Consumers' League* <http://www.nclnet.org/history> [accessed 12 July 2022].

Hood, Thomas, 'The Song of the Shirt', *Punch, or The London Charivari*, 16 December 1843, reprinted on *The Victorian Web* <https://www.vic torianweb.org/authors/hood/shirt.html> [accessed 15 February 2021].

Huneault, Kristina, *Difficult Subjects: Working Women and Visual Culture, Britain 1880–1914* (Aldershot: Ashgate, 2002).

Kelley, Florence, 'Aims and Principles of the Consumers' League', *American Journal of Sociology*, 5.3 (1899), 289–304 <https://jstor.org/stable/2761531> [accessed 30 March 2020].

——, *Some Ethical Gains through Legislation* (New York: Macmillan, 1905).

——, 'The Ten Hours Law for Working Women', *Pensacola Journal*, 19 April 1908, p. 14.

Klein, Naomi, *No Logo* (London: Flamingo, 2001 [2000]).

Leydesdorff, Selma, *Verborgen Arbeid, Vergeten Arbeid: Een verkenning van de vrouwenarbeid rond negentienhonderd* (Assen and Amsterdam: Van Gorcum, 1977).

Livesey, Ruth, *Socialism, Sex, and the Culture of Aestheticism in Britain, 1880–1914* (Oxford: Oxford University Press, 2007).

MacDonald, Margaret, 'The "Daily News" Sweated Home Industries Exhibition', *Women's Industrial News*, June 1906, p. 558.

McWilliam, Rohan, 'The Melodramatic Seamstress: Interpreting a Victorian Penny Dreadful', in *Famine and Fashion: Needlewomen in the Nineteenth Century*, ed. Beth Harris (Aldershot: Ashgate, 2005), pp. 99–114.

Mappen, Ellen, 'Introduction', in *Helping Women at Work: The Women's Industrial Council 1889–1914*, ed. Mappen (London: Hutchinson, 1985), pp. 11–30.

Marx, Karl, and Friedrich Engels, 'The Manifesto of the Communist Party', trans. Samuel Moore, transcribed from *Marx/Engels Selected Works*, vol. 1 (Moscow: Progress Publishers, 1969), pp. 98–137 <https://www.marxists.org/archive/marx/works/download/pdf/Manifesto.pdf> [accessed 9 February 2020].

Meyer, Mrs Carl [Adele], and Clementina Black, *Makers of our Clothes: A Case for Trade Boards* (London: Duckworth, 1909).

Mitchell, Ian, 'Ethical Shopping in Late Victorian and Edwardian Britain', *Journal of Historical Research in Marketing*, 7.3 (2015), 310–29 <https://doi.org/10.1108/JHRM-08-2014-0021>.

Money, L. G. Chiozza, 'Match Box Making', in *Handbook of the 'Daily News' Sweated Industries' Exhibition*, compiled by Richard Mudie-Smith (London: Burt, 1906), pp. 95–8 <https://archive.org/stream/handbookofdailynoomudi_o#page/n75/mode/1up> [accessed 24 July 2016].

Mudie-Smith, Richard, compiler, *Handbook of the 'Daily News' Sweated Industries' Exhibition* (London: Burt, 1906) <https://archive.org/stream/handbookofdailynoomudi_o#page/n6/mode/1up> [accessed 24 July 2016].

Nathan, Maud, *The Story of an Epoch-Making Movement* (London: Heinemann, 1926).

Noel, Gerard, 'Ena, princess of Battenberg (1887–1969)', *Oxford Dictionary of National Biography* (Oxford: Oxford University Press, 2004) <http://www.oxforddnb.com/view/article/36656> [accessed 27 February 2017].

Peralta, Paola, 'Why some gig workers are struggling to access their sick pay', *Employee Benefit News*, 9 February 2022 <https://www.benefitnews.com/news/delivery-drivers-dont-have-access-to-their-covid-sick-pay> [accessed 10 September 2022].

Pollack, Ervin H., ed., *The Brandeis Reader* (New York: Oceana, 1956).

Ruskin, John, 'The Nature of Gothic', in *The Stones of Venice*, vol. 2 (New York: National Library Association, n.d. [1853]), pp. 151–230.

'The Salvation Army Bakery', *Darkest England Gazette*, 20 January 1894, p. 12.

'She Escaped Starvation', *The Sun*, 21 January 1890, p. 5.

Skocpol, Theda, *Protecting Soldiers and Mothers* (Cambridge, MA: Harvard University Press, 1992).

Smith, Adam, *An Inquiry into the Nature and Causes of the Wealth of Nations* (Oxford: Oxford University Press, 2006 [1776]).

Smith, H. W., 'The German Home-Work Exhibition, Berlin, 1906', in *Handbook of the 'Daily News' Sweated Industries' Exhibition*, compiled by Richard Mudie-Smith (London: Burt, 1906), pp. 19–22 <https://archive.org/stream/handbookofdailynoomudi_o#page/n15/mode/1up> [accessed 24 July 2016].

Storrs, Landon R. Y., *Civilizing Capitalism: The National Consumers' League, Women's Activism, and Labor Standards in the New Deal Era* (Chapel Hill: University of North Carolina Press, 2000).

'"Sweated Industries" and High-Placed Hypocrisy', *Justice*, 5 May 1906, p. 1.

'Sweating Exhibition', *Daily News*, 4 May 1906, p. 7.

Thomas, Dana, *Fashionopolis: The Price of Fast Fashion and the Future of Clothes* (London: Head of Zeus, 2019).

The Times, 27 October 1843, p. 4.

Trentmann, Frank, 'Knowing Consumers – Histories, Identities, Practices: An Introduction', in *The Making of the Consumer*, ed. Trentmann (Oxford: Berg, 2006), pp. 1–27.

——, 'The Politics of Everyday Life', in *The Oxford Handbook of the History of Consumption*, ed. Trentmann (Oxford: Oxford University Press, 2012), pp. 521–47.

Tuckwell, Gertrude, 'Preface', in *Handbook of the 'Daily News' Sweated Industries' Exhibition*, compiled by Richard Mudie-Smith (London: Burt, 1906), pp. 12–19 <https://archive.org/stream/hand bookofdailynoomudi_o#page/n11/mode/1up> [accessed 24 July 2016].

Vadillo, Ana Parejo, *Women Poets and Urban Aestheticism: Passengers of Modernity* (Basingstoke: Palgrave Macmillan, 2005).

Veblen, Thorstein, *The Theory of the Leisure Class: An Economic Study in the Evolution of Institutions* (London: Macmillan, 1899).

Webb, Catherine, *The Woman with the Basket: The History of the Women's Co-operative Guild 1883–1927* (Manchester: Co-operative Wholesale Society's Printing Works, 1927).

Which?: Your Consumer Champion <https://www.which.co.uk/> [accessed 12 January 2023].

Woloch, Nancy, *A Class by Herself: Protective Laws for Women Workers, 1890s–1990s* (Princeton: Princeton University Press, 2015).

Woodbridge, Alice L., *Report on the Condition of Working Women in New York Retail Stores* (New York: Freytag, 1893), 8pp., *LSE Selected Pamphlets* <https://www.jstor.org/stable/60218789> [accessed 30 March 2020].

Index